Treasures

of

VERSE

A Collection Of
The World's Most Famous And
Familiar Poems

**BRISTOL
PARK
BOOKS**

Edited With An Introduction By
Sarah Anne Stuart

First Bristol Park Books edition published in 2019

Bristol Park Books
252 W.38th Street
NYC, NY 10018

Bristol Park Books is a registered trademark
of Bristol Park Books, Inc.

Library of Congress Control Number 2019947516

ISBN: 978-0-88486-732-6

Text and cover design by Elizabeth Sheehan Design

Printed in the United States of America

CONTENTS

v

FOREWORD

Putting one's thoughts into words can sometimes be frustrating. At times, words can become a limitation — we are left thinking how we felt so much more than we were able to convey.

However, words can also challenge us into thinking a new way — pushing the limits of our individual scope and opening us up to a larger world.

Poetry captures in a few words the thoughts and emotions that reach to the heart of human experience, flashing insight on the universal truths that unite all of us. In a unique way, poetry is able to break the boundaries of unspoken feelings, helping the reader feel that he or she is not alone; uniting the reader with the world around him.

The poems in this collection celebrate the variety of beliefs, visions, and hopes that we share with others-and sometimes stand alone to defrnd. In this volume arc poems of joy, oflove, of faith; poems of sacrifice, truth, and romance; poems that celebrate living, tell a story, reaffirm the soul. Many of them will be famil iar; many are works by poets you have enjoyed through the years:

Walt Whitman, Robert Frost, Amy Lowell, Carl Sandburg, William Wordsworth, Edgar Allan Poe, John Keats, Tennyson, Shakespeare, Shelley, Byron, Longfellow, and many more. New poets and poems may be waiting to be discovered. Each is a complete portrait, a painting in words which is framed by your own thoughts, memories, and feelings about life. Some you will be able to identify with; some will make you laugh; some will make you think; but all the poems within these pages were chosen because they are the kind of poems that will stay with you, become a part of you-the kind you will want to read again and again. This is a book which you will treasure as a source of beauty, inspiration, and renewal for years to come.

Sarah Anne Stuart

AGING

Growing Old

The days grow shorter, the nights grow longer;
  The headstones thicken along the way;
And life grows sadder, but love grows stronger
  For those who walk with us day by day.

The tear comes quicker, the laugh comes slower;
  The courage is lesser to do and dare;
And the tide of joy in the heart falls lower,
  And seldom covers the reefs of care.

But all true things in the world seem truer,
  And the better things of earth seem best,
And friends are dearer, as friends are fewer,
  And love is all as our sun dips west.

Then let us clasp hands as we walk together,
  And let us speak softly in low, sweet tone,
For no man knows on the morrow whether
  We two pass on—or but one alone.

ELLA WHEELER WILCOX

The Oak

Live thy Life,
  Young and old,
Like yon oak,
Bright in spring,
  Living gold;

Summer-rich
  Then; and then
Autumn-changed,
Soberer-hued
  Gold again.

All his leaves
  Fallen at length,
Look, he stands,
Trunk and bough,
  Naked strength.
                ALFRED, LORD TENNYSON

The Old Familiar Faces

I have had playmates, I have had companions,
In my days of childhood, in my joyful school-days,
All, all are gone, the old familiar faces.

I have been laughing, I have been carousing,
Drinking late, sitting late, with my bosom cronies,
All, all are gone, the old familiar faces.

I loved a love once, fairest among women;
Closed are her doors on me, I must not see her—
All, all are gone, the old familiar faces.

I have a friend, a kinder friend has no man;
Like an ingrate, I left my friend abruptly;
Left him, to muse on the old familiar faces.

4

Ghost-like I paced round the haunts of my childhood.
Earth seemed a desert I was bound to traverse,
Seeking to find the old familiar faces.

Friend of my bosom, thou more than a brother,
Why wert not thou born in my father's dwelling?
So might we talk of the old familiar faces—

How some they have died, and some they have left me,
And some are taken from me; all are departed;
All, all are gone, the old familiar faces.

CHARLES LAMB

'Tis the Last Rose of Summer

'Tis the last rose of summer
    Left blooming alone;
All her lovely companions
    Are faded and gone;
No flower of her kindred,
    No rosebud, is nigh,
To reflect back her blushes,
    To give sigh for sigh.

I'll not leave thee, thou lone one,
    To pine on the stem;
Since the lovely are sleeping,
    Go sleep thou with them.
Thus kindly I scatter
    Thy leaves o'er the bed,
Where thy mates of the garden
    Lie scentless and dead.

So soon may I follow
   When friendships decay,
And from Love's shining circle
   The gems drop away!
When true hearts lie wither'd,
      And fond ones are flown,
Oh! who would inhabit
   This bleak world alone?

THOMAS MOORE

The Old Song

When all the world is young, lad,
   And all the trees are green;
And every goose a swan, lad,
   And every lass a queen;
Then hey for boot and horse, lad,
   And round the world away!
Young blood must have its course, lad,
   And every dog his day.

When all the world is old, lad,
   And all the trees are brown;
And all the sport is stale, lad,
   And all the wheels run down;
Creep home, and take your place there
   The spent and maim'd among;
God grant you find one face there
   You loved when all was young!

CHARLES KINGSLEY

When You Are Old

When you are old and gray and full of sleep,
And nodding by the fire, take down this book,
And slowly read, and dream of the soft look
Your eyes had once, and of their shadows deep;

How many loved your moments of glad grace,
And loved your beauty with love false or true;
But one man loved the pilgrim soul in you,
And loved the sorrows of your changing face.

And bending down beside the glowing bars,
Murmur, a little sadly, how love fled
And paced upon the mountains overhead
And hid his face amid a crowd of stars.

WILLIAM BUTLER YEATS

Terminus

It is time to be old,
To take in sail:—
The god of bounds,
Who sets to seas a shore,
Came to me in his fatal rounds,
And said: 'No more!
No farther shoot
Thy broad ambitious branches, and thy root,
Fancy departs: no more invent,
Contract thy firmament
To compass of a tent.

There's not enough for this and that,
Make thy option which of two;
Economize the failing river,
Nor the less revere the Giver,
Leave the many and hold the few.
Timely wise accept the terms,
Soften the fall with wary foot;
A little while
Still plan and smile,
And, fault of novel germs,
Mature the unfallen fruit.
Bad husbands of their fires,
Who, when they gave thee breath,
Failed to bequeath
The needful sinew stark as once,
The Baresark marrow to thy bones,
But left a legacy of ebbing veins,
Inconstant heat and nerveless reins,—
Amid the Muses, left thee deaf and dumb,
Amid the gladiators, halt and numb.'

As the bird trims her to the gale,
I trim myself to the storm of time,
I man the rudder, reef the sail,
Obey the voice at eve obeyed at prime:
'Lowly faithful, banish fear,
Right onward drive unharmed;
The port well worth the cruise, is near,
And every wave is charmed.'

RALPH WALDO EMERSON

BEAUTY

She Walks in Beauty

She walks in beauty, like the night
Of cloudless climes and starry skies,
And all that's best of dark and bright
Meet in her aspect and her eyes;
Thus mellowed to that tender light
Which heaven to gaudy day denies.

One shade the more, one ray the less,
Had half impaired the nameless grace
Which waves in every raven tress
Or softly lightens o'er her face,
Where thoughts serenely sweet express
How pure, how dear their dwelling-place.

And on that cheek and o'er that brow
So soft, so calm, yet eloquent,
The smiles that win, the tints that glow
But tell of days in goodness spent,
A mind at peace with all below,
A heart whose love is innocent.

GEORGE GORDON, LORD BYRON

Beauty Is Not Bound

Give beauty all her right!
She's not to one form tied;
Each shape yields fair delight Where
her perfections bide: Helen, I grant,
might pleasing be, And Rosamond
was as sweet as she.

11

Some the quick eye commends,
Some swelling lips and red;
Pale looks have many friends,
Through sacred sweetness bred:
Meadows have flowers that pleasures move,
Though roses are the flowers of love.

Free beauty is not bound
To one unmovèd clime;
She visits every ground
And favors every time.
Let the old loves with mine compare;
My sovereign is as sweet and fair.

THOMAS CAMPION

Shall I Compare Thee to a Summer's Day?

Shall I compare thee to a summer's day?
Thou art more lovely and more temperate:
Rough winds do shake the darling buds of May,
And summer's lease hath all too short a date:
Sometime too hot the eye of heaven shines,
And often is his gold complexion dimm'd;
And every fair from fair sometime declines,
By chance, or nature's changing course untrimm'd;
But thy eternal summer shall not fade,
Nor lose possession of that fair thou ow'st,
Nor shall death brag thou wander'st in his shade,
When in eternal lines to time thou grow'st;

So long as men can breathe, or eyes can see,
So long lives this, and this gives life to thee.
WILLIAM SHAKESPEARE

Ode on a Grecian Urn

I

Thou still unravish'd bride of quietness.
    Thou foster-child of silence and slow time,
Sylvan historian, who canst thus express
    A flowery tale more sweetly than our rhyme:
What leaf-fring'd legend haunts about the shape
    Of deities or mortals, or of both,
        In Tempe or the dales of Arcady?
    What men or gods are these? What maidens loth?
What mad pursuit? What struggle to escape?
    What pipes and timbrels? What wild ecstasy?

II

Heard melodies are sweet, but those unheard
    Are sweeter; therefore, ye soft pipes, play on;
Not to the sensual ear, but, more endear'd,
    Pipe to the spirit ditties of no tone:
Fair youth, beneath the trees, thou canst not leave
    Thy song, nor ever can those trees be bare;
        Bold Lover, never, never canst thou kiss,
Though winning near the goal—yet, do not grieve;
    She cannot fade, though thou hast not thy bliss,
        For ever wilt thou love, and she be fair!

Ah, happy, happy boughs! that cannot shed
   Your leaves, nor ever bid the Spring adieu;
And, happy melodist, unwearied,
   Forever piping songs forever new;
More happy love! more happy, happy love!
   Forever warm and still to be enjoy'd,
     Forever panting, and forever young;
All breathing human passion far above,
   That leaves a heart high-sorrowful and cloy'd,
     A burning forehead, and a parching tongue.

IV

Who are these coming to the sacrifice?
   To what green altar, O mysterious priest,
Lead'st thou that heifer lowing at the skies,
   And all her silken flanks with garlands drest?
What little town by river or sea shore,
   Or mountain-built with peaceful citadel,
     Is emptied of this folk, this pious morn
And, little town, thy streets for evermore
   Will silent be; and not a soul to tell
     Why thou art desolate, can e'er return.

V

O Attic shape! Fair attitude! with brede
   Of marble men and maidens overwrought,
With forest branches and the trodden weed;
   Thou, silent form, dost tease us out of thought
As doth eternity: Cold Pastoral!
   When old age shall this generation waste,
     Thou shalt remain, in midst of other woe
Than ours, a friend to man, to whom thou say'st,
   'Beauty is truth, truth beauty,'—that is all
     Ye know on earth, and all ye need to know.

JOHN KEATS

BEREAVEMENT

Death, Be Not Proud

Death, be not proud, though some have called thee
  Mighty and dreadful, for thou art not so;
  For those whom thou think'st thou dost overthrow
Die not, poor Death, nor yet canst thou kill me.
From rest and sleep, which but thy pictures be,
  Much pleasure; then from thee much more must flow,
And soonest our best men with thee do go,
Rest of their bones, and soul's delivery.

Thou art slave to fate, chance, kings, and desperate men,
  And dost with poison, war, and sickness dwell;
  And poppy or charms can make us sleep as well
And better than thy stroke; why swell'st thou then?
  One short sleep past, we wake eternally,
  And death shall be no more; Death, thou shalt die.

JOHN DONNE

Requiescat

Strew on her roses, roses,
  And never a spray of yew:
In quiet she reposes;
  Ah, would that I did too!

Her mirth the world required;
  She bathed it in smiles of glee.
But her heart was tired, tired,
  And now they let her be.

Her life was turning, turning,
    In mazes of heat and sound.
But for peace her soul was yearning,
    And now peace laps her round.

Her cabined, ample spirit,
    It fluttered and failed for breath;
Tonight it doth inherit
    The vasty hall of death.

MATTHEW ARNOLD

The Stone

"And you will cut a stone for him,
To set above his head?
And will you cut a stone for him—
A stone for him?" she said.

Three days before, a splintered rock
Had struck her lover dead—
Had struck him in the quarry dead,
Where, careless of the warning call,
He loitered, while the shot was fired—
A lively stripling, brave and tall,
And sure of all his heart desired . . .
A flash, a shock,
A rumbing fall . . .
And, broken 'neath the broken rock,
A lifeless heap, with face of clay;
And still as any stone he lay,
With eyes that saw the end of all.

I went to break the news to her;
And I could hear my own heart beat
With dread of what my lips might say
But, some poor fool had sped before;
And flinging wide her father's door,
Had blurted out the news to her,
Had struck her lover dead for her,
Had struck the girl's heart dead in her,
Had struck life lifeless at a word,
And dropped it at her feet:
Then hurried on his witless way,
Scarce knowing she had heard.

And when I came, she stood alone,
A woman turned to stone:
And, though no word at all she said,
I knew that all was known.
Because her heart was dead,
She did not sigh nor moan.
His mother wept;
She could not weep.
Her lover slept:
She could not sleep.
Three days, three nights,
She did not stir:
Three days, three nights,
Were one to her,
Who never closed her eyes
From sunset to sunrise,
From dawn to evenfall:
Her tearless, staring eyes,
That seeing naught, saw all.
The fourth night when I came from work,
I found her at my door.
"And will you cut a stone for him?"

She said: and spoke no more:
But followed me, as I went in,
And sank upon a chair;
And curdled the warm blood in me,
Those eyes that cut me to the bone,
And pierced my marrow like cold steel.

And so I rose, and sought a stone;
And cut it, smooth and square:
And, as I worked, she sat and watched,
Beside me, in her chair.
Night after night, by candlelight,
I cut her lover's name:
Night after night, so still and white,
And like a ghost she came;
And sat beside me in her chair;
And watched with eyes aflame.
She eyed each stroke;
And hardly stirred:
She never spoke
A single word:
And not a sound or murmur broke
The quiet, save the mallet-stroke.
With still eyes ever on my hands,
With eyes that seemed to burn my hands,
My wincing, overwearied hands,
She watched, with bloodless lips apart,
And silent, indrawn breath:
And every stroke my chisel cut,
Death cut still deeper in her heart:
The two of us were chiseling,
Together, I and death.

And when at length the job was done,
And I had laid the mallet by,
As if, at last, her peace were won,
She breathed his name; and, with a sigh,
Passed slowly through the open door:
And never crossed my threshold more.

Next night I labored late, alone.
To cut her name upon the stone.

WILFRID WILSON GIBSON

Requiescat

Tread lightly, she is near
    Under the snow,
Speak gently, she can hear
    The daisies grow.

All her bright golden hair
    Tarnished with rust,
She that was young and fair
    Fallen to dust.

Lily-like, white as snow,
    She hardly knew
She was a woman, so
    Sweetly she grew.

Coffin-board, heavy stone,
  Lie on her breast;
I vex my heart alone,
  She is at rest.

Peace, peace; she cannot hear
  Lyre or sonnet;
All my life's buried here.
  Heap earth upon it.

OSCAR WILDE

BETRAYAL

I Am

I am: yet what I am none cares or knows,
  My friends forsake me like a memory lost;
I am the self-consumer of my woes,
  They rise and vanish in oblivious host,
Like shades in love and death's oblivion lost;
And yet I am, and live with shadows tost

Into the nothingness of scorn and noise,
  Into the living sea of waking dreams,
Where there is neither sense of life nor joys,
  But the vast shipwreck of my life's esteems;
And e'en the dearest—that I loved the best—
Are strange—nay, rather stranger than the rest.

I long for scenes where man has never trod;
  A place where woman never smiled or wept;
There to abide with my Creator, God,
  And sleep as I in childhood sweetly slept:
Untroubling and untroubled where I lie;
The grass below—above the vaulted sky.

JOHN CLARE

Then Hate Me When Thou Wilt

Then hate me when thou wilt; if ever, now;
Now, while the world is bent my deeds to cross,
Join with the spite of fortune, make me bow,
And do not drop in for an after-loss:
Ah! do not, when my heart hath 'scaped this sorrow,
Come in the rearward of a conquered woe;
Give not a windy night a rainy morrow,
To linger out a purposed overthrow.
If thou wilt leave me, do not leave me last,
When other petty griefs have done their spite,
But in the onset come; so shall I taste
At first the very worst of fortune's might;
   And other strains of woe, which now seem woe,
   Compared with loss of thee will not seem so.

WILLIAM SHAKESPEARE

BROTHERHOOD

The Human Touch

'Tis the human touch in this world that counts,
 The touch of your hand and mine,
Which means far more to the fainting heart
 Than shelter and bread and wine;
For shelter is gone when the night is o'er,
 And bread lasts only a day,
But the touch of the hand and the sound of the voice
 Sing on in the soul alway.

SPENCER MICHAEL FREE

The House by the Side of the Road

There are hermit souls that live withdrawn
 In the peace of their self-content;
There are souls, like stars, that dwell apart,
 In a fellowless firmament;
There are pioneer souls that blaze their paths
 Where highways never ran;
But let me live by the side of the road
 And be a friend to man.

Let me live in a house by the side of the road,
 Where the race of men go by—
The men who are good and the men who are bad,
 As good and as bad as I.
I would not sit in the scorner's seat,
 Or hurl the cynic's ban;

Let me live in a house by the side of the road
   And be a friend to man.

I see from my house by the side of the road,
   By the side of the highway of life,
The men who press with the ardor of hope,
   The men who are faint with the strife.
But I turn not away from their smiles
      nor their tears—
   Both parts of an infinite plan;
Let me live in my house by the side of the road
   And be a friend to man.

Let me live in my house by the side of the road
   Where the race of men go by—
They are good, they are bad, they are weak,
      they are strong,
   Wise, foolish—so am I.
Then why should I sit in the scorner's seat
   Or hurl the cynic's bar?—
Let me live in my house by the side of the road
   And be a friend to man.

SAM WALTER FOSS

What Was His Creed?

What was his creed?
I do not know his creed, I only know
That here below, he walked the common road
And lifted many a load, lightened the task,
Brightened the day for others toiling on a weary way:
This, his only meed; I do not know his creed.

His creed? I care not what his creed;
Enough that never yielded he to greed,
But served a brother in his daily need;
Plucked many a thorn and planted many a flower;
Glorified the service of each hour;
Had faith in God, himself, and fellow-men;—
Perchance he never thought in terms of creed,
I only know he lived a life, in deed!

H.N. FIFER

The Voice of God

I sought to hear the voice of God,
  And climbed the topmost steeple.
But God declared: "Go down again,
  I dwell among the people."
LOUIS I. NEWMAN

Plea for Tolerance

If we but knew what forces helped to mold
   The lives of others from their earliest years—
   Knew something of their background, joys and tears,
And whether or not their youth was drear and cold,
Or if some dark belief had taken hold
   And kept them shackled, torn with doubts and fears
   So long it crushed the force that perseveres
And made their hearts grow prematurely old,—

Then we might judge with wiser, kindlier sight,
   And learn to put aside our pride and scorn . . .
Perhaps no one can ever quite undo
   His faults or wholly banish some past blight—
The tolerant mind is purified, reborn,
   And lifted upward to a saner view.

MARGARET E. BRUNER

Outwitted

He drew a circle that shut me out—
Heretic, rebel, a thing to flout.
But Love and I hat the wit to win:
We drew a circle that took him in!

EDWIN MARKHAM

Who Are My People?

My people? Who are they?
I went into the church where the congregation
Worshipped my God. Were they my people?
I felt no kinship to them as they knelt there.
My people? Where are they?
I went into the land where I was born,
Where men spoke my language . . .
I was a stranger there.
"My people," my soul cried. "Who are my people?"

Last night in the rain I met an old man
Who spoke a language I do not speak,
Which marked him as one who does not
        know my God.
With apologetic smile he offered me
The shelter of his patched umbrella.
I met his eyes . . . And then I knew. . . .

ROSA ZAGNONI MARINONI

CELEBRATION

Ring Out, Wild Bells

Ring out, wild bells, to the wild sky,
    The flying cloud, the frosty light:
    The year is dying in the night;
Ring out, wild bells, and let him die.

Ring out the old, ring in the new,
    Ring, happy bells, across the snow:
    The year is going, let him go;
Ring out the false, ring in the true.
            ALFRED, LORD TENNYSON

Trees

I think that I shall never see
A poem lovely as a tree.

A tree whose hungry mouth is prest
Against the earth's sweet flowing breast;

A tree that looks at God all day,
And lifts her leafy arms to pray;

A tree that may in Summer wear
A nest of robins in her hair;

Upon whose bosom snow has lain;
Who intimately lives with rain.

Poems are made by fools like me,
But only God can make a tree.
JOYCE KILMER

The Daffodils

I wandered lonely as a cloud
   That floats on high o'er vales and hills,
When all at once I saw a crowd,
   A host, of golden daffodils,
Beside the lake, beneath the trees,
Fluttering and dancing in the breeze.

Continuous as the stars that shine
   And twinkle on the milky way,
They stretched in never-ending line
   Along the margin of a bay:
Ten thousand saw I at a glance
Tossing their heads in sprightly dance.

The waves beside them danced, but they
   Out-did the sparkling waves in glee:
A Poet could not but be gay
   In such a jocund company!
I gazed—and gazed—but little thought
What wealth the show to me had brought:

For oft, when on my couch I lie
   In vacant or in pensive mood,
They flash upon that inward eye
   Which is the bliss of solitude;

And then my heart with pleasure fills,
And dances with the daffodils.
WILLIAM WORDSWORTH

Holidays

The holiest of all holidays are those
Kept by ourselves in silence and apart;
The secret anniversaries of the heart.
HENRY WADSWORTH LONGFELLOW

A Thing of Beauty

A thing of beauty is a joy for ever:
Its loveliness increases; it will never
Pass into nothingness; but still will keep
A bower quiet for us, and a sleep
Full of sweet dreams, and health, and quiet breathing.
Therefore, on every morrow, are we wreathing
A flowery band to bind us to the earth,
Spite of despondence, of the inhuman dearth
Of noble natures, of the gloomy days,
Of all the unhealthy and o'er-darkened ways
Made for our searching: yes, in spite of all,
Some shape of beauty moves away the pall
From our dark spirits.

JOHN KEATS

Sea-Fever

I must go down to the seas again, to the lonely sea
    and the sky,
And all I ask is a tall ship and a star to steer her by,
And the wheel's kick and the wind's song and the
    white sail's shaking,
And a gray mist on the sea's face and a gray dawn
    breaking.

I must go down to the seas again, for the call of the
    running tide
Is a wild call and a clear call that may not be denied;
And all I ask is a windy day with the white clouds
    flying,
And the flung spray and the blown spume, and the
    sea-gulls crying.

I must go down to the seas again to the vagrant gypsy
    life.
To the gull's way and the whale's way where the
    wind's like a whetted knife;
And all I ask is a merry yarn from a laughing fellow-
    rover,
And quiet sleep and a sweet dream when the long
    trick's over.

JOHN MASEFIELD

There Is No Death

There is no death! The stars go down
   To rise upon some other shore,
And bright in heaven's jeweled crown
   They shine for evermore.

There is no death! The dust we tread
   Shall change beneath the summer showers
To golden grain or mellow fruit
   Or rainbow-tinted flowers.

There is no death! The leaves may fall,
   The flowers may fade and pass away—

They only wait, through wintry hours,
   The coming of the May.

The bird-like voice, whose joyous tones
   Made glad this scene of sin and strife,
Sings now an everlasting song
   Amid the tree of life.

And ever near us, though unseen,
   The dear immortal spirits tread;
For all the boundless universe
   Is Life—there are no dead!

JOHN LUCKEY McCREERY

The Village Blacksmith

Under a spreading chestnut tree
    The village smithy stands;
The smith, a mighty man is he,
    With large and sinewy hands;
And the muscles of his brawny arms
    Are strong as iron bands.

His hair is crisp, and black, and long,
    His face is like the tan;
His brow is wet with honest sweat,
    He earns whate'er he can,
And looks the whole world in the face,
    For he owes not any man.

Week in, week out, from morn till night,
    You can hear his bellows blow;
You can hear him swing his heavy sledge,
    With measured beat and slow,
Like a sexton ringing the village bell,
    When the evening sun is low.

And children coming home from school
    Look in at the open door;
They love to see the flaming forge,
    And hear the bellows roar,
And catch the burning sparks that fly
    Like chaff from a threshing floor.

He goes on Sunday to the church,
  And sits among his boys;
He hears the parson pray and preach,
  He hears his daughter's voice,
Singing in the village choir,
  And it makes his heart rejoice.

It sounds to him like her mother's voice,
  Singing in Paradise!
He needs must think of her once more,
  How in the grave she lies;
And with his hard, rough hand he wipes
  A tear out of his eyes.

Toiling,—rejoicing,—sorrowing,
  Onward through life he goes;
Each morning sees some task begin,
  Each evening sees it close;
Something attempted, something done,
  Has earned a night's repose.

Thanks, thanks to thee, my worthy friend,
  For the lesson thou hast taught!
Thus at the flaming forge of life
  Our fortunes must be wrought;
Thus on its sounding anvil shaped
  Each burning deed and thought!
              HENRY WADSWORTH LONGFELLOW

Chicago

Hog Butcher for the World,
Tool Maker, Stacker of Wheat,
Player with Railroads and the Nation's Freight
    Handler;
Stormy, husky, brawling,
City of the Big Shoulders:

They tell me you are wicked and I believe them,
    for I have seen your painted women under the
    gas lamps luring the farm boys.
And they tell me you are crooked and I answer:
    Yes, it is true I have seen the gunman kill and
    go free to kill again.
And they tell me you are brutal and my reply is:
    On the faces of women and children I have
    seen the marks of wanton hunger.
And having answered so I turn once more to
    those who sneer at this my city, and I give
    them back the sneer and say to them:
Come and show me another city with lifted head
    singing so proud to be alive and coarse and
    strong and cunning.
Flinging magnetic cures amid the toil of piling
    job on job, here is a tall bold slugger set vivid
    against the little soft cities;
Fierce as a dog with tongue lapping for action,
    cunning as a savage pitted against the
    wilderness,

Bareheaded,
Shoveling,
Wrecking,
Planning,
Building, breaking, rebuilding
Under the smoke, dust all over his mouth,
    laughing with white teeth,
Under the terrible burden of destiny laughing as a
    young man laughs,
Laughing even as an ignorant fighter laughs who
    has never lost a battle,
Bragging and laughing that under his wrist is the
    pulse, and under his ribs the heart of the
    people.
                    Laughing!
Laughing the stormy, husky, brawling laughter
    of Youth, half-naked, sweating, proud to be
    Hog Butcher, Tool Maker, Stacker of Wheat,
    Player with Railroads and Freight Handler to
    the Nation.

                                CARL SANDBURG

CHARACTER

The Inner Man

Beauty depends on simplicity—I mean the true simplicity
   of a rightly and nobly ordered mind and character.
He is a fool who seriously inclines to weigh the beautiful by
   any other standard than that of the good.
The good is the beautiful.
Grant me to be beautiful in the inner man.

PLATO

The Noble Nature

It is not growing like a tree
   In bulk, doth make man better be;
Or standing long an oak, three hundred year,
To fall a log at last, dry, bald, and sear:
   A lily of a day
   Is fairer far in May,
Although it fall and die that night,—
It was the plant and flower of Light.
In small proportions we just beauties see,
And in short measures life may perfect be.

BEN JONSON

My Mind to Me a Kingdom Is

My mind to me a kingdom is;
   Such present joys therein I find
That it excels all other bliss
   That earth affords or grows by kind.
Though much I want which most would have,
Yet still my mind forbids to crave.

No princely pomp, no wealthy store,
   No force to win the victory,
No wily wit to salve a sore,
   No shape to feed a loving eye;
To none of these I yield as thrall—
For why? My mind doth serve for all.

I see how plenty surfeits oft,
   And hasty climbers soon do fall;
I see that those which are aloft
   Mishap doth threaten most of all;
They get with toil, they keep with fear—
Such cares my mind could never bear.

Content to live, this is my stay;
   I seek no more than may suffice;
I press to bear no haughty sway;
   Look, what I lack my mind supplies.
Lo, thus I triumph like a king,
Content with that my mind doth bring.

Some have too much, yet still do crave;
   I little have, and seek no more.

They are but poor, though much they have,
    And I am rich with little store.
They poor, I rich; they beg, I give;
They lack, I leave; they pine, I live.

I laugh not at another's loss;
    I grudge not at another's pain;
No worldly waves my mind can toss;
    My state at one doth still remain.
I fear no foe, I fawn no friend;
I loathe not life, nor dread my end.

Some weigh their pleasure by their lust,
    Their wisdom by their rage of will;
Their treasure is their only trust;
    A cloakèd craft their store of skill.
But all the pleasure that I find
Is to maintain a quiet mind.

My wealth is health and perfect ease;
    My conscience clear my chief defense;
I neither seek by bribes to please,
    Nor by deceit to breed offense.
Thus do I live; thus will I die;
Would all did so as well as I!

SIR EDWARD DYER

In Men Whom Men Condemn as Ill

In men whom men condemn as ill
I find so much of goodness still,
In men whom men pronounce divine
I find so much of sin and blot,
I do not dare to draw a line
Between the two, where God has not.

JOAQUIN MILLER

We Will Speak Out

We will speak out, we will be heard,
   Though all earth's systems crack;
We will not bate a single word,
   Nor take a letter back.
Let liars fear, let cowards shrink,
   Let traitors turn away;
Whatever we have dared to think
   That dare we also say.
We speak the truth, and what care we
   For hissing and for scorn,
While some faint gleamings we can see
   Of Freedom's coming morn?

JAMES RUSSELL LOWELL

A Psalm of Life

Tell me not, in mournful numbers,
   Life is but an empty dream!—
For the soul is dead that slumbers,
   And things are not what they seem.

Life is real! Life is earnest!
   And the grave is not its goal;
Dust thou art, to dust returnest,
   Was not spoken of the soul.

Not enjoyment, and not sorrow,
   Is our destined end or way;
But to act, that each to-morrow
   Finds us farther than to-day.

Art is long, and Time is fleeting,
   And our hearts, though stout and brave,
Still, like muffled drums, are beating
   Funeral marches to the grave.

In the world's broad field of battle,
   In the bivouac of Life,
Be not like dumb, driven cattle!
   Be a hero in the strife!

Trust no Future, howe'er pleasant!
   Let the dead Past bury its dead!
Act,—act in the living Present!
   Heart within, and God o'erhead!

Lives of great men all remind us
    We can make our lives sublime,
And, departing, leave behind us
    Footprints on the sands of time;

Footprints, that perhaps another,
    Sailing o'er life's solemn main,
A forlorn and shipwrecked brother,
    Seeing, shall take heart again.

Let us, then, be up and doing,
    With a heart for any fate;
Still achieving, still pursuing,
    Learn to labor and to wait.

        HENRY WADSWORTH LONGFELLOW

COMPASSION

Life Lesson

There! little girl; don't cry!
  They have broken your doll, I know;
    And your tea-set blue,
    And your play-house, too,
  Are things of the long ago;
    But childish troubles will soon pass by
    There! little girl; don't cry!

There! little girl; don't cry!
  They have broken your slate, I know;
    And the glad, wild ways
    of your school-girl days
  Are things of the long ago;
    But life and love will soon come by.
    There! little girl; don't cry!

There! little girl; don't cry!
  They have broken your heart, I know;
    And the rainbow gleams
    Of your youthful dreams
  Are things of the long ago;
    But heaven holds all for which you sigh.
    There! little girl; don't cry!

          JAMES WHITCOMB RILEY

Song of the Shirt

With fingers weary and worn,
   With eyelids heavy and red,
A woman sat in unwomanly rags,
   Plying her needle and thread—
Stitch! stitch! stitch!
   In poverty, hunger, and dirt,
And still with a voice of dolorous pitch
   She sang the "Song of the Shirt!"

"Work—work—work
   Till the brain begins to swim;
Work—work—work
   Till the eyes are heavy and dim!
Seam, and gusset, and band,
   Band, and gusset, and seam,
Till over the buttons I fall asleep,
   And sew them on in a dream!

"O men, with sisters dear!
   O men, with mothers and wives!
It is not linen you're wearing out,
   But human creatures' lives!
Stitch—stitch—stitch!
   In poverty, hunger, and dirt—
Sewing at once, with a double thread,
   A shroud as well as a shirt!

"But why do I talk of Death—
   That phantom of grisly bone?

I hardly fear his terrible shape,
   It seems so like my own,—
It seems so like my own
   Because of the fasts I keep;
O God! that bread should be so dear,
   And flesh and blood so cheap!

"Work! work! work!
   My labor never flags;
And what are its wages? A bed of straw,
   A crust of bread—and rags.
That shattered roof—and this naked floor—
   A table—a broken chair—
And a wall so bland, my shadow I thank
   For sometimes falling there!

"Work—work—work!
   From weary chime to chime!
Work—work—work!
   As prisoners work for crime!
Band, and gusset, and seam,
   Seam, and gusset, and band—
Till the heart is sick and the brain benumbed,
   As well as the weary hand.

"Work—work—work!
   In the dull December light!
And work—work—work!
   When the weather is warm and bright!
While underneath the eaves
   The brooding swallows cling,
As if to show me their sunny backs,
   And twit me with the spring.

"Oh, but for one short hour—
    A respite, however brief!
No blessed leisure for love or hope,
    But only time for grief!
A little weeping would ease my heart;
    But in their briny bed
My tears must stop, for every drop
    Hinders needle and thread!"

With fingers weary and worn,
    With eyelids heavy and red,
A woman sat in unwomanly rags,
    Plying her needle and thread—
Stitch! stitch! stitch!
    In poverty, hunger, and dirt;
And still with a voice of dolorous pitch—
Would that its tone could reach the rich!—
    She sang this "Song of the Shirt."
                              THOMAS HOOD

Charity

There is so much good in the worst of us,
And so much bad in the best of us,
That it ill behooves any of us
To find fault with the rest of us.
                              AUTHOR UNKNOWN

Fleurette

My leg? It's off at the knee.
Do I miss it? Well, some. You see
I've had it since I was born;
And lately a devilish corn.
(I rather chuckle with glee
To think how I've fooled that corn.)

But I'll hobble around all right.
It isn't that, it's my face.
Oh I know I'm a hideous sight,
Hardly a thing in place;
Sort of gargoyle, you'd say.
Nurse won't give me a glass,
But I see the folks as they pass
Shudder and turn away;
Turn away in distress . . .
Mirror enough, I guess.

I'm gay! You bet I *am* gay;
But I wasn't a while ago.
If you'd seen me even to-day,
The darndest picture of woe,
With this Caliban mug of mine,
So ravaged and raw and red,
Turned to the wall—in fine,
Wishing that I was dead. . . .

So over the blanket's rim
I raised my terrible face,
And I saw—how I envied him!

A girl of such delicate grace;
Sixteen, all laughter and love;
As gay as a linnet, and yet
As tenderly sweet as a dove;
Half woman, half child—Fleurette.

What has happened since then,
Since I lay with my face to the wall,
The most despairing of men?
Listen! I'll tell you all.
That *poilu* across the way,
With the shrapnel wound in his head,
Has a sister: she came to day
To sit awhile by his bed.
All morning I heard him fret:
"Oh, when will she come, Fleurette?"

Then sudden, a joyous cry;
The tripping of little feet;
The softest, tenderest sigh;
A voice so fresh and sweet;
Clear as a silver bell,
Fresh as the morning dews:
"C'est toi, c'est toi, Marcel!
Mon frère, comme je suis heureuse!"

Then I turned to the wall again.
(I was awfully blue, you see,)
And I thought with a bitter pain:
"Such visions are not for me."

So there like a log I lay,
All hidden, I thought, from view,
When sudden I heard her say:
"Ah! Who is that *malheureux?"*

Then briefly I heard him tell
(However he came to know)
How I'd smothered a bomb that fell
Into the trench, and so
None of my men were hit,
Though it busted me up a bit.

Well, I didn't quiver an eye,
And he chattered and there she sat;
And I fancied I heard her sigh—
But I wouldn't just swear to that.
And maybe she wasn't so bright,
Though she talked in a merry strain,
And I closed my eyes ever so tight,
Yet I saw her ever so plain:
Her dear little tilted nose,
Her delicate, dimpled chin,
Her mouth like a budding rose,
And the glistening pearls within;
Her eyes like the violet:
Such a rare little queen—Fleurette.

And at last when she rose to go,
The light was a little dim,
And I ventured to peep, and so
I saw her, graceful and slim,
And she kissed him and kissed him, and oh
How I envied and envied him!

So when she was gone I said
In rather a dreary voice
To him of the opposite bed:
"Ah, friend, how you must rejoice!

But me, I'm a thing of dread.
For me nevermore the bliss,
The thrill of a woman's kiss."

Then I stopped, for lo! she was there,
And a great light shone in her eyes.
And me! I could only stare,
I was taken so by surprise,
When gently she bent her head:
"May I kiss you, Sergeant?" she said.

Then she kissed my burning lips
With her mouth like a scented flower,
And I thrilled to the finger-tips,
And I hadn't even the power
To say: "God bless you, dear!"
And I felt such a precious tear
Fall on my withered cheek,
And darn it! I couldn't speak.
And so she went sadly away,
And I knew that my eyes were wet.
Ah, not to my dying day
Will I forget, forget!
Can you wonder now I am gay?
God bless her, that little Fleurette!

ROBERT SERVICE

The Rime of the
Ancient Mariner

PART I

It is an ancient Mariner,
   And he stoppeth one of three.
'By thy long grey beard and glittering eye,
   Now wherefore stopp'st thou me?

The Bridegroom's doors are opened wide,
   And I am next of kin;
The guests are met, the feast is set:
   May'st hear the merry din.'

He holds him with his skinny hand,
   'There was a ship,' quoth he.
'Hold off! unhand me, grey-beard loon!'
   Eftsoons his hand dropt he.

He holds him with his glittering eye—
   The Wedding-Guest stood still,
And listens like a three years' child:
   The Mariner hath his will.

The Wedding-Guest sat on a stone:
   He cannot choose but hear;
And thus spake on that ancient man,
   The bright-eyed Mariner.

'The ship was cheered, the harbour cleared,
   Merrily did we drop
Below the kirk, below the hill,
   Below the lighthouse top.

The Sun came up upon the left,
    Out of the sea came he!
And he shone bright, and on the right
    Went down into the sea.

Higher and higher every day,
    Till over the mast at noon—
The Wedding-Guest here beat his breast,
    For he heard the loud bassoon.

The bride hath paced into the hall,
    Red as a rose is she;
Nodding their heads before her goes
    The merry minstrelsy.

The Wedding-Guest he beat his breast,
    Yet he cannot choose but hear;
And thus spake on that ancient man,
    The bright-eyed Mariner.

'And now the Storm-blast came, and he
    Was tyrannous and strong:
He struck with his o'ertaking wings,
    And chased us south along.

With sloping masts and dipping prow,
    As who pursued with yell and blow
Still treads the shadow of his foe,
    And forward bends his head,
The ship drove fast, loud roared the blast,
    And southward aye we fled.

And now there came both mist and snow,
    And it grew wondrous cold:
And ice, mast-high, came floating by,
    As green as emerald.

And through the drifts the snowy clifts
　　Did send a dismal sheen:
Nor shapes of men nor beasts we ken—
　　The ice was all between.

The ice was here, the ice was there,
　　The ice was all around:
It cracked and growled, and roared and howled,
　　Like noises in a swound!

At length did cross an Albatross,
　　Thorough the fog it came;
As if it had been a Christian soul,
　　We hailed it in God's name.

It ate the food it ne'er had eat,
　　And round and round it flew.
The ice did split with a thunder-fit;
The helmsman steer'd us through!

And a good south wind sprung up behind;
　　The Albatross did follow,
And every day, for food or play,
　　Came to the mariners' hollo!

In mist or cloud, on mast or shroud,
　　It perched for vespers nine;
Whiles all the night, through fog-smoke white,
　　Glimmered the whole moonshine.'

'God save thee, ancient Mariner,
　　From the fiends, that plague thee thus!—
Why look'st thou so?'—'With my crossbow
　　I shot the Albatross.

PART II

'The Sun now rose upon the right:
    Out of the sea came he,
Still hid in mist, and on the left
    Went down into the sea.

And the good south wind still blew behind,
    But no sweet bird did follow,
Nor any day for food or play
    Came to the mariners' hollo!

And I had done a hellish thing,
    And it would work 'em woe:
For all averred I had killed the bird
    That made the breeze to blow.
Ah wretch! said they, the bird to slay,
    That made the breeze to blow!

Nor dim nor red, like God's own head,
    The glorious Sun uprist:
Then all averred I had killed the bird
    That brought the fog and mist.
'Twas right, said they, such birds to slay
    That bring the fog and mist.

The fair breeze blew, the white foam flew,
    The furrow followed free;
We were the first that ever burst
    Into that silent sea.

Down dropt the breeze, the sails dropt down
    'Twas sad as sad could be;
And we did speak only to break
    The silence of the sea!

All in a hot and copper sky,
   The bloody Sun, at noon,
Right up above the mast did stand,
   No bigger than the Moon.

Day after day, day after day,
   We stuck, nor breath nor motion;
As idle as a painted ship
   Upon a painted ocean.

Water, water, everywhere,
   And all the boards did shrink;
Water, water everywhere
   Nor any drop to drink.

The very deep did rot: O Christ!
   That ever this should be!
Yea, slimy things did crawl with legs
   Upon the slimy sea.

About, about, in reel and rout
   The death-fires danced at night;
The water, like a witch's oils,
   Burnt green, and blue, and white.

And some in dreams assured were
   Of the Spirit that plagued us so;
Nine fathom deep he had followed us
   From the land of mist and snow.

And every tongue, through utter drought,
   Was withered at the root;
We could not speak, no more than if
   We had been choked with soot.

Ah! well a-day! what evil looks
   Had I from old and young!
Instead of the cross, the Albatross
   About my neck was hung.

PART III

'There passed a weary time. Each throat
   Was parched, and glazed each eye.
A weary time! a weary time!
   How glazed each weary eye!
When, looking westward, I beheld
   A something in the sky.

At first it seemed a little speck,
   And then it seemed a mist;
It moved and moved, and took at last
   A certain shape, I wist.

A speck, a mist, a shape, I wist!
   And still it neared and neared:
As if it dodged a water-sprite,
   It plunged, and tacked and veered.

With throats unslaked, with black lips baked,
   We could nor laugh nor wail;
Through utter drought all dumb we stood!
   I bit my arm, I sucked the blood.
And cried, A sail! a sail!

With throats unslaked, with black lips baked,
   Agape they heard me call:
Gramercy! they for joy did grin,
   And all at once their breath drew in,
As they were drinking all.

See! see! (I cried) she tacks no more!
    Hither to work us weal—
Without a breeze, without a tide,
    She steadies with upright keel!

The western wave was all aflame,
    The day was well nigh done!
Almost upon the western wave
    Rested the broad, bright Sun;
When that strange shape drove suddenly
    Betwixt us and the Sun.

And straight the Sun was flecked with bars
    (Heaven's Mother send us grace!),
As if through a dungeon-grate he peered
    With broad and burning face.

Alas! (thought I, and my heart beat loud)
    How fast she nears and nears!
Are those *her* sails that glance in the Sun,
    Like restless gossameres?

Are those *her* ribs through which the Sun
    Did peer, as through a grate?
And is that Woman all her crew?
    Is that a Death? and are there two?
Is Death that Woman's mate?

Her lips were red, her looks were free,
    Her locks were yellow as gold:
Her skin was as white as leprosy,
    The Nightmare Life-in-Death was she,
Who thicks man's blood with cold.

The naked hulk alongside came,
    And the twain were casting dice;
"The game is done! I've won! I've won!"
    Quoth she, and whistles thrice.

The Sun's rim dips; the stars rush out:
    At one stride comes the dark;
With far-heard whisper, o'er the sea,
    Off shot the spectre-bark.

We listened and looked sideways up!
    Fear at my heart, as at a cup,
My life-blood seemed to sip!
    The stars were dim, and thick the night,
The steerman's face by his lamp gleamed white;
    From the sails the dew did drip—
Till clomb above the eastern bar
    The horned Moon, with one bright star
Within the nether tip.

One after one, by the star-dogged Moon,
    Too quick for groan or sigh,
Each turned his face with a ghastly pang,
    And cursed me with his eye.

Four times fifty living men
    (And I heard nor sigh nor groan),
With heavy thump, a lifeless lump,
    They dropped down one by one.

The souls did from their bodies fly—
    They fled to bliss or woe!

And every soul, it passed me by
  Like the whizz of my cross-bow!'

PART IV

'I fear thee, ancient Mariner!
  I fear thy skinny hand!
And thou art long, and lank, and brown,
  As is the ribbed sea-sand.

I fear thee and thy glittering eye,
  And thy skinny hand so brown.'—
'Fear not, fear not, thou Wedding Guest!
  This body dropt not down.

Alone, alone, all, all alone
  Alone on a wide, wide sea!
And never a saint took pity on
  My soul in agony.

The many men, so beautiful!
  And they all dead did lie:
And a thousand thousand slimy things
  Lived on; and so did I.

I looked upon the rotting sea,
  And drew my eyes away;
I looked upon the rotting deck,
  And there the dead men lay.

I looked to heaven, and tried to pray;
  But or ever a prayer had gusht,
A wicked whisper came, and made
  My heart as dry as dust.

I closed my lids, and kept them close,
  And the balls like pulses beat;
But the sky and the sea, and the sea and the sky,
  Lay like a load on my weary eye,
And the dead were at my feet.

The cold sweat melted from their limbs,
  Nor rot nor reek did they:
The look with which they looked on me
  Had never passed away.

An orphan's curse would drag to hell
  A spirit from on high;
But oh! more horrible than that
  Is the curse in a dead man's eye!
Seven days, seven nights, I saw that curse,
  And yet I could not die.

The moving Moon went up the sky,
  And nowhere did abide;
Softly she was going up,
  And a star or two beside—

Her beams bemocked the sultry main,
  Like April hoar-frost spread;
But where the ship's huge shadow lay,
  The charmed water burnt alway
A still and awful red.

Beyond the shadow of the ship,
  I watched the water-snakes:
They moved in tracks of shining white,
  And when they reared, the elfish light
Fell off in hoary flakes.

Within the shadow of the ship
    I watched their rich attire:
Blue, glossy green, and velvet black,
    They coiled and swam; and every track
Was a flash of golden fire.

O happy living things! no tongue
    Their beauty might declare:
A spring of love gushed from my heart,
    And I blessed them unaware:
Sure my kind saint took pity on me,
    And I blessed them unaware.

The selfsame moment I could pray;
    And from my neck so free
The Albatross fell off, and sank
    Like lead into the sea.

PART V

'O sleep! it is a gentle thing,
    Beloved from pole to pole!
To Mary Queen the praise be given!
    She sent the gentle sleep from Heaven,
That slid into my soul.

The silly buckets on the deck,
    That had so long remained,
I dreamt that they were filled with dew;
    And when I awoke, it rained.

My lips were wet, my throat was cold,
    My garments all were dank;
Sure I had drunken in my dreams,
    And still my body drank.

75

I moved, and could not feel my limbs:
    I was so light—almost
I thought that I had died in sleep,
    And was a blessed ghost.

And soon I heard a roaring wind:
    It did not come anear;
But with its sound it shook the sails,
    That were so thin and sere.

The upper air burst into life;
    And a hundred fire-flags sheen;
To and fro they were hurried about!
    And to and fro, and in and out,
The wan stars danced between.

And the coming wind did roar more loud,
    And the sails did sigh like sedge;
And the rain poured down from one black cloud;
    The Moon was at its edge.

The thick black cloud was cleft, and still
    The Moon was at its side;
Like waters shot from some high crag,
    The lightning fell with never a jag,
A river steep and wide.

The loud wind never reached the ship,
    Yet now the ship moved on!
Beneath the lightning and the Moon
    The dead men gave a groan.

They groaned, they stirred, they all uprose,
    Nor spake, nor moved their eyes;
It had been strange, even in a dream,
    To have seen those dead men rise.

The helmsman steered, the ship moved on;
 Yet never a breeze up-blew;
The mariners all 'gan work the ropes,
 Where they were wont to do;
They raised their limbs like lifeless tools—
 We were a ghastly crew.

The body of my brother's son
 Stood by me, knee to knee:
The body and I pulled at one rope,
 But he said naught to me.'

'I fear thee, ancient Mariner!'
 'Be calm, thou Wedding-Guest!
'Twas not those souls that fled in pain,
 Which to their corses came again,
But a troop of spirits blest:

For when it dawned—they dropped their arms,
 And clustered round the mast;
Sweet sounds rose slowly through their mouths,
 And from their bodies passed.

Around, around, flew each sweet sound,
 Then darted to the Sun;
Slowly the sounds came back again,
 Now mixed, now one by one.

Sometimes a-dropping from the sky
 I heard the skylark sing;
Sometimes all little birds that are,
 How they seemed to fill the sea and air
With their sweet jargoning!

And now 'twas like all instruments,
  Now like a lonely flute;
And now it is an angel's song,
  That makes the Heavens be mute.

It ceased; yet still the sails made on
  A pleasant noise till noon,
A noise like of a hidden brook
  In the leafy month of June,
That to the sleeping woods all night
  Singeth a quiet tune.

Till noon we quietly sailed on,
  Yet never a breeze did breathe:
Slowly and smoothly went the ship,
  Moved onward from beneath.

Under the keel nine fathom deep,
  From the land of mist and snow,
The Spirit slid: and it was he
  That made the ship to go.
The sails at noon left off their tune,
  And the ship stood still also.

The Sun, right up above the mast,
  Had fixed her to the ocean:
But in a minute she 'gan stir,
  With a short uneasy motion—
Backwards and forwards half her length
  With a short uneasy motion.

Then like a pawing horse let go,
  She made a sudden bound:
It flung the blood into my head,
  And I fell down in a swound.

How long in that same fit I lay,
    I have not to declare;
But ere my living life returned,
    I heard, and in my soul discerned
Two voices in the air.

"Is it he?" quoth one, "is this the man?
    By Him who died on cross,
With his cruel bow he laid full low
    The harmless Albatross.

The Spirit who bideth by himself
    In the land of mist and snow,
He loved the bird that loved the man
    Who shot him with his bow."

The other was a softer voice,
    As soft as honey-dew:
Quoth he, "The man hath penance done,
    And penance more will do."

PART VI

First Voice:
"But tell me, tell me! speak again,
    Thy soft response renewing—
What makes that ship drive on so fast?
    What is the Ocean doing?"

Second Voice:
"Still as a slave before his lord,
    The Ocean hath no blast;
His great bright eye most silently
    Up to the Moon is cast—

If he may know which way to go;
    For she guides him smooth or grim.
See, brother, see! how graciously
    She looketh down on him."

"But why drives on that ship so fast,
    Without or wave or wind?"

"The air is cut away before,
    And closes from behind.

Fly, brother, fly! more high, more high!
    Or we shall be belated:
For slow and slow that ship will go,
    When the Mariner's trance is abated."

I woke, and we were sailing on
    As in a gentle weather:
'Twas night, calm night, the Moon was high;
    The dead men stood together.

All stood together on the deck,
    For a charnel-dungeon fitter:
All fixed on me their stony eyes,
    That in the Moon did glitter.

The pang, the curse, with which they died,
    Had never passed away:
I could not draw my eyes from theirs,
    Nor turn them up to pray.

And now this spell was snapt: once more
  I viewed the ocean green,
And looked far forth, yet little saw
  Of what had else been seen—

Like one that on a lonesome road
  Doth walk in fear and dread,
And having once turned round, walks on,
  And turns no more his head;
Because he knows a frightful fiend
  Doth close behind him tread.

But soon there breathed a wind on me
  Nor sound nor motion made:
Its path was not upon the sea,
  In ripple or in shade.

It raised my hair, it fanned my cheek
  Like a meadow-gale of spring—
It mingled strangely with my fears,
  Yet it felt like a welcoming.

Swiftly, swiftly flew the ship,
  Yet she sailed softly too:
Sweetly, sweetly blew the breeze—
  On me alone it blew.

O dream of joy! is this indeed
  The lighthouse top I see?
Is this the hill? is this the kirk?
  Is this mine own countree?

We drifted o'er the harbour-bar,
  And I with sobs did pray—

O let me be awake, my God!
  Or let me sleep alway.

The harbour-bay was clear as glass,
  So smoothly it was strewn!
And on the bay the moonlight lay,
  And the shadow of the Moon.

The rock shone bright, the kirk no less
  That stands above the rock:
The moonlight steeped in silentness
  The steady weathercock.

And the bay was white with silent light
  Till rising from the same,
Full many shapes, that shadows were,
  In crimson colours came.

A little distance from the prow
  Those crimson shadows were:
I turned my eyes upon the deck—
  O Christ! what saw I there!

Each corse lay flat, lifeless and flat,
  And, by the holy rood!
A man all light, a seraph-man,
  On every corse there stood.

This seraph-band, each waved his hand:
  It was a heavenly sight!
They stood as signals to the land,
  Each one a lovely light.

This seraph-band, each waved his hand,
  No voice did they impart—

No voice; but O, the silence sank
   Like music on my heart.

But soon I heard the dash of oars,
   I heard the Pilot's cheer;
My head was turned perforce away,
   And I saw a boat appear.

The Pilot and the Pilot's boy,
   I heard them coming fast:
Dear Lord in Heaven! it was a joy
   The dead men could not blast.

I saw a third—I heard his voice:
   It is the Hermit good!
He singeth loud his godly hymns
   That he makes in the wood.
He'll shrieve my soul, he'll wash away
   The Albatross's blood.

PART VII

'This hermit good lives in that wood
   Which slopes down to the sea.
How loudly his sweet voice he rears!
   He loves to talk with marineres
That come from a far countree.

He kneels at morn, and noon, and eve—
   He hath a cushion plump.
It is the moss that wholly hides
   The rotted old oak-stump.

The skiff-boat neared: I heard them talk,
   "Why, this is strange, I trow!
Where are those lights so many and fair,
   That signal made but now?"

"Strange, by my faith!" the Hermit said—
    "And they answered not our cheer!
The planks look warped! and see those sails
    How thin they are and sere!
I never saw aught like to them,
    Unless perchance it were

Brown skeletons of leaves that lag
    My forest-brook along;
When the ivy-tod is heavy with snow,
    And the owlet whoops to the wolf below,
That eats the she-wolf's young."

"Dear Lord! it hath a fiendish look—
    (The Pilot made reply)
I am a-feared."—"Push on, push on!"
    Said the Hermit cheerily.

The boat came closer to the ship,
    But I nor spake nor stirred;
The boat came close beneath the ship,
    And straight a sound was heard.

Under the water it rumbled on
    Still louder and more dread:
It reached the ship, it split the bay;
    The ship went down like lead.

Stunned by that loud and dreadful sound,
    Which sky and ocean smote,
Like one that hath been seven days drowned
    My body lay afloat;
But swift as dreams, myself I found
    Within the Pilot's boat.

Upon the whirl, where sank the ship,
　　The boat spun round and round;
And all was still, save that the hill
　　Was telling of the sound.

I moved my lips—the Pilot shriek'd
　　And fell down in a fit;
The holy Hermit raised his eyes,
　　And prayed where he did sit.

I took the oars: the Pilot's boy,
　　Who now doth crazy go,
Laughed loud and long, and all the while
　　His eyes went to and fro.
"Ha! ha!" quoth he, "full plain I see
　　The Devil knows how to row."

And now, all in my own countree,
　　I stood on the firm land!
The Hermit stepped forth from the boat,
　　And scarcely he could stand.

"O shrieve me, shrieve me, holy man!"
　　The Hermit crossed his brow.
"Say quick," quoth he, "I bid thee say—
　　What manner of man art thou?"

Forthwith this frame of mine was wrenched
　　With a woful agony
Which forced me to begin my tale;
　　And then it left me free.

Since then, at an uncertain hour,
　　That agony returns:

And till my ghastly tale is told,
   This heart within me burns.

I pass, like night, from land to land;
   I have strange power of speech;
That moment that his face I see,
   I know the man that must hear me:
To him my tale I teach.

What loud uproar bursts from that door!
   The wedding-guests are there:
But in the garden-bower the bride
   And bride-maids singing are:
And hark, the little vesper bell,
   Which biddeth me to prayer!

O Wedding-Guest! this soul hath been
   Alone on a wide, wide sea:
So lonely 'twas, that God Himself
   Scarce seemed there to be.

O sweeter than the marriage-feast,
   'Tis sweeter far to me,
To walk together to the kirk
   With a goodly company!—

To walk together to the kirk,
   And all together pray
While each to his great Father bends,
   Old men, and babes, and loving friends,
And youths and maidens gay!

Farewell, farewell! but this I tell
   To thee, thou Wedding-Guest!

He prayeth well, who loveth well
 Both man and bird and beast.

He prayeth best, who loveth best
 All things both great and small;
For the dear God who loveth us,
 He made and loveth all.'

The Mariner, whose eye is bright,
 Whose beard with age is hoar,
Is gone: and now the Wedding-Guest
 Turned from the bridegroom's door.

He went like one that hath been stunn'd,
 And is of sense forlorn:
A sadder and a wiser man
 He rose the morrow morn.
SAMUEL TAYLOR COLERIDGE

Prayer for Shut-ins

Because, dear Lord, their way is rough and steep,
And some are sore perplexed, and some do weep,
We come to ask that Thou wilt show the way
And give Thy rod and staff to be their stay.

Especially, dear Lord, for these we ask,
Who have not strength to meet their task;
And for all weary on the road
Please give fresh courage, ease their load.
RUTH WINANT WHEELER

CONSEQUENCES

The Road Not Taken

Two roads diverged in a yellow wood,
And sorry I could not travel both
And be one traveler, long I stood
And looked down one as far as I could
To where it bent in the undergrowth;

Then took the other, as just as fair,
And having perhaps the better claim,
Because it was grassy and wanted wear;
Though as for that the passing there
Had worn them really about the same,

And both that morning equally lay
In leaves no step had trodden black.
Oh, I kept the first for another day!
Yet knowing how way leads on to way,
I doubted if I should ever come back.

I shall be telling this with a sigh
Somewhere ages and ages hence:
Two roads diverged in a wood, and I—
I took the one less traveled by,
And that has made all the difference.

ROBERT FROST

You Never Can Tell

You never can tell when you send a word
   Like an arrow shot from a bow
By an archer blind, be it cruel or kind,
   Just where it may chance to go.
It may pierce the breast of your dearest friend,
   Tipped with its poison or balm,
To a stranger's heart in life's great mart
   It may carry its pain or its calm.

ELLA WHEELER WILCOX

COURAGE

It Can be Done

The man who misses all the fun
Is he who says, "It can't be done."
In solemn pride he stands aloof
And greets each venture with reproof.
Had he the power he'd efface
The history of the human race;
We'd have no radio or motor cars,
No streets lit by electric stars;
No telegraph nor telephone,
We'd linger in the age of stone.
The world would sleep if things were run
By men who say, "It can't be done."

AUTHOR UNKNOWN

Invictus

Out of the night that covers me,
   Black as the Pit from pole to pole,
I thank whatever gods may be
   For my unconquerable soul.

In the fell clutch of circumstance
   I have not winced nor cried aloud.
Under the bludgeonings of chance
   My head is bloody, but unbowed.

Beyond this place of wrath and tears
   Looms but the horror of the shade,
And yet the menace of the years
   Finds, and shall find me, unafraid.

It matters not how strait the gate,
   How charged with punishments the scroll,
I am the master of my fate:
   I am the captain of my soul.

               WILLIAM ERNEST HENLEY

Defeat

No one is beat till he quits,
   No one is through till he stops,
No matter how hard Failure hits,
   No matter how often he drops,
A fellow's not down till he lies
In the dust and refuses to rise.

Fate can slam him and bang him around,
   And batter his frame till he's sore,
But she never can say that he's downed
   While he bobs up serenely for more.
A fellow's not dead till he dies,
Nor beat till no longer he tries.

               EDGAR GUEST

You Mustn't Quit

When things go wrong, as they sometimes will,
When the road you're trudging seems all uphill,
When the funds are low and the debts are high
And you want to smile, but you have to sigh,
When care is pressing you down a bit,
Rest! if you must—but never quit.

Life is queer, with its twists and turns,
As every one of us sometimes learns,
And many a failure turns about
When he might have won if he'd stuck it out;
Stick to your task, though the pace seems slow—
You may succeed with one more blow.

Success is failure turned inside out—
The silver tint of the clouds of doubt—
And you never can tell how close you are,
It may be near when it seems afar;
So stick to the fight when you're hardest hit—
It's when things seem worst that YOU MUSTN'T QUIT.

AUTHOR UNKNOWN

If—

If you can keep your head when all about you
    Are losing theirs and blaming it on you;
If you can trust yourself when all men doubt you,
    But make allowance for their doubting too;

If you can wait and not be tired by waiting,
   Or, being lied about, don't deal in lies,
Or, being hated, don't give way to hating,
   And yet don't look too good, nor talk too wise;

If you can dream—and not make dreams your
      master;
If you can think—and not make thoughts your
      aim;
If you can meet with triumph and disaster
   And treat those two impostors just the same;
If you can bear to hear the truth you've spoken
   Twisted by knaves to make a trap for fools,
Or watch the things you gave your life to broken,
   And stoop and build 'em up with worn out tools;

If you can make one heap of all your winnings
   And risk it on one turn of pitch-and-toss,
And lose, and start again at your beginnings
   And never breathe a word about your loss;
If you can force your heart and nerve and sinew
   To serve your turn long after they are gone,
And so hold on when there is nothing in you
   Except the Will which says to them: "Hold on!"

If you can talk with crowds and keep your virtue,
   Or walk with kings—nor lose the common touch;
If neither foes nor loving friends can hurt you;
   If all men count with you, but none too much;
If you can fill the unforgiving minute
   With sixty seconds' worth of distance run—
Yours is the Earth and everything that's in it,
   And—which is more—you'll be a Man, my son!

RUDYARD KIPLING

Curfew Must Not Ring Tonight

Slowly England's sun was setting o'er the hilltops far
    away,
Filling all the land with beauty at the close of one sad
    day;
And the last rays kissed the forehead of a man and a
    maiden fair,
He with footsteps slow and weary, she with sunny
    floating hair;
He with bowed head, sad and thoughtful, she with
    lips all cold and white,
Struggling to keep back the murmur, "Curfew must
    not ring tonight!"

"Sexton," Bessie's white lips faltered, pointing to the
    prison old,
With its turrets tall and gloomy, with its walls, dark,
    damp and cold—
"I've a lover in the prison, doomed this very night to
    die
At the ringing of the curfew, and no earthly help is
    nigh!
Cromwell will not come till sunset"; and her face
    grew strangely white
As she breathed the husky whisper, "Curfew must not
    ring tonight!"

"Bessie," calmly spoke the sexton—and his accents
    pierced her heart
Like the piercing of an arrow, like a deadly poisoned
    dart—

"Long, long years I've rung the curfew from that
     gloomy, shadowed tower;
Every evening, just at sunset, it has told the twilight
     hour;
I have done my duty ever, tried to do it just and
     right—
Now I'm old I still must do it: Curfew, girl, must ring
     tonight!"

Wild her eyes and pale her features, stern and white
     her thoughtful brow,
And within her secret bosom Bessie made a solemn
     vow.
She had listened while the judges read, without a tear
     or sigh,
"At the ringing of the curfew, Basil Underwood must
     die."
And her breath came fast and faster, and her eyes grew
     large and bright,
As in undertone she murmured, "Curfew must not
     ring tonight!"

With quick step she bounded forward, sprang within
     the old church door,
Left the old man threading slowly paths he'd often
     trod before;
Not one moment paused the maiden, but with eye and
     cheek aglow
Mounted up the gloomy tower, where the bell swung
     to and fro
As she climbed the dusty ladder, on which fell no ray
     of light,
Up and up, her white lips saying, "Curfew shall not
     ring tonight!"

She has reached the topmost ladder, o'er her hangs
  the great dark bell:
Awful is the gloom beneath her, like the pathway
  down to hell!
Lo, the ponderous tongue is swinging.
  'Tis the hour of curfew now,
And the sight has chilled her bosom, stopped her
  breath and paled her brow;
Shall she let it ring? No, never! Flash her eyes with
  sudden light,
And she springs and grasps it firmly:
  "Curfew shall not ring tonight!"

Out she swung, far out; the city seemed a speck of
  light below;
She 'twixt heaven and earth suspended as the bell
  swung to and fro;
And the sexton at the bell rope, old and deaf, heard
  not the bell,
But he thought it still was ringing fair young Basil's
  funeral knell.
Still the maiden clung more firmly, and, with trem-
  bling lips and white,
Said, to hush her heart's wild beating, "Curfew shall
  not ring tonight!"

It was o'er; the bell ceased swaying, and the maiden
  stepped once more
Firmly on the dark old ladder, where for hundred
  years before
Human foot had not been planted; but the brave deed
  she had done
Should be told long ages after—often as the setting
  sun

Should illume the sky with beauty, aged sires, with
    heads of white,
Long should tell the little children, "Curfew did not
    ring that night."

O'er the distant hills came Cromwell; Bessie sees him,
    and her brow,
Full of hope and full of gladness, has no anxious
    traces now.
At his feet she tells her story, shows her hands all
    bruised and torn;
And her face so sweet and pleading, yet with sorrow
    pale and worn,
Touched his heart with sudden pity—lit his eye with
    misty light;
"Go, your lover lives!" said Cromwell; "Curfew shall
    not ring tonight!"

Wide they flung the massive portals, led the prisoner
    forth to die,
All his bright young life before him. 'Neath the
    darkening English sky
Bessie came with flying footsteps, eyes aglow with
    love-light sweet;
Kneeling on the turf beside him, laid a pardon at his
    feet.
In his brave, strong arms he clasped her, kissed the
    face upturned and white,
Whispered, "Darling, you have saved me; curfew will
    not ring tonight."

ROSE HARTWICK THORPE

The Hell-Gate of Soissons

My name is Darino, the poet. You have heard?
 Oui, Comédie Française.
Perchance it has happened, *mon ami,* you know of
 my unworthy lays.
Ah, then you must guess how my fingers are itching
 to talk to a pen;
For I was at Soissons, and saw it, the death of the
 twelve Englishmen.

My leg, *malheureusement,* I left it behind on the
 banks of the Aisne.
Regret? I would pay with the other to witness their
 valor again.
A trifle, indeed, I assure you, to give for the honor to
 tell
How that handful of British, undaunted, went into the
 Gateway of Hell.

Let me draw you a plan of the battle. Here we French
 and your Engineers stood;
 Over there a detachment of German sharpshooters lay
 hid in a wood.
A *mitrailleuse* battery planted on top of this well-
 chosen ridge
Held the road for the Prussians and covered the direct
 approach to the bridge.

It was madness to dare the dense murder that spewed
 from those ghastly machines.
(Only those who have danced to its music can know
 what the *mitrailleuse* means.)

But the bridge on the Aisne was a menace; our safety
     demanded its fall:
"Engineers—volunteers!" In a body, the Royals stood
     out at the call.

Death at best was the fate of that mission—to their
     glory not one was dismayed.
A party was chosen—and seven survived till the
     powder was laid.
And *they* died with their fuses unlighted. Another
     detachment! Again
A sortie is made—all too vainly. The bridge still
     commanded the Aisne.

We were fighting two foes—Time and Prussia—the
     moments were worth more than troops.
We *must* blow up the bridge. A lone soldier darts out
     from the Royals and swoops
For the fuse! Fate seems with us. We cheer him; he
     answers—our hopes are reborn!
A ball rips his visor—his khaki shows red where
     another has torn.

Will he live—will he last—will he make it? *Hélas!*
     And so near to the goal!
A second, he dies! Then a third one! A fourth! Still the
     Germans take toll!
A fifth, *magnifique!* It is magic! How does he escape
     them? He may . . .
Yes, he *does!* See, the match flares! A rifle rings out
     from the wood and says "Nay!"

Six, seven, eight, nine take their places; six, seven,
     eight, nine brave their hail:

Six, seven, eight, nine—how we count them! But the
    sixth, seventh, eighth, and ninth fail!
A tenth! *Sacré nom!* But these English are soldiers—
    they know how to try;
(He fumbles the place where his jaw was)—they
    show, too, how heroes can die.

Ten we count—ten who ventured unquailing—ten
    there were—and ten are no more!
Yet another salutes and superbly essays where the ten
    failed before.
God of Battles, look down and protect him! Lord, his
    heart is as Thine—let him live!
But the *mitrailleuse* splutters and stutters, and riddles
    him into a sieve.

Then I thought of my sins, and sat waiting the charge
    that we could not withstand.
And I thought of my beautiful Paris, and gave a
    last look at the land,
At France, my *belle France,* in her glory of blue sky
    and green field and wood.
Death with honor, but never surrender. And to die
    with such men—it was good.

They are forming—the bugles are blaring—they will
    cross in a moment and then—
When out of the line of the Royals (your island, *mon
    ami,* breeds men)
Bursts a private, a tawny-haired giant—it was
    hopeless, but *ciel* how he ran!
Bon Dieu please remember the pattern, and make
    many more on his plan!

No cheers from our ranks, and the Germans, they
    halted in wonderment, too;
See, he reaches the bridge; ah! he lights it! I am
    dreaming, it *cannot* be true.
Screams of rage! *Fusillade!* They have killed him! Too
    late though, the good work is done.
By the valor of twelve English martyrs, the Hell-Gate
    of Soissons is won!

HERBERT KAUFMAN

Horatius

Lars Porsena of Clusium
    By the Nine Gods he swore
That the great house of Tarquin
    Should suffer wrong no more.
By the Nine Gods he swore it,
    And named a trysting day,
And bade his messengers ride forth,
East and west and south and north,
    To summon his array.

East and west and south and north
    The messengers ride fast,
And tower and town and cottage
    Have heard the trumpet's blast.
Shame on the false Etruscan
    Who lingers in his home
When Porsena of Clusium
    Is on the march for Rome.

And now hath every city
   Sent up her tale of men;
The foot are fourscore thousand,
   The horse are thousands ten.
Before the gates of Sutirum
   Is met the great array.
A proud man was Lars Porsena
   Upon the trysting day.

Now from the rock Tarpeian,
   Could the wan burghers spy
The line of blazing villages
   Red in the midnight sky.
The fathers of the City,
   They sat all night and day,
For every hour some horseman came
   With tidings of dismay.

I wis, in all the Senate,
   There was no heart so bold,
But sore it ached, and fast it beat,
   When that ill news was told.
Forthwith up rose the Consul,
   Up rose the Fathers all;
In haste they girded up their gowns,
   And hied them to the wall.

They held a council standing
   Before the River-gate;
Short time was there, ye well may guess,
   For musing or debate.
Out spake the Consul roundly:
   "The bridge must straight go down;
For, since Janiculum is lost,
   Naught else can save the town."

Just then a scout came flying,
    All wild with haste and fear:
"To arms! to arms! Sir Consul;
    Lars Porsena is here."
On the low hills to westward
    The Consul fixed his eye,
And saw the swarthy storm of dust
    Rise fast along the sky.

And the Consul's brow was sad,
    And the Consul's speech was low,
And darkly looked he at the wall,
    And darkly at the foe.
"Their van will be upon us
    Before the bridge goes down;
And if they once may win the bridge,
    What hope to save the town?"

Then out spake brave Horatius,
    The Captain of the gate:
"To every man upon this earth
    Death cometh soon or late.
And how can man die better
    Than facing fearful odds,
For the ashes of his fathers
    And the temples of his Gods!

"Hew down the bridge, Sir Consul,
    With all the speed ye may;
I, with two more to help me,
    Will hold the foe in play.
In yon strait path a thousand
    May well be stopped by three.
Now who will stand on either hand,
    And keep the bridge with me?"

Then out spake Spurius Lartius;
    A Ramnian proud was he:
"Lo, I will stand at thy right hand,
    And keep the bridge with thee."
And out spake strong Herminius;
    Of Titan blood was he:
"I will abide on thy left side,
    And keep the bridge with thee."

Now while the Three were tightening
    Their harness on their backs,
The Consul was the foremost man
    To take in hand an axe:
And Fathers mixed with Commons
    Seized hatchet, bar, and crow,
And smote upon the planks above,
    And loosed the props below.

The Three stood calm and silent
    And looked upon the foes,
And a great shout of laughter
    From all the vanguard rose:
And forth three chiefs came spurring
    Before that deep array;
To earth they sprang, their swords they drew,
And lifted high their shields, and flew
    To win the narrow way;

Aunus from green Tifernum,
    Lord of the Hill of Vines;
And Seius, whose eight hundred slaves
    Sicken in Ilva's mines;
And Picus, long to Clusium
    Vassal in peace and war,

Who led to fight his Umbrian powers
From that gray crag where, girt with towers,
The fortress of Nequinum lowers
   O'er the pale waves of Nar.

Stout Lartius hurled down Aunus
   Into the stream beneath:
Herminius struck at Seius,
   And clove him to the teeth:
At Picus brave Horatius
   Darted one fiery thrust;
And the proud Umbrian's gilded arms
   Clashed in the bloody dust.

Then Ocnus of Falerii
   Rushed on the Roman Three;
And Lausulus of Urgo,
   The rover of the sea;
And Aruns of Volsinium,
   Who slew the great wild boar,
The great wild boar that had his den
Amidst the reeds of Cosa's fen,
And wasted fields, and slaughtered men,
   Along Albinia's shore.

Herminius smote down Aruns:
   Lartius laid Ocnus low:
Right to the heart of Lausulus
   Horatius sent a blow.
"Lie there," he cried, "fell pirate!
   No more, aghast and pale,
From Ostia's walls the crowd shall mark
The track of thy destroying bark.

No more Campania's hinds shall fly
To woods and caverns when they spy
   Thy thrice accursed sail."

But now no sound of laughter
   Was heard among the foes.
A wild and wrathful clamor
   From all the vanguard rose.
Six spears' lengths from the entrance
   Halted that deep array,
And for a space no man came forth
   To win the narrow way.

But hark! the cry is Astur:
   And lo! the ranks divide;
And the great Lord of Luna
   Comes with his stately stride.
Upon his ample shoulders
   Clangs loud the four-fold shield,
And in his hand he shakes the brand
   Which none but he can wield.

He smiled on those bold Romans
   A smile serene and high;
He eyed the flinching Tuscans,
   And scorn was in his eye.
Quoth he, "The she-wolf's litter
   Stand savagely at bay:
But will ye dare to follow,
   If Astur clears the way?"

Then, whirling up his broadsword
   With both hands to the height,
He rushed against Horatius,
   And smote with all his might.

With shield and blade Horatius
　　Right deftly turned the blow.
The blow, though turned, came yet too nigh;
It missed his helm, but gashed his thigh:
The Tuscans raised a joyful cry
　　To see the red blood flow.

He reeled, and on Herminius
　　He leaned one breathing-space;
Then, like a wild cat mad with wounds,
　　Sprang right at Astur's face.
Through teeth, and skull, and helmet,
　　So fierce a thrust he sped,
The good sword stood a hand-breadth out
　　Behind the Tuscan's head.

And the great Lord of Luna
　　Fell at that deadly stroke,
As falls on Mount Alvernus
　　A thunder-smitten oak.
Far o'er the crashing forest
　　The giant arms lie spread;
And the pale augurs, muttering low,
　　Gaze on the blasted head.

On Astur's throat Horatius
　　Right firmly pressed his heels,
And thrice and four times tugged amain,
　　Ere he wrenched out the steel.
"And see," he cried, "the welcome,
　　Fair guests, that waits you here!
What noble Lucomo comes next,
　　To taste our Roman cheer?"

But at this haughty challenge
   A sullen murmur ran,
Mingled of wrath, and shame, and dread,
   Along that glittering van.
There lacked not men of prowess,
   Nor men of lordly race;
For all Etruria's noblest
   Were round the fatal place.

Was none who would be foremost
   To lead such dire attack;
But those behind cried "Forward!"
   And those before cried "Back!"
And backward now and forward
   Wavers the deep array;
And on the tossing sea of steel,
To and fro the standards reel;
And the victorious trumpet-peal
   Dies fitfully away.

But meanwhile axe and lever
   Have manfully been plied,
And now the bridge hangs tottering
   Above the boiling tide.
"Come back, come back, Horatius!"
   Loud cried the Fathers all.
"Back, Lartius! back, Herminius!
   Back, ere the ruin fall!"

Back darted Spurius Lartius;
   Herminius darted back:
And, as they passed, beneath their feet
   They felt the timbers crack.

But when they turned their faces,
    And on the farther shore
Saw brave Horatius stand alone,
    They would have crossed once more.

Alone stood brave Horatius,
    But constant still in mind;
Thrice thirty thousand foes before,
    And the broad flood behind.
"Down with him!" cried false Sextus,
    With a smile on his pale face.
"Now yield thee," cried Lars Porsena,
    "Now yield thee to our grace."

Round turned he, as not deigning
    Those craven ranks to see;
Naught spake he to Lars Porsena,
    To Sextus naught spake he:
But he saw on Palatinus
    The white porch of his home;
And he spake to the noble river
    That rolls by the towers of Rome.

"Oh, Tiber! Father Tiber!
    To whom the Romans pray,
A Roman's life, a Roman's arms,
    Take thou in charge this day!"
So he spake, and speaking sheathed
    The good sword by his side,
And with his harness on his back,
    Plunged headlong in the tide.

No sound of joy or sorrow
　　Was heard from either bank;
But friends and foes in dumb surprise,
With parted lips and straining eyes,
　　Stood gazing where he sank;
And when above the surges
　　They saw his crest appear,
All Rome sent forth a rapturous cry,
And even the ranks of Tuscany
　　Could scarce forbear to cheer.

But fiercely ran the current,
　　Swollen high by months of rain:
And fast his blood was flowing;
　　And he was sore in pain,
And heavy with his armor,
　　And spent with changing blows:
And oft they thought him sinking,
　　But still again he rose.

Never, I ween, did swimmer,
　　In such an evil case,
Struggle through such a raging flood
　　Safe to the landing-place:
But his limbs were borne up bravely
　　By the brave heart within,
And our good Father Tiber
　　Bore bravely up his chin.

"Curse on him!" quoth false Sextus:
　　"Will not the villain drown?
But for this stay, ere close of day
　　We should have sacked the town!"

"Heaven help him!" quoth Lars Porsena,
  "And bring him safe to shore;
For such a gallant feat of arms
  Was never seen before."

And now he feels the bottom;
  Now on dry earth he stands;
Now round him throng the Fathers
  To press his gory hands;
And now, with shouts and clapping,
  And noise of weeping loud,
He enters through the River-gate,
  Borne by the joyous crowd.

They gave him of the corn-land
  That was of public right
As much as two strong oxen
  Could plough from morn till night;
And they made a molten image,
  And set it up on high,
And there it stands unto this day
  To witness if I lie.

It stands in the Comitium,
  Plain for all folk to see;
Horatius in his harness,
  Halting upon one knee:
And underneath is written,
  In letters all of gold,
How valiantly he kept the bridge
  In the brave days of old.

                    THOMAS BABINGTON MACAULAY

CREED

At Set of Sun

If you sit down at set of sun
And count the acts that you have done,
   And, counting, find
One self-denying deed, one word
That eased the heart of him who heard,
   One glance most kind
That fell like sunshine where it went—
Then you may count that day well spent.

But if, through all the livelong day,
You've cheered no heart, by yea or nay—
   If, through it all
You've nothing done that you can trace
That brought the sunshine to one face—
   No act most small
That helped some soul and nothing cost—
Then count that day as worse than lost.

GEORGE ELIOT

For This Is Wisdom

For this is Wisdom; to love, to live,
To take what Fate, or the Gods, may give,
To ask no question, to make no prayer,
To kiss the lips and caress the hair,
Speed passion's ebb as you greet its flow,—
To have,—to hold,—and,—in time,—let go!

LAURENCE HOPE

Perseverance

If a task is once begun
Never leave it till it's done.
Be the labor great or small,
Do it well or not at all.

AUTHOR UNKNOWN

John Wesley's Rule

Do all the good you can,
By all the means you can,
In all the ways you can,
In all the places you can,
At all the times you can,
To all the people you can,
As long as ever you can.

ELLA WHEELER WILCOX

With Every Rising of the Sun

With every rising of the sun
Think of your life as just begun.

The past has shrived and buried deep
All yesterdays—there let them sleep . . . .

Concern yourself with but today,
Woo it and teach it to obey,

Your wish and will. Since time began
Today has been the friend of man . . . .

You and today! a soul sublime
And the great pregnant hour of time.

With God between to bind the twain—
Go forth I say—attain—attain.

ELLA WHEELER WILCOX

DISILLUSIONMENT

Pity Me Not

Pity me not because the light of day
At close of day no longer walks the sky;
Pity me not for beauties passed away
From field and thicket as the year goes by;
Pity me not the waning of the moon,
Nor that the ebbing tide goes out to sea,
Nor that a man's desire is hushed so soon,
And you no longer look with love on me.
This have I known always: Love is no more
Than the wide blossom which the wind assails,
Than the great tide that treads the shifting shore,
Strewing fresh wreckage gathered in the gales;
Pity me that the heart is slow to learn
What the swift mind beholds at every turn.

EDNA ST. VINCENT MILLAY

ELEGY

The Martyr

*Indicative of the Passion of the People
on the 15th of April 1865*

Good Friday was the day
  Of the prodigy and crime,
When they killed him in his pity,
  When they killed him in his prime
Of clemency and calm—
    When with yearning he was filled
    To redeem the evil-willed,
And, though conqueror, be kind;
  But they killed him in his kindness,
  In their madness and their blindness,
And they killed him from behind.

There is sobbing of the strong,
  And a pall upon the land;
But the People in their weeping
    Bare the iron hand:
Beware the People weeping
  When they bare the iron hand.

He lieth in his blood—
  The father in his face;
They have killed him, the Forgiver—
  The Avenger takes his place,
The Avenger wisely stern,
    Who in righteousness shall do
    What the heavens call him to,
And the parricides remand;

For they killed him in his kindness,
   In their madness and their blindness,
And his blood is on their hand.

There is sobbing of the strong,
   And a pall upon the land;
But the People in their weeping
   Bare the iron hand:
Beware the People weeping
   When they bare the iron hand.

HERMAN MELVILLE

To an Athlete Dying Young

The time you won your town the race
We chaired you through the market-place;
Man and boy stood cheering by,
And home we brought you shoulder-high.

Today, the road all runners come,
Shoulder-high we bring you home,
And set you at your threshold down,
Townsman of a stiller town.

Smart lad, to slip betimes away
From fields where glory does not stay,
And early though the laurel grows
It withers quicker than the rose.

Eyes the shady night has shut
Cannot see the record cut,
And silence sounds no worse than cheers
After death has stopped the ears:

Now you will not swell the rout
Of lads that wore their honors out,
Runners whom renown outran
And the name died before the man.

So set, before its echoes fade,
The fleet foot on the sill of shade,
And hold to the low lintel up
The still-defended challenge-cup.

And round that early-laureled head
Will flock to gaze the strengthless dead,
And find unwithered on its curls
The garland briefer than a girl's.

A. E. HOUSMAN

When Lilacs Last in the Dooryard Bloomed

1

When lilacs last in the dooryard bloomed,
And the great star early drooped in the western sky in the
   night,
I mourned, and yet shall mourn with ever-returning spring.

Ever-returning spring, trinity sure to me you bring,
Lilac blooming perennial and drooping star in the west,
And thought of him I love.

2

O powerful western fallen star!
O shades of night—O moody, tearful night!
O great star disappeared—O the black murk that hides the
   star!
O cruel hands that hold me powerless—O helpless soul of
   me!
O harsh surrounding cloud that will not free my soul.

3

In the dooryard fronting an old farmhouse near the white-
   washed palings,
Stands the lilac bush tall-growing with heart-shaped leaves
   of rich green,
With many a pointed blossom rising delicate, with the per-
   fume strong I love,
With every leaf a miracle—and from this bush in the door-
   yard,
With delicate-colored blossoms and heart-shaped leaves of
   rich green,
A sprig with its flower I break.

4

In the swamp in secluded recesses,
A shy and hidden bird is warbling a song.

Solitary the thrush,
The hermit withdrawn to himself, avoiding the settle-
   ments,
Sings by himself a song.

Song of the bleeding throat,
Death's outlet song of life (for well dear brother I know,
If thou wast not granted to sing thou wouldst surely die).

5

Over the breast of the spring, the land, amid cities,
Amid lanes and through old woods, where lately the violets
   peeped from the ground, spotting the gray debris,
Amid the grass in the fields each side of the lanes, passing
   the endless grass,
Passing the yellow-speared wheat, every grain from its
   shroud in the dark-brown fields uprisen,
Passing the apple-tree blows of white and pink in the
   orchards,
Carrying a corpse to where it shall rest in the grave,
Night and day journeys a coffin.

6

Coffin that passes through lanes and streets,
Through day and night with the great cloud darkening the
   land,
With the pomp of the inlooped flags with the cities draped
   in black,
With the show of the States themselves as of crape-veiled
   women standing,
With processions long and winding and the flambeaus of
   the night,
With the countless torches lit, with the silent sea of faces
   and the unbared heads,
With the waiting depot, the arriving coffin, and the somber
   faces,
With dirges through the night, with the thousand voices
   rising strong and solemn,

With all the mournful voices of the dirges poured around
　　the coffin,
The dim-lit churches and the shuddering organs—where
　　amid these you journey,
With the tolling tolling bells' perpetual clang,
Here, coffin that slowly passes,
I give you my sprig of lilac.

7

(Nor for you, for one alone,
Blossoms and branches green to coffins all I bring,
For fresh as the morning, thus would I chant a song for you
　　O sane and sacred death,
All over bouquets of roses,
O death, I cover you over with roses and early lilies,
But mostly and now the lilac that blooms the first,
Copious I break, I break the sprigs from the bushes,
With loaded arms I come, pouring for you,
For you and the coffins all of you O death.)

8

O western orb sailing the heaven,
Now I know what you must have meant as a month since I
　　walked,
As I walked in silence the transparent shadowy night,
As I saw you had something to tell as you bent to me night
　　after night,
As you drooped from the sky low down as if to my side
　　(while the other stars all looked on),
As we wandered together the solemn night (for something
　　I know not what kept me from sleep),
As the night advanced, and I saw on the rim of the west
　　how full you were of woe,

As I stood on the rising ground in the breeze in the cool
    transparent night,
As I watched where you passed and was lost in the nether-
    ward black of the night,
As my soul in its trouble dissatisfied sank, as where you sad
    orb,
Concluded, dropped in the night, and was gone.

9

Sing on there in the swamp,
O singer bashful and tender, I hear your notes, I hear your
    call,
I hear, I come presently, I understand you,
But a moment I linger, for the lustrous star has detained
    me,
The star my departing comrade holds and detains me.

10

O how shall I warble myself for the dead one there I loved?
And how shall I deck my song for the large sweet soul that
    has gone?
And what shall my perfume be for the grave of him I love?
Sea winds blown from east and west,
Blown from the Eastern sea and blown from the Western
    sea, till there on the prairies meeting,
These and with these and the breath of my chant,
I perfume the grave of him I love.

11

O what shall I hang on the chamber walls?
And what shall the pictures be that I hang on the walls,
To adorn the burial house of him I love?
Pictures of growing spring and farms and homes,

With the Fourth-month eve at sundown, and the gray
smoke lucid and bright,
With floods of the yellow gold of the gorgeous, indolent,
sinking sun, burning, expanding the air
With the fresh sweet herbage underfoot, and the pale green
leaves of the trees prolific,
In the distance the flowing glaze, the breast of the river,
with a wind dapple here and there,
With ranging hills on the banks, with many a line against
the sky, and shadows,
And the city at hand with dwellings so dense, and stacks of
chimneys,
And all the scenes of life and the workshops, and the work-
men homeward returning.

12

Lo, body and soul—this land,
My own Manhattan with spires, and the sparkling and
hurrying tides, and the ships,
The varied and ample land, the South and the North in the
light, Ohio's shores and flashing Missouri,
And ever the far-spreading prairies covered with grass and
corn.
Lo, the most excellent sun so calm and haughty,
The violet and purple morn with just-felt breezes,
The gentle soft-born measureless light,
The miracle spreading bathing all, the fulfilled moon,
The coming eve delicious, the welcome night and the stars,
Over my cities shining all, enveloping man and land.

13

Sing on, sing on you gray-brown bird,
Sing from the swamps, the recesses, pour your chant from
the bushes,

Limitless out of the dusk, out of the cedars and pines.
Sing on dearest brother, warble your reedy song,
Loud human song, with voice of uttermost woe.
O liquid and free and tender!
O wild and loose to my soul—O wondrous singer!
You only I hear—yet the star holds me (but will soon depart),
Yet the lilac with mastering odor holds me.

14

Now while I sat in the day and looked forth,
In the close of the day with its light and the fields of spring,
and the farmers preparing their crops,
In the large unconscious scenery of my land with its lakes
and forests,
In the heavenly aerial beauty (after the perturbed winds
and the storms),
Under the arching heavens of the afternoon swift passing,
and the voices of children and women,
The many-moving sea tides, and I saw the ships how they
sailed,
And the summer approaching with richness, and the fields
all busy with labor,
And the infinite separate houses, how they all went on,
each with its meals and minutia of daily usages,
And the streets how their throbbings throbbed, and the
cities pent—lo, then and there,
Falling upon them all and among them all, enveloping me
with the rest,
Appeared the cloud, appeared the long black trail,
And I knew death, its thought, and the sacred knowledge of
death.

Then with the knowledge of death as walking one side of
me,

And the thought of death close-walking the other side of
    me,
And I in the middle as with companions, and as holding the
    hands of companions,
I fled forth to the hiding receiving night that talks not,
Down to the shores of the water the path by the swamp in
    the dimness,
To the solemn shadowy cedars and ghostly pines so still.

And the singer so shy to the rest received me,
The gray-brown bird I know received us comrades three,
And he sang the carol of death, and a verse for him I love.

From deep secluded recesses
From the fragrant cedars and the ghostly pines so still,
Came the carol of the bird.

And the charm of the carol rapt me,
As I held as if by their hands my comrades in the night,
And the voice of my spirit tallied the song of the bird.

Come lovely and soothing death,
Undulate round the world, serenely arriving, arriving,
In the day, in the night, to all, to each,
Sooner or later delicate death.

Praised be the fathomless universe,
For life and joy, and for objects and knowledge curious,
And for love, sweet love—but praise! praise! praise!
For the sure-enwinding arms of cool-enfolding death.

Dark mother always gliding near with soft feet,
Have none chanted for thee a chant of fullest welcome?
Then I chant it for thee, I glorify thee above all,

I bring thee a song that when thou must indeed come, come
  unfalteringly.

Approach strong deliveress,
When it is so, when thou hast taken them I joyously sing the dead,
Lost in the loving floating ocean of thee,
Laved in the flood of thy bliss O death.

From me to thee glad serenades,
Dances for thee I propose saluting thee, adornments and feastings
  for thee,
And the sights of the open landscape and the high-spread sky are
  fitting,
And life and the fields, and the huge and thoughtful night.

The night in silence under many a star,
The ocean shore and the husky whispering wave whose voice I know,
And the soul turning to thee O vast and well-veiled death,
And the body gratefully nestling close to thee.

Over the treetops I float thee a song,
Over the rising and sinking waves, over the myriad fields and the
  prairies wide,
Over the dense-packed cities all and the teeming wharves and ways,
I float this carol with joy, with joy to thee O death.

15

To the tally of my soul,
Loud and strong kept up the gray-brown bird,
With pure deliberate notes spreading filling the night.

Loud in the pines and cedars dim,
Clear in the freshness moist and the swamp perfume,
And I with my comrades there in the night.

While my sight that was bound in my eyes unclosed,
As to long panoramas of visions.

And I saw askant the armies,
I saw as in noiseless dreams hundreds of battle flags,
Borne through the smoke of the battles and pierced with
    missiles I saw them,
And carried hither and yon through the smoke, and torn
    and bloody,
And at last but a few shreds left on the staffs (and all in
    silence),
And the staffs all splintered and broken.

I saw battle corpses, myriads of them,
And the white skeletons of young men, I saw them,
I saw the debris and debris of all the slain soldiers of the
    war,
But I saw they were not as was thought,
They themselves were fully at rest, they suffered not,
The living remained and suffered, the mother suffered,
And the wife and the child and the musing comrade suf-
    fered,
And the armies that remained suffered.

16

Passing the visions, passing the night,
Passing, unloosing the hold of my comrades' hands,
Passing the song of the hermit bird and the tallying song of
    my soul,
Victorious song, death's outlet song, yet varying ever-
    altering song,
As low and wailing, yet clear the notes, rising and falling,
    flooding the night,

Sadly sinking and fainting, as warning and warning, and yet
    again bursting with joy,
Covering the earth and filling the spread of the heaven,
As that powerful psalm in the night I heard from recesses,
Passing, I leave thee lilac with heart-shaped leaves,
I leave thee there in the dooryard, blooming, returning with
    spring.

I cease from my song for thee,
From my gaze on thee in the west, fronting the west,
    communing with thee,
O comrade lustrous with silver face in the night.
Yet each to keep and all, retrievements out of the night,
The song, the wondrous chant of the gray-brown bird,
And the tallying chant, the echo aroused in my soul,
With the lustrous and drooping star with the countenance
    full of woe,
With the holders holding my hand nearing the call of the
    bird,
Comrades mine and I in the midst, and their memory ever
    to keep, for the dead I loved so well,
For the sweetest, wisest soul of all my days and lands—and
    this for his dear sake,
Lilac and star and bird twined with the chant of my soul,
There in the fragrant pines and the cedars dusk and dim.

WALT WHITMAN

ETERNITY

Song's Eternity

What is song's eternity?
   Come and see.
Can it noise and bustle be?
   Come and see.

Praises sung or praises said
   Can it be?
Wait awhile and these are dead—
   Sigh, sigh;
Be they high or lowly bred
   They die.

What is song's eternity?
   Come and see.
Melodies of earth and sky,
   Here they be.

Song once sung to Adam's ears
   Can it be?
Ballads of six thousand years
   Thrive, thrive;
Songs awaken with the spheres
   Alive.

Mighty songs that miss decay,
   What are they?
Crowds and cities pass away
   Like a day.

Books are out and books are read;
   What are they?

Years will lay them with the dead—
    Sigh, sigh;
Trifles unto nothing wed,
    They die.

Dreamers, mark the honey bee;
    Mark the tree
Where the blue cap *"tootle tee"*
    Sings a glee

Sung to Adam and to Eve—
    Here they be.
When floods covered every bough,
    Noah's ark
Heard that ballad singing now;
    Hark, hark,

"Tootle tootle tootle tee"—
    Can it be
Pride and fame must shadows be?
    Come and see—

Every season owns her own;
    Bird and bee
Sing creation's music on;
    Nature's glee
Is in every mood and tone
    Eternity.

JOHN CLARE

FACING DEATH

Dirge in Woods

A wind sways the pines,
        And below
Not a breath of wild air;
Still as the mosses that glow
On the flooring and over the lines
Of the roots here and there.
The pine tree drops its dead;
They are quiet, as under the sea.
Overhead, overhead
Rushes life in a race,
As the clouds the clouds chase;
        And we go,
And we drop like the fruits of the tree,
        Even we,
        Even so.

GEORGE MEREDITH

When I Have Fears

When I have fears that I may cease to be
Before my pen has glean'd my teeming brain,
Before high-piled books, in charact'ry
Hold like rich garners the full-ripen'd grain;

When I behold, upon the night's starr'd face,
Huge cloudy symbols of a high romance,
And think that I may never live to trace
Their shadows, with the magic hand of chance

And when I feel, fair Creature of an hour!
That I shall never look upon thee more,
Never have relish in the faery power
Of unreflecting love—then on the shore

Of the wide world I stand alone, and think
Till Love and Fame to nothingness do sink.
                                        JOHN KEATS

A Slumber Did My Spirit Seal

A slumber did my spirit seal;
    I had o human fears:
She seemed a thing that could not feel
    The touch of earthly years.

No motion has she now, no force;
    She neither hears nor sees;
Rolled round in earth's diurnal course,
    With rocks, and stones, and trees.
                        WILLIAM WORDSWORTH

A Parting Guest

What delightful hosts are they—
  Life and Love!
Lingeringly I turn away,
  This late hour, yet glad enough
They have not withheld from me
  Their high hospitality.
So, with face lit with delight
  And all gratitude, I stay
  Yet to press their hands and say,
"Thanks,—So fine a time! Good night."
JAMES WHITCOMB RILEY

Requiem

Under the wide and starry sky,
Dig the grave and let me lie.
Glad did I live and gladly die,
  And I laid me down with a will.

This be the verse you grave for me:
Here he lies where he longd to be;
Home is the sailor, home from sea,
  And the hunter home from the hill.
ROBERT LOUIS STEVENSON

Nature

As a fond mother, when the day is o'er,
   Leads by the hand her little child to bed,
   Half willing, half reluctant to be led,
   And leave his broken playthings on the floor,
Still gazing at them through the open door,
   Nor wholly reassured and comforted
   By promises of others in their stead,
   Which, though more splendid, may not please him more;
So Nature deals with us, and takes away
   Our playthings one by one, and by the hand
   Leads us to rest so gently, that we go
Scarce knowing if we wish to go or stay,
   Being too full of sleep to understand
   How far the unknown transcends the what we know.

HENRY WADSWORTH LONGFELLOW

The Last Invocation

At the last, tenderly,
From the walls of the powerful fortress'd house,
From the clasp of the knitted locks, from the keep of the
   well-closed doors,
Let me be wafted.

Let me glide noiselessly forth;
With the key of softness unlock the locks—with a whisper,
Set ope the doors O soul.

Tenderly—be not impatient,
(Strong is your hold O mortal flesh.
Strong is your hold O love.)
WALT WHITMAN

When I Am Dead,
My Dearest

When I am dead, my dearest,
  Sing no sad songs for me;
Plant thou no roses at my head,
  Nor shady cypress-tree:
Be the green grass above me
  With showers and dewdrops wet;
And if thou wilt, remember,
  And if thou wilt, forget.

I shall not see the shadows,
  I shall not feel the rain;
I shall not hear the nightingale
  Sing on, as if in pain:
And dreaming through the twilight
  That doth not rise nor set,
Haply I may remember,
  And haply may forget.

CHRISTINA ROSSETTI

Remember

Remember me when I am gone away,
Gone far away into the silent land;
When you can no more hold me by the hand,
Nor I half turn to go, yet turning stay.
Remember me when no more, day by day,
You tell me of our future that you planned;
Only remember me; you understand
It will be late to counsel then or pray.

Yet if you should forget me for a while
And afterwards remember, do not grieve;
For if the darkness and corruption leave
A vestige of the thoughts that once I had,
Better by far you should forget and smile
Than that you should remember and be sad.

CHRISTINA ROSSETTI

Thanatopsis

To him who in the love of Nature holds
Communion with her visible forms, she speaks
A various language; for his gayer hours
She has a voice of gladness, and a smile
And eloquence of beauty, and she glides
Into his darker musings, with a mild
Ant healing sympathy that steals away
Their sharpness, ere he is aware. When thoughts
Of the last bitter hour come like a blight
Over the spirit, and sad images

Of the stern agony, and shroud, and pall,
And breathless darkness, and the narrow house,
Make thee to shudder, and grow sick at heart;—
Go forth, under the open sky, and list
To Nature's teachings, while from all around—
Earth and her waters, and the depths of air—
Comes a still voice—Yet a few days, and thee
The all-beholding sun shall see no more
In all his course; nor yet in the cold ground,
Where thy pale form was laid, with many tears,
Nor in the embrace of ocean, shall exist
Thy image. Earth, that nourished thee, shall claim
Thy growth, to be resolved to earth again,
And, lost each human trace, surrendering up
Thine individual being, shalt thou go
To mix for ever with the elements,
To be a brother to the insensible rock
And to the sluggish clod, which the rude swain
Turns with his share, and treads upon. The oak
Shall send his roots abroad, and pierce thy mould.

Yet not to thine eternal resting-place
Shalt thou retire alone, nor couldst thou wish
Couch more magnificent. Thou shalt lie down
With patriarchs of the infant world—with kings,
The powerful of the earth—the wise, the good,
Fair forms, and hoary seers of ages past,
All in one mighty sepulchre. The hills
Rock-ribbed and ancient as the sun,—the vales
Stretching in pensive quietness between;
The venerable woods—rivers that move
In majesty, and the complaining brooks
That make the meadows green; and, poured round all,
Old Ocean's gray and melancholy waste,—

Are but the solemn decorations all
Of the great tomb of man. The golden sun,
The planets, all the infinite host of heaven,
Are shining on the sad abodes of death,
Through the still lapse of ages. All that tread
The globe are but a handful to the tribes
That slumber in its bosom.—Take the wings
Of morning, pierce the Barcan wilderness,
Or lose thyself in the continuous woods
Where rolls the Oregon, and hears no sound,
Save his own dashings—yet the dead are there:
And millions in those solitudes, since first
The flight of years began, have laid them down
In their last sleep—the dead reign there alone.

So shalt thou rest, and what if thou withdraw
In silence from the living, and no friend
Take note of thy departure? All that breathe
Will share thy destiny. The gay will laugh
When thou art gone, the solemn brood of care
Plod on, and each one as before will chase
His favorite phantom; yet all these shall leave
Their mirth and their employments, and shall come
And make their bed with thee. As the long train
Of ages glide away, the sons of men,
The youth in life's green spring, and he who goes
In the full strength of years, matron and maid,
The speechless babe, and the gray-headed man—
Shall one by one be gathered to thy side,
By those, who in their turn shall follow them.

So live, that when thy summons comes to join
The innumerable caravan, which moves
To that mysterious realm, where each shall take

His chamber in the silent halls of death,
Thou go not, like the quarry-slave at night,
Scourged to his dungeon, but, sustained and soothed
By an unfaltering trust, approach thy grave,
Like one who wraps the drapery of his couch
About him, and lies down to pleasant dreams.

WILLIAM CULLEN BRYANT

Good-Bye

Good-bye, proud world! I'm going home:
Thou art not my friend, and I'm not thine.
Long through thy weary crowds I roam;
A river-ark on the ocean brine,
Long I've been tossed like the driven foam;
But now, proud world! I'm going home.

Good-bye to Flattery's fawning face;
To Grandeur with his wise grimace;
To upstart Wealth's averted eye;
To supple Office, low and high;
To crowded halls, to court and street;
To frozen hearts and hasting feet;
To those who go, and those who come;
Good-bye, proud world! I'm going home.

I am going to my own hearth-stone,
Bosomed in yon green hills alone—
A secret nook in a pleasant land,
Whose groves the frolic fairies planned;
Where arches green, the livelong day,

Echo the blackbird's roundelay,
And vulgar feet have never trod
A spot that is sacred to thought and God.

O, when I am safe in my sylvan home,
I tread on the pride of Greece and Rome;
And when I am stretched beneath the pines,
Where the evening star so holy shines,
I laugh at the lore and the pride of man,
At the sophist schools and the learned clan;
For what are they all, in their high conceit,
When man in the bush with God may meet?

RALPH WALDO EMERSON

He Is Not Dead

I cannot say, and I will not say
That he is dead. He is just away.
With a cheery smile, and a wave of the hand,
He has wandered into an unknown land
And left us dreaming how very fair
It needs must be, since he lingers there.
And you—oh, you, who the wildest yearn
For an old-time step, and the glad return,
Think of him faring on, as dear
In the love of There as the love of Here.
Think of him still as the same. I say,
He is not dead—he is just away.

JAMES WHITCOMB RILEY

I Shall Not Care

When I am dead and over me bright April
    Shakes out her rain-drenched hair,
Though you should lean above me broken-hearted,
    I shall not care.

I shall have peace, as leafy trees are peaceful
    When rain bends down the bough;
And I shall be more silent and cold-hearted
    Than you are now.

SARA TEASDALE

Crossing the Bar

Sunset and evening star,
    And one clear call for me!
And may there be no moaning of the bar,
    When I put out to sea.

But such a tide as moving seems asleep,
    Too full for sound and foam,
When that which drew from out the boundless deep
    Turns again home.

Twilight and evening bell,
    And after that the dark!
And may there be no sadness of farewell,
    When I embark;

For tho' from out our bourne of Time and Place
　　The flood may bear me far,
I hope to see my Pilot face to face
　　When I have crost the bar.

ALFRED, LORD TENNYSON

The Ballad of Reading Gaol

I never saw a man who looked
　　With such a wistful eye
Upon that little tent of blue
　　Which prisoners call the sky,
And at every drifting cloud that went
　　With sails of silver by.

I walked, with other souls in pain,
　　Within another ring,
And was wondering if the man had done
　　A great or little thing,
When a voice behind me whispered low,
　　"That fellow's got to swing."

Dear Christ! the very prison walls
　　Suddenly seemed to reel,
And the sky above my head became
　　Like a casque of scorching steel;
And, though I was a soul in pain,
　　My pain I could not feel.

I only knew what hunted thought
    Quickened his step, and why
    He looked upon the garish day
    With such a wistful eye;
The man had killed the thing he loved,
    And so he had to die.

Yet each man kills the thing he loves,
    By each let this be heard,
Some do it with a bitter look,
    Some with a flattering word,
The coward does it with a kiss,
    The brave man with a sword!

Some kill their love when they are young,
    And some when they are old;
Some strangle with the hands of Lust,
    Some with the hands of Gold:
The kindest use a knife, because
    The dead so soon grow cold.

Some love too little, some too long,
    Some sell, and others buy;
Some do the deed with many tears,
    And some without a sigh:
For each man kills the thing he loves,
    Yet each man does not die.

He does not die a death of shame
    On a day of dark disgrace,
Nor have a noose about his neck,
    Nor a cloth upon his face,
Nor drop feet foremost through the floor
    Into an empty space.

He does not sit with silent men
  Who watch him night and day;
Who watch him when he tries to weep,
  And when he tries to pray;
Who watch him lest himself should rob
  The prison of its prey.

He does not wake at dawn to see
  Dread figures throng his room,
The shivering Chaplain robed in white,
  The Sheriff stern with gloom,
And the Governor all in shiny black,
  With the yellow face of Doom.

He does not rise in piteous haste
  To put on convict-clothes,
While some coarse-mouthed Doctor gloats, and notes
  Each new and nerve-twitched pose,
Fingering a watch whose little ticks
  Are like horrible hammer-blows.

He does not know that sickening thirst
  That sands one's throat, before
The hangman with his gardener's gloves
  Slips through the padded door,
And binds one with three leathern thongs,
  That the throat may thirst no more.

He does not bend his head to hear
  The Burial Office read,
Nor, while the terror of his soul
  Tells him he is not dead,
Cross his own coffin, as he moves
  Into the hideous shed.

He does not stare upon the air
   Through a little roof of glass:
He does not pray with lips of clay
   For his agony to pass;
Nor feel upon his shuddering cheek
   That kiss of Caiaphas.

It is sweet to dance to violins
   When Love and Life are fair:
To dance to flutes, to dance to lutes
   Is delicate and rare:
But it is not sweet with nimble feet
   To dance upon the air!

OSCAR WILDE

In Memoriam

A late lark twitters from the quiet skies;
And from the west,
Where the sun, his day's work ended,
Lingers as in content,
There falls on the old, gray city
An influence luminous and serene,
A shining peace.

The smoke ascends
In a rosy-and-golden haze. The spires
Shine, and are changed. In the valley
Shadows rise. The lark sings on. The sun,
Closing his benediction,
Sinks, and the darkening air
Thrills with a sense of the triumphing night—
Night with her train of stars
And her great gift of sleep.

So be my passing!
My task accomplished and the long day done,
My wages taken, and in my heart
Some late lark singing,
Let me be gathered to the quiet west,
The sundown splendid and serene,
Death.

WILLIAM ERNEST HENLEY

I Have a Rendezvous with Death

I have a rendezvous with Death
  At some disputed barricade,
   When Spring comes back with rustling shade
     And apple blossoms fill the air—
I have a rendezvous with Death
     When Spring brings back blue days and fair.

It may be he shall take my hand,
And lead me into his dark land,
   And close my eyes and quench my breath—
It may be I shall pass him still.
   I have a rendezvous with Death
On some scarred slope of battered hill,
   When Spring comes round again this year
   And the first meadow flowers appear.

God knows 'twere better to be deep
Pillowed in silk and scented down,
Where Love throbs out in blissful sleep,
Pulse nigh to pulse, and breath to breath,
Where hushed awakenings are dear . . .
But I've a rendezvous with Death
At midnight in some flaming town,
When Spring trips north again this year;
And I to my pledged word am true,
I shall not fail that rendezvous.

ALAN SEEGER

FACING LIFE

Take the World as It Is

Take the world as it is!—with its smiles and its
    sorrow,
    Its love and its friendship—its falsehood and
      truth—
Its schemes that depend on the breath of tomorrow!
  Its hopes which pass by like the dreams of our
      youth—
Yet, oh! whilst the light of affection may shine,
  The heart in itself hath a fountain of bliss!
In the *worst* there's some spark of a nature divine,
  And the wisest and best *take the world as it is.*

CHARLES SWAIN

On His Blindness

When I consider how my light is spent
  Ere half my days in this dark world and wide,
  And that one talent which is death to hide
Lodged with me useless, though my soul more bent
To serve therewith my Maker, and present
  My true account, lest he returning chide,
  "Doth God exact day-labor, light denied?"
I fondly ask. But Patience, to prevent
That murmur, soon replies, "God doth not need
  Either man's work or his own gifts. Who best
  Bear his mild yoke, they serve him best. His state
Is kingly: thousands at his bidding speed,
  And post o'er land and ocean without rest;
  They also serve who only stand and wait."

JOHN MILTON

One Year to Live

If I had but one year to live;
One year to help; one year to give;
One year to love; one year to bless;
One year of better things to stress;
One year to sing; one year to smile;
To brighten earth a little while;
I think that I would spend each day,
In just the very self-same way
That I do now. For from afar
The call may come to cross the bar
At any time, and I must be
Prepared to meet eternity.
So if I have a year to live,
Or just a day in which to give
A pleasant smile, a helping hand,
A mind that tries to understand
A fellow-creature when in need,
'Tis one with me,—I take no heed;
But try to live each day He sends
To serve my gracious Master's ends.

MARY DAVIS REED

High Resolve

I'll hold my candle high, and then
Perhaps I'll see the hearts of men
Above the sordidness of life,
Beyond misunderstandings, strife.

Though many deeds that others do
Seem foolish, rash and sinful too,
Just who am I to criticize
What I perceive with my dull eyes?
I'll hold my candle high, and then,
Perhaps I'll see the hearts of men.

AUTHOR UNKNOWN

The Junk Box

My father often used to say:
"My boy don't throw a thing away:
You'll find a use for it some day."

So in a box he stored up things,
Bent nails, old washers, pipes and rings,
And bolts and nuts and rusty springs.

Despite each blemish and each flaw,
Some use for everything he saw;
With things material, this was law.

And often when he'd work to do,
He searched the junk box through and through
And found old stuff as good as new.

And I have often thought since then,
That father did the same with men;
He knew he'd need their help again.

It seems to me he understood
That men, as well as iron and wood,
May broken be and still be good.

Despite the vices he'd display
He never threw a man away,
But kept him for another day.

A human junk box is this earth
And into it we're tossed at birth,
To wait the day we'll be of worth.

Though bent and twisted, weak of will,
And full of flaws and lacking skill,
Some service each can render still.

EDGAR GUEST

Worthwhile

It is easy enough to be pleasant,
  When life flows by like a song,
But the man worthwhile is one who will smile,
  When everything goes dead wrong.
For the test of the heart is trouble,
  And it always comes with the years,
And the smile that is worth the praises of earth
  Is the smile that shines through tears.

It is easy enough to be prudent,
  When nothing tempts you to stray,
When without or within no voice of sin
  Is luring your soul away;

But it's only a negative virtue
    Until it is tried by fire,
And the life that is worth the honor on earth
    Is the one that resists desire.

By the cynic, the sad, the fallen,
    Who had no strength for the strife,
The world's highway is cumbered today;
    They make up the sum of life.
But the virtue that conquers passion,
    And the sorrow that hides in a smile,
It is these that are worth the homage on earth
    For we find them but once in a while.

ELLA WHEELER WILCOX

A Bag of Tools

Isn't it strange
    That princes and kings,
And clowns that caper
    In sawdust rings,
And common people
    Like you and me
    Are builders for eternity?

Each is given a bag of tools,
    A shapeless mass,
A book of rules;
    And each must make—
Ere life is flown—
    A stumbling block
Or a steppingstone.

R.L. SHARPE

Then Laugh

Build for yourself a strong box,
　Fashion each part with care;
When it's strong as your hand can make it,
　Put all your troubles there;
Hide there all thought of your failures,
　And each bitter cup that you quaff;
Lock all your heartaches within it,
　Then sit on the lid and laugh.

Tell no one else its contents,
　Never its secrets share;
When you've dropped in your care and worry
　Keep them forever there;
Hide them from sight so completely
　That the world will never dream half;
Fasten the strong box securely—
　Then sit on the lid and laugh.

BERTHA ADAMS BACKUS

FAITH

After-Thought

I thought of Thee, my partner and my guide,
As being past away.—Vain sympathies!
For, backward, Duddon! as I cast my eyes,
I see what was, and is, and will abide;
Still glides the Stream, and shall for ever glide;
The Form remains, the Function never dies;
While we, the brave, the mighty, and the wise,
We Men, who in our morn of youth defied
The elements, must vanish;-be it so!
Enough, if something from our hands have power
To live, and act, and serve the future hour;
And if, as toward the silent tomb we go,
Through love, through hope, and faith's transcendent dower,
We feel that we are greater than we know.

WILLIAM WORDSWORTH

God

I see Thee in the distant blue;
But in the violet's dell of dew,
Behold, I *breathe and touch* Thee too.

JOHN BANISTER TABB

Surprised by Joy

Surprised by joy—impatient as the Wind
I turned to share the transport—Oh! with whom
But Thee, deep buried in the silent tomb,
That spot which no vicissitude can find?
Love, faithful love, recalled thee to my mind—
But how could I forget thee? Through what power,
Even for the least division of an hour,
Have I been so beguiled as to be blind
To my most grievous loss!—That thought's return
Was the worst pang that sorrow ever bore,
Save one, one only, when I stood forlorn,
Knowing my heart's best treasure was no more;
That neither present time, nor years unborn
Could to my sight that heavenly face restore.

WILLIAM WORDSWORTH

O Never Star Was Lost

O never star
Was lost; here
We all aspire to heaven and there is heaven
Above us.
If I stoop
Into a dark tremendous sea of cloud,
It is but for a time; I press God's lamp
Close to my breast; its splendor soon or late
Will pierce the gloom. I shall emerge some day.

ROBERT BROWNING

Obedience

I said, "Let me walk in the fields."
   He said, "No, walk in the town."
I said, "There are no flowers there."
   He said, "No flowers, but a crown."

I said, "But the skies are black;
   There is nothing but noise and din."
And He wept as he sent me back:
   "There is more," He said; "there is sin."

I said, "But the air is thick,
   And fogs are veiling the sun."
He answered, "Yet souls are sick,
   And souls in the dark undone."

I said, "I shall miss the light,
   And friends will miss me, they say."
He answered, "Choose to-night,
   If *I* am to miss you, or they."

I pleaded for time to be given.
   He said, "Is it hard to decide?
It will not seem hard in heaven
   To have followed the steps of your Guide."

I cast one look at the fields,
　　Then set my face to the town:
He said, "My child, do you yield?
　　Will you leave the flowers for the crown?"

Then into His hand went mine,
　　And into my heart came He;
And I walk in a light divine
　　The path I had feared to see.

GEORGE MACDONALD

My Church

My church has but one temple,
　　Wide as the world is wide,
Set with a million stars,
　　Where a million hearts abide.

My church has no creed to bar
　　A single brother man
But says, "Come thou and worship"
　　To every one who can.

My church has no roof nor walls,
　　Nor floors save the beautiful sod—
For fear, I would seem to limit
　　The love of the illimitable God.

AUTHOR UNKNOWN. SIGNED E.O.G.

What Thomas an Buile
Said in a Pub

I saw God. Do you doubt it?
  Do you dare to doubt it?
I saw the Almighty Man. His hand
Was resting on a mountain, and
He looked upon the World and all about it:
I saw Him plainer than you see me now,
  You mustn't doubt it.

He was not satisfied;
  His look was all dissatisfied.
His beard swung on a wind far out of sight
Behind the world's curve, and there was light
Most fearful from His forehead, and He sighed,
"That star went always wrong, and from the start
  I was dissatisfied."

He lifted up His hand—
  I say He heaved a dreadful hand
Over the spinning Earth. Then I said, "Stay,
You must not strike it, God; I'm in the way;
And I will never move from where I stand."
He said, "Dear child, I feared that you were dead,"
  And stayed His hand.

JAMES STEPHENS

Faith

I will not doubt, though all my ships at sea
    Come drifting home with broken masts and sails;
    I shall believe the Hand which never fails,
From seeming evil worketh good to me;
    And, though I weep because those sails are
        battered,
    Still will I cry, while my best hopes lie shattered,
        "I trust in Thee."

I will not doubt, though all my prayers return
    Unanswered from the still, white realm above;
    I shall believe it is an all-wise Love
Which has refused those things for which I yearn;
    And though, at times, I cannot keep from
        grieving,
    Yet the pure ardor of my fixed believing
        Undimmed shall burn.

I will not doubt, though sorrows fall like rain,
    And troubles swarm like bees about a hive;
    I shall believe the heights for which I strive,
Are only reached by anguish and by pain;
    And, though I groan and tremble with my crosses,
    I yet shall see, through my severest losses,
        The greater gain.

I will not doubt; well anchored in the faith,
　　Like some stanch ship, my soul braves every gale,
　　So strong its courage that it will not fail
To breast the mighty, unknown sea of death.
　　Oh, may I cry when body parts with spirit,
　　"I do not doubt," so listening worlds may hear it
　　　　　With my last breath.

ELLA WHEELER WILCOX

A Prayer for Faith

God, give me back the simple faith
　　that I so long have clung to,
　　My simple faith in peace and hope,
　　in loveliness and light—
Because without this faith of mine,
　　the rhythms I have sung to
　　Become as empty as the sky upon a starless night.

God, let me feel that right is right,
　　that reason dwells with reason,
　　And let me feel that something grows
　　whenever there is rain—
And let me sense that splendid truth
　　that season follows season,
　　And let me dare to dream
　　that there is tenderness in pain.

God, give me back my simple faith
    because my soul is straying
Away from all the little creeds
    that I so long have known;
Oh, answer me while still I have
    at least the strength for praying,
For if the prayer dies from my heart

MARGARET E. SANGSTER

There Is No Unbelief

There is no unbelief;
Whoever plants a seed beneath the sod
And waits to see it push away the clod,
    He trusts in God.
            I will be quite alone.

There is no unbelief;
Whoever says, when clouds are in the sky,
"Be patient, heart; light breaketh by and by,"
    Trusts the Most High.

There is no unbelief;
Whoever sees, 'neath winter's field of snow,
The silent harvest of the future grow—
    God's power must know.

There is no unbelief;
\Whoever lies down on his couch to sleep,
Content to lock each sense in slumber deep,
   Knows God will keep.

There is no unbelief;
The heart that looks on when dear eyelids close,
And dares to live when life has only woes,
   God's comfort knows.

LIZZIE YORK CASE

FAREWELL

Farewell

Farewell! if ever fondest prayer
   For other's weal availed on high,
Mine will not all be lost in air,
   But waft thy name beyond the sky.
'Twere vain to speak, to weep, to sigh:
   Oh! more than tears of blood can tell,
When wrung from guilt's expiring eye,
   Are in that word—Farewell!—Farewell!

These lips are mute, these eyes are dry;
   But in my breast and in my brain,
Awake the pangs that pass not by,
   The thought that ne'er shall sleep again.
My soul nor deigns nor dares complain,
   Though grief and passion there rebel:
I only know we loved in vain;
   I only feel—Farewell!—Farewell!

            GEORGE GORDON, LORD BYRON

Farewell! Thou Art Too Dear

Farewell! thou art too dear for my possessing,
And like enough thou know'st thy estimate:
The charter of thy worth gives thee releasing;
My bonds in thee are all determinate.
For how do I hold thee but by thy granting?
And for that riches where is my deserving?

189

The cause of this fair gift in me is wanting,
And so my patent back again is swerving.
Thyself thou gav'st, thy own worth then not knowing,
Or me, to whom thou gav'st it, else mistaking;
So thy great gift, upon misprison growing,
Comes home again, on better judgment making.
Thus have I had thee, as a dream doth flatter
In sleep a king; but waking, no such matter.

WILLIAM SHAKESPEARE

April Love

We have walked in Love's land a little way,
   We have learnt his lesson a little while,
And shall we not part at the end of day,
   With a sigh, a smile?

A little while in the shine of the sun,
   We were twined together, joined lips, forgot
How the shadows fall when the day is done,
   And when Love is not.

We have made no vows—there will none be broke,
   Our love was free as the wind on the hill,
There was no word said we need wish unspoke,
   We have wrought no ill.

So shall we not part at the end of day,
   Who have loved and lingered a little while,
Join lips for the last time, go our way,
   With a sigh, a smile?

ERNEST DOWSON

from *Idea*

Dear, why should you command me to my rest
When now the night doth summon all to sleep?
Methinks this time becometh lovers best;
Night was ordained together friends to keep.
How happy are all other living things
Which, though the day disjoin by several flight,
The quiet evening yet together brings,
And each returns unto his love at night.
O thou, that art so courteous else to all,
Why shouldst thou, Night, abuse me only thus,
That every creature to his kind doth call
And yet 'tis thou dost only sever us.
Well could I wish it would be ever day
If when night comes you bid me go away.

MICHAEL DRAYTON

FATHERS

Only a Dad

Only a dad with a tired face,
Coming home from the daily race,
Bringing little of gold or fame
To show how well he has played the game;
But glad in his heart that his own rejoice
To see him come and to hear his voice.

Only a dad with a brood of four,
One of ten million men or more
Plodding along in the daily strife,
Bearing the whips and the scorns of life,
With never a whimper of pain or hate,
For the sake of those who at home await.
Only a dad, neither rich nor proud,
Merely one of the surging crowd,
Toiling, striving from day to day,
Facing whatever may come his way,
Silent whenever the harsh condemn,
And bearing it all for the love of them.

Only a dad but he gives his all,
To smooth the way for his children small,
Doing with courage stern and grim
The deeds that his father did for him.
This is the line that for him I pen:
Only a dad, but the best of men.

EDGAR GUEST

Father

Used to wonder just why father
  Never had much time for play,
Used to wonder why he'd rather
  Work each minute of the day.
Used to wonder why he never
  Loafed along the road an' shirked;
Can't recall a time whenever
  Father played while others worked.

Father didn't dress in fashion,
  Sort of hated clothing new;
Style with him was not a passion;
  He had other things in view.
Boys are blind to much that's going
  On about 'em day by day,
And I had no way of knowing
  What became of father's pay.

All I knew was when I needed
  Shoes I got 'em on the spot;
Everything for which I pleaded,
  Somehow, father always got.
Wondered, season after season,
  Why he never took a rest,
And that *I* might be the reason
  Then I never even guessed.

Father set a store on knowledge;
  If he'd lived to have his way
He'd have sent me off to college
  And the bills been glad to pay.

That, I know, was his ambition:
  Now and then he used to say
He'd have done his earthly mission
  On my graduation day.

Saw his cheeks were getting paler,
  Didn't understand just why;
Saw his body growing frailer,
  Then at last I saw him die.
Rest had come! His tasks were ended
  Calm was written on his brow;
Father's life was big and splendid,
  And I understand it now.

EDGAR GUEST

FRIENDSHIP

Love

I love you,
Not only for what you are,
But for what I am
When I am with you.

I love you,
Not only for what
You have made of yourself,
But for what
You are making of me.

I love you
For the part of me
That you bring out;
I love you
For putting your hand
Into my heaped-up heart
And passing over
All the foolish, weak things
That you can't help
Dimly seeing there,
And for drawing out
Into the light
All the beautiful belongings
That no one else had looked
Quite far enough to find.

I love you because you
Are helping me to make
Of the lumber of my life
Not a tavern
But a temple;
Out of the works
Of my every day
Not a reproach
But a song.
I love you
Because you have done
More than any creed
Could have done
To make me good,
And more than any fate
Could have done
To make me happy.

You have done it
Without a touch,
Without a word,
Without a sign.
You have done it
By being yourself.
Perhaps that is what
Being a friend means,
After all.

ROY CROFT

Accept My Full Heart's Thanks

Your words came just when needed.
Like a breeze,
Blowing and bringing from the wide salt sea
Some cooling spray, to meadow scorched with heat
And choked with dust and clouds of sifted sand
That hateful whirlwinds, envious of its bloom,
Had tossed upon it. But the cool sea breeze
Came laden with the odors of the sea
And damp with spray, that laid the dust and sand
And brought new life and strength to blade and
        bloom
So words of thine came over miles to me,
Fresh from the mighty sea, a true friend's heart,
And brought me hope, and strength, and swept away
The dusty webs that human spiders spun
Across my path. Friend—and the word means
        much—
So few there are who reach like thee, a hand
Up over all the barking curs of spite
And give the clasp, when most its need is felt,
Friend, newly found, accept my full heart's thanks.

ELLA WHEELER WILCOX

Confide in a Friend

When you're tired and worn at the close of day
And things just don't seem to be going your way,
When even your patience has come to an end,
Try taking time out and confide in a friend.

Perhaps he too may have walked the same road
With a much troubled heart and burdensome load,
To find peace and comfort somewhere near the end,
When he stopped long enough to confide in a friend.

For then are most welcome a few words of cheer,
For someone who willingly lends you an ear.
No troubles exist that time cannot mend,
But to get quick relief, just confide in a friend.

AUTHOR UNKNOWN

On Friendship

And let your best be for your friend.
If he must know the ebb of your tide, let him know
    its flood also.
For what is your friend that you should seek him with
    hours to kill?
Seek him always with hours to live.
For it is his to fill your need, but not your emptiness.
And in the sweetness of friendship let there be
    laughter, and sharing of pleasures.
For in the dew of little things the heart finds its
    morning and is refreshed.

Your friend is your needs answered.
He is your field which you sow with love and reap
    with thanksgiving.
And he is your board and your fireside.
For you come to him with your hunger, and you seek
    him for peace.

KAHLIL GIBRAN

The Arrow and the Song

I shot an arrow into the air,
It fell to earth, I knew not where;
For, so swiftly it flew, the sight
Could not follow it in its flight.

I breathed a song into the air,
It fell to earth, I knew not where;
For who has sight so keen and strong,
That it can follow the flight of song?

Long, long afterward, in an oak
I found the arrow, still unbroke;
And the song, from beginning to end,
I found again in the heart of a friend.

HENRY WADSWORTH LONGFELLOW

New Friends and
Old Friends

Make new friends, but keep the old;
Those are silver, these are gold.

New-made friendships, like new wine,
Age will mellow and refine.
Friendships that have stood the test—
Time and change—are surely best;
Brow may wrinkle, hair grow gray;
Friendship never knows decay.
For 'mid old friends, tried and true,
Once more we our youth renew.
But old friends, alas! may die;
New friends must their place supply.
Cherish friendship in your breast—
New is good, but old is best;
Make new friends, but keep the old;
Those are silver, these are gold.

JOSEPH PARRY

To My Friend

I have never been rich before,
   But you have poured
Into my heart's high door
   A golden hoard.

My wealth is the vision shared,
   The sympathy,
The feast of the soul prepared
   By you for me.

Together we wander through
   The wooded ways.
Old beauties are green and new
   Seen through your gaze.

I look for no greater prize
Than your soft voice.
The steadiness of your eyes
Is my heart's choice.

I have never been rich before,
But I divine
Your step on my sunlit floor
And wealth is mine!

ANNE CAMPBELL

God Bless You

I seek in prayerful words, dear friend,
My heart's true wish to send you,
That you may know that, far or near,
My loving thoughts attend you.

I cannot find a truer word,
Nor better to address you;
Nor song, nor poem have I heard
Is sweeter than God bless you!

God bless you! So I've wished you all
Of brightness life possesses;
For can there any joy at all
Be yours unless God blesses?

God bless you! So I breathe a charm
Lest grief's dark night oppress you,
For how can sorrow bring you harm
If 'tis God's way to bless you?

And so, "through all thy days
   May shadows touch thee never—"
But this alone—God bless thee—
   Then art thou safe forever.

AUTHOR UNKNOWN

There Is Always a Place for You

There is always a place for you at my table,
   You never need to be invited.
I'll share every crust as long as I'm able,
   And know you will be delighted.
There is always a place for you by my fire,
   And though it may burn to embers,
If warmth and good cheer are your desire
   The friend of your heart remembers!
There is always a place for you by my side,
   And should the years tear us apart,
I will face lonely moments more satisfied
   With a place for you in my heart!

ANNE CAMPBELL

A Poison Tree

I was angry with my friend:
I told my wrath, my wrath did end.
I was angry with my foe:
I told it not, my wrath did grow.

And I watered it in fears
Night and morning with my tears,
And I sunned it with smiles
And with soft deceitful wiles.

And it grew both day and night,
Till it bore an apple bright,
And my foe beheld it shine,
And he knew that it was mine—

And into my garden stole
When the night had veiled the pole;
In the morning, glad, I see
My foe outstretched beneath the tree.

WILLIAM BLAKE

Around the Corner

Around the corner I have a friend,
In this great city that has no end;
Yet days go by, and weeks rush on,
And before I know it a year is gone,
And I never see my old friend's face,
For Life is a swift and terrible race.
He knows I like him just as well
As in the days when I rang his bell
And he rang mine. We were younger then,
And now we are busy, tired men:
Tired with trying to make a name.
"Tomorrow," I say, "I will call on Jim,
Just to show that I'm thinking of him."

But tomorrow comes—and tomorrow goes,
And the distance between us grows and grows
Around the corner!—yet miles away. . . .
"Here's a telegram, sir. . . ."

Jim died today."
And that's what we get, and deserve in the end:
Around the corner, a vanished friend.
CHARLES HANSON TOWNE

Friendship

Friendship needs no studied phrases,
   Polished face, or winning wiles;
Friendship deals no lavish praises,
   Friendship dons no surface smiles.

Friendship follows Nature's diction,
   Shuns the blandishments of Art,
Boldly severs truth from fiction,
   Speaks the language of the heart.

Friendship favors no condition,
   Scorns a narrow-minded creed,
Lovingly fulfills its mission,
   Be it word or be it deed.

Friendship cheers the faint and weary,
   Makes the timid spirit brave,
Warns the erring, lights the dreary,
   Smooths the passage to the grave.

Friendship—pure, unselfish friendship,
  All through life's allotted span,
Nurtures, strengthens, widens, lengthens,
  Man's relationship with man.
                    AUTHOR UNKNOWN

Fellowship

When a feller hasn't got a cent
And is feelin' kind of blue,
And the clouds hang thick and dark
And won't let the sunshine thro'
It's a great thing, oh my brethren,
For a feller just to lay
His hand upon your shoulder
   in a friendly sort o' way.

It make a man feel queerish,
It makes the tear-drops start.
And you kind o' feel a flutter
In the region of your heart.
You can't look up and meet his eye,
You don't know what to say
When a hand is on your shoulder
   in a friendly sort o' way.

Oh this world's a curious compound
With its honey and its gall;
Its cares and bitter crosses,
But a good world after all.

And a good God must have made it,
Leastwise that is what I say,
When a hand is on your shoulder
  in a friendly sort o' way.
AUTHOR UNKNOWN

To Know All Is To Forgive All

If I knew you and you knew me—
If both of us could clearly see,
And with an inner sight divine
The meaning of your heart and mine—
I'm sure that we would differ less
And clasp our hands in friendliness;
Our thoughts would pleasantly agree
If I knew you, and you knew me.

If I knew you and you knew me,
As each one knows his own self, we
Could look each other in the face
And see therein a truer grace.

Life has so many hidden woes,
So many thorns for every rose;
The "why" of things our hearts would see,
If I knew you and you knew me.
NIXON WATERMAN

from *Devotions XVII*

No man is an island, entire of itself;
every man is a piece of the continent,
   a part of the main;
. . . any man's death diminishes me, because
   I am involved in mankind;
and therefore never send to know for whom the bell tolls;
it tolls for thee.

JOHN DONNE

Friendship Is Love
Without His Wings

Why should my anxious breast repine,
   Because my youth is fled?
Days of delight may still be mine;
   Affection is not dead.
In tracing back the years of youth,
One firm record, one lasting truth
   Celestial consolation brings;
Bear it, ye breezes, to the seat
Where first my heart responsive beat,—
   "Friendship is Love without his wings!"

GEORGE GORDON, LORD BYRON

FRUSTRATION

My Love Is Like to Ice

My love is like to ice, and I to fire:
How comes it then that this her cold so great
Is not dissolved through my so hot desire,
But harder grows the more I her entreat?
Or how comes it that my exceeding heat
Is not allayed by her heart-frozen cold,
But that I burn much more in boiling sweat,
And feel my flames augmented manifold?
What more miraculous thing may be told,
That fire, which all things melts, should harden
   ice,
And ice, which is congealed with senseless cold,
Should kindle fire by wonderful device?
Such is the power of love in gentle mind,
That it can alter all the course of kind.

EDMUND SPENSER

Villanelle of the Poet's Road

Wine and woman and song,
   Three things garnish our way:
Yet is day over long.

Lest we do our youth wrong,
   Gather them while we may:
   Wine and woman and song.

Three things render us strong,
　　Vine leaves, kisses and bay:
Yet is day over long.

Unto us they belong,
　　Us the bitter and gay,
Wine and woman and song.

We, as we pass along,
　　Are sad that they will not stay;
Yet is day over long.

Fruits and flowers among,
　　What is better than they:
Wine and woman and song?
Yet is day over long.

ERNEST DOWSON

FULFILLMENT

Today

I have spread wet linen
On lavender bushes,
I have swept rose petals
From a garden walk.
I have labeled jars of raspberry jam,
I have baked a sunshine cake;
I have embroidered a yellow duck
On a small blue frock.
I have polished andirons,
Dusted the highboy,
Cut sweets peas for a black bowl,
Wound the tall clock,
Pleated a lace ruffle . . .
To-day
I have lived a poem.

ETHEL ROMIG FULLER

The Day Is Done

The day is done, and the darkness
  Falls from the wings of Night,
As a feather is wafted downward
  From an eagle in his flight.

I see the lights of the village
  Gleam through the rain and the mist,
And a feeling of sadness comes o'er me
  That my soul cannot resist:

A feeling of sadness and longing,
   That is not akin to pain,
And resembles sorrow only
   As the mist resembles the rain.

Come, read to me some poem,
   Some simple and heartfelt lay,
That shall soothe this restless feeling,
   And banish the thoughts of day.

Not from the grand old masters,
   Not from the bards sublime,
Whose distant footsteps echo
   Through the corridors of Time.

For, like strains of martial music,
   Their mighty thoughts suggest
Life's endless toil and endeavor;
   And tonight I long for rest.

Read from some humbler poet,
   Whose songs gushed from his heart,
As showers from the clouds of summer,
   Or tears from the eyelids start;

Who, through long days of labor,
   And nights devoid of ease,
Still heard in his soul the music
   Of wonderful melodies.

Such songs have power to quiet
   The restless pulse of care,
And come like the benediction
   That follows after prayer.

Then read from the treasured volume
    The poem of thy choice,
And lend to the rhyme of the poet
    The beauty of thy voice.

And the night shall be filled with music,
    And the cares, that infest the day,
Shall fold their tents, like the Arabs,
    And as silently steal away.
        HENRY WADSWORTH LONGFELLOW

Thanks Be to God

I do not thank Thee, Lord,
That I have bread to eat while others starve;
Nor yet for work to do
While empty hands solicit Heaven;
Nor for a body strong
While other bodies flatten beds of pain.
No, not for these do I give thanks!

But I am grateful, Lord,
Because my meager loaf I may divide;
For that my busy hands
May move to meet another's need;
Because my doubled strength
I may expend to steady one who faints.
Yes, for all these do I give thanks!

For heart to share, desire to bear
And will to lift,
Flamed into one by deathless Love—
Thanks be to God for this!
Unspeakable! His Gift!

JANIE ALFORD

Better than Gold

Better than grandeur, better than gold,
Than rank and titles a thousandfold,
Is a healthy body and a mind at ease,
And simple pleasures that always please.
A heart that can feel for another's woe,
And share his joys with a genial glow;
With sympathies large enough to enfold
All men as brothers, is better than gold.

Better than gold is a conscience clear,
Though toiling for bread in an humble sphere,
Doubly blessed with content and health,
Untried by the lusts and cares of wealth,
Lowly living and lofty thought
Adorn and ennoble a poor man's cot;
For mind and morals in nature's plan
Are the genuine tests of an earnest man.

Better than gold is a peaceful home
Where all the fireside characters come,
The shrine of love, the heaven of life,

Hallowed by mother, or sister, or wife.
However humble the home may be,
Or tried with sorrow by heaven's decree,
The blessings that never were bought or sold,
And center there, are better than gold.

ABRAM J. RYAN

Life Owes Me Nothing

Life owes me nothing. Let the years
Bring clouds or azure, joy or tears;
   Already a full cup I've quaffed;
   Already wept and loved and laughed,
And seen, in ever-endless ways,
New beauties overwhelm the days.

Life owes me nought. No pain that waits
Can steal the wealth from memory's gates;
   No aftermath of anguish slow
   Can quench the soul fire's early glow.
I breathe, exulting, each new breath,
Embracing Life, ignoring Death.

Life owes me nothing. One clear morn
Is boon enough for being born;
   And be it ninety years or ten,
   No need for me to question when.
While Life is mine, I'll find it good,
And greet each hour with gratitude.

AUTHOR UNKNOWN

A Thankful Heart

Lord, Thou hast given me a cell
   Wherein to dwell,
A little house whose humble roof
   Is weatherproof . . .
Low is my porch as is my fate,
   Both void of state,
And yet the threshold of my door
   Is worn by the poor
Who hither come and freely get
   Good words or meat.
'Tis Thou that crown'st my glittering hearth
   With guileless mirth.
All these and better Thou dost send
   Me to this end,
That I should render for my part
   A thankful heart.

ROBERT HERRICK

Fulfillment

Lo, I have opened unto you the gates of my being,
And like a tide, you have flowed into me.
The innermost recesses of my spirit are full of you
And all the channels of my soul are grown sweet with
    your presence
For you have brought me peace;
  The peace of great tranquil waters,
And the quiet of the summer sea.

Your hands are filled with peace as
The noon-tide is filled with light;
  About your head is bound the eternal
Quiet of the stars, and in your heart dwells the calm
    miracle of twilight.

I am utterly content.
In all my being is no ripple of unrest
  For I have opened unto you
The wide gates of my being
  And like a tide, you have flowed into me.

AUTHOR UNKNOWN

I Have Found Such Joy

I have found such joy in simple things;
  A plain, clean room, a nut-brown loaf of bread,
A cup of milk, a kettle as it sings,
  The shelter of a roof above my head,
And in a leaf-laced square along the floor,
Where yellow sunlight glimmers through a door.

I have found such joy in things that fill
  My quiet days: a curtain's blowing grace,
A potted plant upon my window sill,
  A rose, fresh-cut and placed within a vase;
A table cleared, a lamp beside a chair,
And books I long have loved beside me there.

Oh, I have found such joys I wish I might
   Tell every woman who goes seeking far
For some elusive, feverish delight,
   That very close to home the great joys are:
The elemental things—old as the race,
Yet never, through the ages, commonplace.

GRACE NOLL CROWELL

FUN

Epigram

You beat your pate, and fancy wit will come:
Knock as you please, there's nobody at home.

ALEXANDER POPE

The Moron

See the happy moron,
He doesn't give a damn!
I wish I were a moron—
My God! Perhaps I am!

AUTHOR UNKNOWN

Explanation

I hate to be a kicker,
   I always long for peace,
But the wheel that does the squeaking,
   Is the one that gets the grease.

JOSH BILLINGS

Don't Copy Cat

Don't, like the cat, try to get more out
of an experience than there is in it.
The cat, having sat upon a hot stove lid,
Will not sit upon a hot stove lid again.
Nor upon a cold stove lid.

MARK TWAIN

The Pessimist

Nothing to do but work,
Nothing to eat but food,
Nothing to wear but clothes
To keep one from going nude.

Nothing to breathe but air,
Quick as a flash 'tis gone;
Nowhere to fall but off,
Nowhere to stand but on.

Nothing to comb but hair
Nowhere to sleep but in bed,
Nothing to weep but tears,
Nothing to bury but dead.

Nothing to sing but songs,
Ah, well, alas! alack!
Nowhere to go but out,
Nowhere to come but back.

Nothing to see but sights,
Nothing to quench but thirst,
Nothing to have but what we've got;
Thus thro' life we are cursed.

Nothing to strike but a gait;
Everything moves that goes.
Nothing at all but common sense
Can ever withstand these woes.

BEN KING

GRIEF

To One in Paradise

Thou wast all that to me, love,
  For which my soul did pine—
A green isle in the sea, love,
  A fountain and a shrine,
All wreathed with fairy fruits and flowers,
  And all the flowers were mine.

Ah, dream too bright to last!
  Ah, starry Hope! that didst arise
But to be overcast!
  A voice from out the Future cries,
"On! on!"—but o'er the Past
  (Dim gulf!) my spirit hovering lies
Mute, motionless, aghast!

For, alas! alas! with me
  The light of Life is o'er!
  No more—no more—no more—
(Such language holds the solemn sea
  To the sands upon the shore)
Shall bloom the thunder-blasted tree,
  Or the stricken eagle soar!

And all my days are trances,
  And all my nightly dreams
Are where thy dark eye glances,
  And where thy footstep gleams—
In what ethereal dances,
  By what eternal streams.

EDGAR ALLAN POE

She Dwelt Among the
Untrodden Ways

She dwelt among the untrodden ways
   Beside the springs of Dove,
A maid whom there were none to praise
   And very few to love:

A violet by a mossy stone
   Half hidden from the eye.
—Fair as a star, when only one
   Is shining in the sky.

She lived unknown, and few could know
   When Lucy ceased to be;
But she is in her grave, and, oh,
   The difference to me!

WILLIAM WORDSWORTH

O Captain! My Captain!

Written Upon Hearing of
the Assassination of President
Abraham Lincoln

O Captain! my Captain! our fearful trip is done,
The ship has weather'd every rack, the prize we
 sought is won,
The port is near, the bells I hear, the people all
 exulting,
While follow eyes the steady keel, the vessel grim and
 daring;
 But O heart! heart! heart!
  O the bleeding drops of red,
   Where on the deck my Captain lies,
    Fallen cold and dead.

O Captain! my Captain! rise up and hear the bells;
Rise up—for you the flag is flung—for you the bugle
 trills,
For you bouquets and ribbon'd wreaths—for you the
 shores a-crowding,
For you they call, the swaying mass, their eager faces
 turning;
 Here Captain! dear father!
  This arm beneath your head!
   It is some dream that on the deck,
    You've fallen cold and dead.

My Captain does not answer, his lips are pale and
    still,
My father does not feel my arm, he has no pulse nor
    will,
The ship is anchor'd safe and sound, its voyage closed
    and done,
From fearful trip the victor ship comes in with object
    won;
    Exult O shores, and ring O bells!
    But I with mournful tread,
      Walk the deck my Captain lies,
      Fallen cold and dead.

WALT WHITMAN

Miss You

I miss you in the morning, dear,
  When all the world is new;
I know the day can bring no joy
  Because it brings not you.
I miss the well-loved voice of you,
  Your tender smile for me,
The charm of you, the joy of your
  Unfailing sympathy.

The world is full of folks, it's true,
  But there was only one of you.

I miss you at the noontide, dear;
　The crowded city street
Seems but a desert now, I walk
　In solitude complete.

I miss your hand beside my own
　The light touch of your hand,
The quick gleam in the eyes of you
　So sure to understand.

The world is full of folks, it's true,
　But there was only one of you.

I miss you in the evening, dear,
　When daylight fades away;
I miss the sheltering arms of you
　To rest me from the day,
I try to think I see you yet
　There where the firelight gleams—
Weary at last, I sleep, and still
　I miss you in my dreams.

The world is full of folks, it's true,
　But there was only one of you.
　　　　　AUTHOR UNKNOWN

Home They Brought
Her Warrior Dead

Home they brought her warrior dead:
  She nor swooned, nor uttered cry:
All her maidens, watching, said,
  "She must weep or she will die."

Then they praised him, soft and low,
  Called him worthy to be loved,
Truest friend and noblest foe;
  Yet she neither spoke nor moved.

Stole a maiden from her place,
  Lightly to the warrior stept,
Took the face-cloth from the face;
  Yet she neither moved nor wept.

Rose a nurse of ninety years,
  Set his child upon her knee—
Like summer tempest came her tears—
  "Sweet my child, I live for thee."
          ALFRED, LORD TENNYSON

Annabel Lee

It was many and many a year ago,
    In a kingdom by the sea,
That a maiden there lived whom you may know
    By the name of Annabel Lee;—
And this maiden she lived with no other thought
    Than to love and be loved by me.

She was a child and I was a child,
    In this kingdom by the sea,
But we loved with a love that was more than love—
    I and my Annabel Lee—
With a love that the winged seraphs of Heaven
    Coveted her and me.

And this was the reason that, long ago,
    In this kingdom by the sea,
A wind blew out of a cloud, by night
    Chilling my Annabel Lee;
So that her highborn kinsmen came
    And bore her away from me,
To shut her up in a sepulchre
    In this kingdom by the sea.

The angels, not half so happy in Heaven,
    Went envying her and me:
Yes! that was the reason (as all men know,
    In this kingdom by the sea)
That the wind came out of the cloud, chilling
    And killing my Annabel Lee.

But our love it was stronger by far than the love
   Of those who were older than we—
   Of many far wiser than we—
And neither the angels in Heaven above
   Nor the demons down under the sea,
Can ever dissever my soul from the soul
   Of the beautiful Annabel Lee:—

For the moon never beams without bringing me
     dreams
   Of the beautiful Annabel Lee;
And the stars never rise but I see the bright eyes
   Of the beautiful Annabel Lee;
And so, all the night-tide, I lie down by the side
Of my darling, my darling, my life and my bridge,
   In her sepulchre there by the sea—
   In her tomb by the sounding sea.

EDGAR ALLAN POE

Joseph Rodman Drame

Green be the turf above thee,
   Friend of my better days!
None knew thee but to love thee,
   Nor named thee but to praise.

Tears fell, when thou wert dying,
   From eyes unused to weep,
And long, where thou art lying,
   Will tears the cold turf steep.

When hearts, whose truth was proven,
    Like thine, are laid in earth,
There should a wreath be woven
    To tell the world their worth;

And I, who woke each morrow
    To clasp thy hand in mine,
Who shared thy joy and sorrow,
    Whose weal and woe were thine,

It should be mine to braid it
    Around thy faded brow,
But I've in vain essayed it,
    And feel I cannot now.

While memory bids me weep thee,
    Nor thoughts nor words are free,
The grief is fixed too deeply
    That mourns a man like thee.

FITZ-GREENE HALLECK

We Kiss'd Again with Tears

As through the land at eve we went,
  And pluck'd the ripen'd ears,
We fell out, my wife and I,
O we fell out I know not why,
  And kiss'd again with tears.
And blessings on the falling out
  That all the more endears,
When we fall out with those we love,
  And kiss again with tears!
For when we came where lies the child
  We lost in other years,
There above the little grave,
O there above the little grave,
  We kiss'd again with tears.

ALFRED, LORD TENNYSON

Patterns

I walk down the garden-paths,
And all the daffodils
Are blowing, and the bright blue squills.
I walk down the patterned garden-paths
In my stiff, brocaded gown.

With my powdered hair and jeweled fan,
I too am a rare
Pattern. As I wander down
The garden-paths.

My dress is richly figured,
And the train
Makes a pink and silver strain
On the gravel, and the thrift
Of the borders.
Just a plate of current fashion,
Tripping by in high-heeled, ribboned shoes.
Not a softness anywhere about me,
Only whalebone and brocade.
And I sink on a seat in the shade
Of a lime-tree. For my passion
Wars against the stiff brocade.
The daffodils and squills
Flutter in the breeze
As they please.
And I weep;
For the lime-tree is in blossom
And one small flower has dropped upon my bosom.

And the plashing of waterdrops
In the marble fountain
Comes down the garden-paths.
The dripping never stops.
Underneath my stiffened gown
Is the softness of a woman bathing in a marble basin,
A basin in the midst of hedges grown
So thick, she cannot see her lover hiding,
But she guesses he is near,
And the sliding of the water
Seems the stroking of a dear
Hand upon her.

What is Summer in a fine brocaded gown!
I should like to see it lying in a heap upon the
    ground.
All the pink and silver crumpled up on the ground.

I would be the pink and silver as I ran along the
    paths,
And he would stumble after,
Bewildered by my laughter.
I should see the sun flashing from his sword-hilt and
    the buckles on his shoes.
I would choose
To lead him in a maze along the patterned paths,
A bright and laughing maze for my heavy-booted lover.
Till he caught me in the shade,
And the buttons of his waistcoat bruised my body as
    he clasped me,
Aching, melting, unafraid.
With the shadows of the leaves and the sundrops,
And the plopping of the waterdrops,
All about us in the open afternoon—
I am very like to swoon
With the weight of this brocade,
For the sun sifts through the shade.

Underneath the fallen blossom
In my bosom
Is a letter I had hid.
It was brought to me this morning by a rider from the
    Duke.
"Madam, we regret to inform you that Lord Hartwell
Died in action Thursday se'nnight."
As I read it in the white, morning sunlight,
The letters squirmed like snakes.
"Any answer, Madam?" said my footman.

"No," I told him.
"See that the messenger takes some refreshment.
No, no answer."
And I walked into the garden,
Up and down the patterned paths,
In my stiff, correct brocade.
The blue and yellow flowers stood up proudly
    in the sun,
Each one.
I stood upright too,
Held rigid to the pattern
By the stiffness of my gown;
Up and down I walked,
Up and down.

In a month he would have been my husband.
In a month, here, underneath this lime,
We would have broke the pattern;
He for me, and I for him,
He as Colonel, I as Lady,
On this shady seat.
He had a whim
That sunlight carried blessing.
And I answered, "It shall be as you have said."
Now he is dead.

In Summer and in Winter I shall walk
Up and down
The patterned garden-paths
In my stiff, brocaded gown.
The squills and daffodils
Will give place to pillared roses, and to asters,
    and to snow.

I shall go
Up and down
In my gown.
Gorgeously arrayed,
Boned and stayed.
And the softness of my body will be guarded
   from embrace
By each button, hook, and lace.
For the man who should loose me is dead,
Fighting with the Duke in Flanders,
In a pattern called a war.
Christ! What are patterns for?

AMY LOWELL

HOME

Home

It takes a heap o' livin' in a house t' make it home,
A heap o' sun an' shadder, an' ye sometimes have t'
  roam
Afore ye really 'preciate the things ye lef' behind,
An' hunger fer 'em somehow, with 'em allus on yer
  mind.
It don't make any differunce how rich ye get t' be,
How much yer chairs an' tables cost, how great yer
  luxury;
It ain't home t' ye, though it be the palace of a king,
Until somehow yer soul is sort o' wrapped round
  everthing.

Home ain't a place that gold can buy or get up in a
  minute;
Afore it's home there's got t' be a heap o' livin' in it;
Within the walls there's got t' be some babies born,
  and then
Right there ye've got t' bring 'em up t' women good,
  an' men;
And gradjerly, as time goes on, ye find ye wouldn't
  part
With anything they ever used—they've grown into yer
  heart:
The old high chairs, the playthings, too, the little
  shoes they wore
Ye hoard; an' if ye could ye'd keep the thumb-marks
  on the door.

Ye've got t' weep t' make it home, ye've got t' sit an'
    sigh
An' watch beside a loved one's bed, an' know that
    Death is nigh;
An' in the stillness o' the night t' see Death's angel
    come,
An' close the eyes o' her that smiled, an' leave her
    sweet voice dumb.
Fer these are scenes that grip the heart, an' when yer
    tears are dried,
Ye find the home is dearer than it was, an' sanctified;
An' tuggin' at ye always are the pleasant memories
O' her that was an' is no more—ye can't escape from
    these.
Ye've got t' sing an' dance fer years, ye've got t' romp
    an' play,
An' learn t' love the things ye have by usin' 'em each
    day;
Even the roses 'round the porch must blossom year by
    year
Afore they 'come a part o' ye, suggestin' someone
    dear
Who used t' love 'em long ago, an' trained 'em jes' t'
    run
the way they do, so's they would get the early
    mornin' sun;
Ye've got t' love each brick an' stone from cellar up t'
    dome:
It takes a heap o' livin' in a house t' make it home.

EDGAR GUEST

No Place to Go

The happiest nights
   I ever know
Are those when I've
   No place to go,
And the missus says
   When the day is through:
"To-night we haven't
   A thing to do."

Oh, the joy of it,
   And the peace untold
Of sitting 'round
   In my slippers old,
With my pipe and book
   In my easy chair,
Knowing I needn't
   Go anywhere.

Needn't hurry
   My evening meal
Nor force the smiles
   That I do not feel,
But can grab a book
   From a near-by shelf,
And drop all sham
   And be myself.

Oh, the charm of it
  And the comfort rare;
Nothing on earth
  With it can compare;
And I'm sorry for him
  Who doesn't know
The joy of having
  No place to go.

EDGAR GUEST

Prayer for This House

May nothing evil cross this door,
And may ill fortune never pry
About these windows; may the roar
  And rain go by.

Strengthened by faith, these rafters will
Withstand the batt'ring of the storm;
This hearth, though all the world grow chill,
  Will keep us warm.

Peace shall walk softly through these rooms,
Touching our lips with holy wine,
Til ev'ry casual corner blooms
  Into a shrine.

Laughter shall drown the raucous shout;
And, though these shelt'ring walls are thin,
May they be strong to keep hate out
  And hold love in.

LOUIS UNTERMEYER

Home

Home!
My very heart's desire is safe
Within thy walls;
The voices of my loved ones, friends who come,
My treasured books that rest in niche serene,
All make more dear to me thy haven sweet.
Nor do my feet
Desire to wander out except that they
May have the glad return at eventide—
Dear Home.

Home!
My very heart's contentment lies
Within thy walls.
No worldly calls hath power to turn my eyes
In longing from thy quietness. Each morn
When I go forth upon the duties of the day
I wend my way
Content to know that eve will bring me
Safely to thy walls again.
Dear Home.

NELLIE WOMACK HINES

Home, Sweet Home

'Mid pleasures and palaces though we may roam,
Be it ever so humble, there's no place like home;
A charm from the sky seems to hallow us there,
Which, seek through the world, is ne'er met with
    elsewhere.
    Home, home, sweet, sweet home!
There's no place like home, oh, there's no place like
    home!

An exile from home, splendor dazzles in vain;
Oh, give me my lowly thatched cottage again!
The birds singing gayly, that came at my call—
Give me them—and the peace of mind, dearer than
    all!
    Home, home, sweet, sweet home!
There's no place like home, oh, there's no place like
    home!

I gaze on the moon as I tread the drear wild,
And feel that my mother now thinks of her child,
As she looks on that moon from our own cottage
    door
Thro' the woodbine, whose fragrance shall cheer me
    no more.
    Home, home, sweet, sweet home!
There's no place like home, oh, there's no place like
    home!

How sweet 'tis to sit 'neath a fond father's smile,
And the caress of a mother to soothe and beguile!

Let others delight 'mid new pleasure to roam,
But give me, oh, give me, the pleasures of home,
  Home, home, sweet, sweet home!
There's no place like home, oh, there's no place like
    home!

To thee I'll return, overburdened with care;
The heart's dearest solace will smile on me there;
No more from that cottage again will I roam;
Be it ever so humble, there's no place like home.
  Home, home, sweet, sweet home!
There's no place like home, oh, there's no place like
    home!

JOHN HOWARD PAYNE

A Prayer for a Little Home

God send us a little home,
To come back to, when we roam.

Low walls and fluted tiles,
Wide windows, a view for miles.

Red firelight and deep chairs,
Small white beds upstairs—

Great talk in little nooks,
Dim colors, rows of books.

One picture on each wall,
Not many things at all.

God send us a little ground,
Tall trees stand round.

Homely flowers in brown sod,
Overhead, thy stars, O God.

God bless thee, when winds blow,
Our home, and all we know.

FLORENCE BONE

Home Is Where There Is One to Love Us

Home's not merely four square walls,
Though with pictures hung and gilded;
Home is where Affection calls—
Filled with shrines the Hearth had builded!
Home! Go watch the faithful dove,
Sailing 'neath the heaven above us.
Home is where there's one to love!
Home is where there's one to love us.

Home's not merely roof and room,
It needs something to endear it;
Home is where the heart can bloom,
Where there's some kind lip to cheer it!
What is home with none to meet,
None to welcome, none to greet us?
Home is sweet, and only sweet,
Where there's one we love to meet us!

CHARLES SWAIN

HOPE

Work Without Hope

All Nature seems at work. Slugs leave their lair—
The bees are stirring—birds are on the wing—
And Winter, slumbering in the open air,
Wears on his smiling face a dream of Spring!
And I, the while, the sole unbusy thing,
Nor honey make, nor pair, nor build, nor sing.

Yet well I ken the banks where amaranths blow,
Have traced the fount whence streams of nectar flow.
Bloom, O ye amaranths! bloom for whom ye may,
For me ye bloom not! Glide, rich streams, away!

With lips unbrighten'd, wreathless brow, I stroll:
And would you learn the spells that drowse my soul?
Work without Hope draws nectar in a sieve,
And Hope without an object cannot live.

SAMUEL TAYLOR COLERIDGE

The Rainy Day

The day is cold, and dark, and dreary;
It rains, and the wind is never weary;
The vine still clings to the moldering wall,
But at every gust the dead leaves fall,
   And the day is dark and dreary.

My life is cold, and dark, and dreary;
It rains, and the wind is never weary;
My thoughts still cling to the moldering Past,
But the hopes of youth fall thick in the blast
   And the days are dark and dreary.

Be still, sad heart! and cease repining;
Behind the clouds is the sun still shining;
   Thy fate is the common fate of all,
Into each life some rain must fall,
   Some days must be dark and dreary.

HENRY WADSWORTH LONGFELLOW

Song

Love laid his sleepless head
On a thorny rosy bed;
And his eyes with tears were red,
And pale his lips as the dead.

And fear and sorrow and scorn
Kept watch by his head forlorn,
Till the night was overworn,
And the world was merry with morn.

And Joy came up with the day,
And kissed Love's lips as he lay,
And the watchers ghostly and gray
Sped from his pillow away.

And his eyes as the dawn grew bright,
And his lips waxed ruddy as light:
Sorrow may reign for a night,
But day shall bring back delight.

ALGERNON CHARLES SWINBURNE

HUMANITY

I Am the People, the Mob

I am the people—the mob—the crowd—the mass.
Do you know that all the great work of the world is done
 through me?
I am the workingman, the inventor, the maker of the
 world's food and clothes.
I am the audience that witnesses history. The Napoleons
 come from me and the Lincolns. They die. And then I
 send forth more Napoleons and Lincolns.
I am the seed ground. I am a prairie that will stand for much
 plowing. Terrible storms pass over me. I forget. The best
 of me is sucked out and wasted. I forget. Everything but
 Death comes to me and makes me work and give up what
 I have. And I forget.
Sometimes I growl, shake myself and spatter a few red
 drops for history to remember. Then—I forget.
When I, the People, learn to remember, when I, the People,
 use the lessons of yesterday and no longer forget who
 robbed me last year, who played me for a fool—then
 there will be no speaker in all the world say the name:
 "The People," with any fleck of a sneer in his voice or any
 far-off smile of derision.
The mob—the crowd—the mass—will arrive then.

CARL SANDBURG

My Days Among the Dead

My days among the dead are past;
  Around me I behold,
Wher'er these casual eyes are cast,
  The mighty minds of old:
My never-failing friends are they,
With whom I converse day by day.

With them I take delight in weal
  And seek relief in woe;
And while I understand and feel
  How much to them I owe,
My cheeks have often been bedewed
With tears of thoughtful gratitude.

My thoughts are with the Dead; with them
  I live in long-past years,
Their virtues love, their faults condemn,
  Partake their hopes and fears;
And from their lessons seek and find
Instruction with an humble mind.

My hopes are with the Dead; anon
  My place with them will be,
And I with them shall travel on
  Through all Futurity;
Yet leaving here a name, I trust,
That will not perish in the dust.

ROBERT SOUTHEY

from *An Essay on Man*

Know then thyself, presume not God to scan,
The proper study of mankind is man.
Placed on this isthmus of a middle state,
A being darkly wise, and rudely great:
With too much knowledge for the sceptic side,
With too much weakness for the stoic's pride,
He hangs between; in doubt to act, or rest;
In doubt to deem himself a god, or beast;
In doubt his mind or body to prefer;
Born but to die, and reasoning but to err;
Alike in ignorance, his reason such,
Whether he thinks too little or too much:
Chaos of thought and passion, all confused;
Still by himself abused or disabused;
Created half to rise and half to fall;
Great lord of all things, yet a prey to all;
Sole judge of truth, in endless error hurled:
The glory, jest, and riddle of the world!

ALEXANDER POPE

The Dead

I see them,—crowd on crowd they walk the earth,
Dry leafless trees no autumn wind laid bare;
And in their nakedness find cause for mirth,
And all unclad would winter's rudeness dare;
No sap doth through their clattering branches flow,
Whence springing leaves and blossoms bright appear;
Their hearts the living God have ceased to know
Who gives the spring-time to th' expectant year.

They mimic life, as if from Him to steal
His glow of health to paint the livid cheek;
They borrow words for thoughts they cannot feel,
That with a seeming heart their tongue may speak;
And in their show of life more dead they live
Than those that to the earth with many tears they give.

JONES VERY

Four Seasons Fill the Measure

Four seasons fill the measure of the year;
There are four seasons in the mind of man:
He has his lusty Spring, when fancy clear
Takes in all beauty with an easy span:
He has his Summer, when luxuriously
Spring's honey'd cud of youthful thought he loves
To ruminate, and by such dreaming nigh
His nearest unto heaven: quiet coves
His soul has in its Autumn, when his wings
He furleth close: contented so to look
On mists in idleness—to let fair things
Pass by unheeded as a threshold brook:
He has his Winter too of pale misfeature,
Or else he would forgo his mortal nature.

JOHN KEATS

IMAGINATION

Aladdin

When I was a beggarly boy,
    And lived in a cellar damp,
I had not a friend nor a toy,
    But I had Aladdin's lamp;
When I could not sleep for the cold,
    I had fire enough in my brain,
And builded, with roofs of gold,
    My beautiful castles in Spain!

Since then I have toiled day and night,
    I have money and power good store,
But I'd give all my lamps of silver bright
    For the one that is mine no more.
Take, Fortune, whatever you choose;
    You gave and may snatch again;
I have nothing 'twould pain me to lose,
    For I own no more castles in Spain!

JAMES RUSSELL LOWELL

Song

Go and catch a falling star,
   Get with child a mandrake root,
Tell me where all past years are,
   Or who cleft the devil's foot,
Teach me to hear mermaids singing,
Or to keep off envy's stinging,
      And find what wind
Serves to advance an honest mind.

If thou beest born to strange sights,
   Things invisible to see,
Ride ten thousand days and nights,
   Till age snow white hairs on thee,
Thou, when thou return'st, wilt tell me
All strange wonders that befell thee,
      And swear no where
Lives a woman true and fair.

If thou find'st one, let me know;
   Such a pilgrimage were sweet.
Yet do not, I would not go,
   Though at next door we might meet.

Though she were true when you met her,
And last till you write your letter,
      Yet she will be
False, ere I come, to two or three.

JOHN DONNE

The Emperor of Ice-Cream

Call the roller of big cigars,
The muscular one, and bid him whip
In kitchen cups concupiscent curds.
Let the wenches dawdle in such dress
As they are used to wear, and let the boys
Bring flowers in last month's newspapers.
Let be be finale of seem.
The only emperor is the emperor of ice-cream.

Take from the dresser of deal,
Lacking the three glass knobs, that sheet
On which she embroidered fantails once
And spread it so as to cover her face.

If her horny feet protrude, they come
To show how cold she is, and dumb.
Let the lamp affix its beam.
The only emperor is the emperor of ice-cream.

WALLACE STEVENS

INSPIRATION

Beyond the Profit of Today

Lord, give me vision that shall see
   Beyond the profit of today
Into the years which are to be,
   That I may take the larger, wiser way.

I seek for fortune, Lord, nor claim
   To scorn the recompense I earn;
But help me, as I play the game,
   To give the world its just return.

Thou mad'st the earth for all of us,
   Teach me through struggle, strain and stress
To win and do my share, for thus
   Can profit lead to happiness.

Guard me from thoughts of little men
   Which blind the soul to greater things;
Save me from smug content and then
   From greed and selfishness it brings.

Aid me to join that splendid clan
   Of Business Men who seek to trace
A calm, considered working-plan
   To make the world a better place.

Teach me to hold this task above
   All lesser thoughts within my ken,
That thus I may be worthy of
   The name of Business Man; Amen!

AUTHOR UNKNOWN

Battle-Hymn of the Republic

Mine eyes have seen the glory of the coming of the
    Lord:
He is trampling out the vintage where the grapes of
    wrath are stored;
He hath loosed the fateful lightning of his terrible
    swift sword:
  His truth is marching on.

I have seen him in the watch-fires of a hundred
    circling camps;
They have builded him an altar in the evening dews
    and damps;
I can read his righteous sentence by the dim and
    flaring lamps:
  His day is marching on.

I have read as fiery gospel, writ in burnished rows of
    steel:
"As ye deal with my contemners, so with you my
    grace shall deal;
Let the Hero, born of woman, crush the serpent with
    his heel,
  Since God is marching on."

He has sounded forth the trumpet that shall never call
    retreat;
He is sifting out the hearts of men before his
    judgment-seat:
O, be swift, my soul, to answer him! be jubilant, my
    feet!
  Our God is marching on.

In the beauty of the lilies Christ was born across the
     sea,
With a glory in his bosom that transfigures you and
     me;
As he died to make men holy, let us die to make men
     free,
  While God is marching on.

                    JULIA WARD HOWE

It Couldn't Be Done

Somebody said that it couldn't be done,
  But he with a chuckle replied
That "maybe it couldn't," but he would be one
  Who wouldn't say so till he'd tried.
So he buckled right in with the trace of a grin
  On his face. If he worried he hid it.
He started to sing as he tackled the thing
  That couldn't be done, and he did it.

Somebody scoffed: "Oh, you'll never do that;
  At least no one ever has done it";
But he took off his coat and he took off his hat,
  And the first thing we knew he'd begun it.
With a lift of his chin and a bit of a grin,
  Without any doubting or quiddit,
He started to sing as he tackled the thing
  That couldn't be done, and he did it.

There are thousands to tell you it cannot be done,
    There are thousands to prophesy failure;
There are thousands to point out to you, one by one,
    The dangers that wait to assail you.
But just buckle in with a bit of a grin,
    Just take off your coat and go to it;
Just start to sing as you tackle the thing
    That "cannot be done," and you'll do it.

                                        EDGAR GUEST

Carry On!

It's easy to fight when everything's right,
And you're mad with the thrill and the glory;
It's easy to cheer when victory's near,
And wallow in fields that are gory.
It's a different song when everything's wrong,
When you're feeling infernally mortal;
When it's ten against one, and hope there is none,
Buck up, little soldier, and chortle:

Carry on! Carry on!
There isn't much punch in your blow.
You're glaring and staring and hitting out blind;
You're muddy and bloody, but never you mind.
Carry on! Carry on!
You haven't the ghost of a show.
It's looking like death, but while you've a breath,
Carry on, my son! Carry on!

And so in the strife of the battle of life
It's easy to fight when you're winning;

It's easy to slave, and starve and be brave,
When the dawn of success is beginning.
But the man who can meet despair and defeat
With a cheer, there's the man of God's choosing;
The man who can fight to Heaven's own height
Is the man who can fight when he's losing.

Carry on! Carry on!
Things never were looming so black.
But show that you haven't a cowardly streak,
And though you're unlucky you never are weak.
Carry on! Carry on!
Brace up for another attack.
It's looking like hell, but—you never can tell:
Carry on, old man! Carry on!

There are some who drift out in the deserts of doubt,
And some who in brutishness wallow;
There are others, I know, who in piety go
Because of a Heaven to follow.
But to labour with zest, and to give of your best,
For the sweetness and joy of the giving;
To help folks along with a hand and a song;
Why, there's the real sunshine of living.

Carry on! Carry on!
Fight the good fight and true;
Believe in your mission, greet life with a cheer;
There's big work to do, and that's why you are here.
Carry on! Carry on!
Let the world be the better for you;
And at last when you die, let this be your cry:
Carry on, my soul! Carry on!

ROBERT SERVICE

Say Not the Struggle
Naught Availeth

Say not the struggle naught availeth,
   The labor and the wounds are vain,
The enemy faints not, nor faileth,
   And as things have been they remain.

If hopes were dupes, fears may be liars;
   It may be, in yon smoke conceal'd,
Your comrades chase e'en now the fliers,
   And, but for you, possess the field.

For while the tired waves, vainly breaking,
   Seem here no painful inch to gain,
Far back, through creeks and inlets making,
   Comes silent, flooding in, the main.

And not by eastern windows only,
   When daylight comes, comes in the light;
In front the sun climbs slow, how slowly.
   But westward, look, the land is bright.

ARTHUR CLOUGH

Hold Fast Your Dreams

Hold fast your dreams!
Within your heart
Keep one still, secret spot
Where dreams may go,

286

And, sheltered so,
May thrive and grow
Where doubt and fear are not.
O keep a place apart,
Within your heart,
For little dreams to go!

Think still of lovely things that are not true.
Let wish and magic work at will in you.
Be sometimes blind to sorrow. Make believe!
Forget the calm that lies
In disillusioned eyes.
Though we all know that we must die,
Yet you and I
May walk like gods and be
Even now at home in immortality.

We see so many ugly things—
Deceits and wrongs and quarrelings;
We know, alas! we know
How quickly fade
The color in the west,
The bloom upon the breast
And youth's blind hour.
Yet keep within your heart
A place apart
Where little dreams may go,
May thrive and grow.
Hold fast—hold fast your dreams!

LOUISE DRISCOLL

Be the Best of
Whatever You Are

If you can't be a pine on the top of the hill,
    Be a scrub in the valley—but be
The best little scrub by the side of the rill;
    Be a bush if you can't be a tree.

If you can't be a bust be a bit of the grass,
    And some highway happier make;
If you can't be a muskie than just be a bass—
    But the liveliest bass in the lake!

We can't all be captains, we've got to be crew,
    There's something for all of us here,
There's big work to do, and there's lesser to do,
    And the task you must do is the near.

If you can't be a highway than just be a trail,
    If you can't be the sun be a star;
It isn't by size that you win or you fail—
    Be the best of whatever you are!

DOUGLAS MALLOCH

The New Jerusalem

And did those feet in ancient time
    Walk upon England's mountains green?
And was the Holy Lamb of God
    On England's pleasant pastures seen?

And did the countenance divine
   Shine forth upon our clouded hills?
And was Jerusalem builded here
Among these dark satanic mills?

Bring me my bow of burning gold!
Bring me my arrows of desire!
Bring me my spear! O clouds, unfold!
   Bring me my chariot of fire!

I will not cease from mental fight,
   Nor shall my sword sleep in my hand,
Till we have built Jerusalem
   In England's green and pleasant land.

WILLIAM BLAKE

JOURNEYS

The Tide Rises, the Tide Falls

The tide rises, the tide falls,
The twilight darkens, the curfew calls;
Along the sea-sands damp and brown
The traveller hastens toward the town,
 And the tide rises, the tide falls.

Darkness settles on roofs and walls,
But the sea, the sea in the darkness calls;
The little waves, with their soft, white hands,
Efface the footprints in the sands,
 And the tide rises, the tide falls.

The morning breaks; the steeds in their stalls
Stamp and neigh, as the hostler calls;
The day returns, but nevermore
Returns the traveller to the shore,
 And the tide rises, the tide falls.
     HENRY WADSWORTH LONGFELLOW

Up-hill

Does the road wind up-hill all the way?
 Yes, to the very end.
Will the day's journey take the whole long day?
 From morn to night, my friend.

But is there for the night a resting-place?
　　A roof for when the slow dark hours begin.
May not the darkness hide it from my face?
　　You cannot miss that inn.

Shall I meet other wayfarers at night?
　　Those who have gone before.
Then must I knock, or call when just in sight?
　　They will not keep you standing at that door.

Shall I find comfort, travel-sore and weak?
　　Of labour you shall find the sum.
Will there be beds for me and all who seek?
　　Yea, beds for all who come.

CHRISTINA ROSSETTI

The Ocean of Life

Ships that pass in the night, and speak
　　each other in passing;
Only a signal shown and a distant
　　voice in the darkness;
So in the ocean of life we pass and
　　speak one another,
Only a look and a voice; then darkness
　　again and a silence.

HENRY WADSWORTH LONGFELLOW

JOY

A Birthday

My heart is like a singing bird
   Whose nest is in a watered shoot:
My heart is like an apple tree
   Whose boughs are bent with thickset fruit;
My heart is like a rainbow shell
   That paddles in a halcyon sea;
My heart is gladder than all these
   Because my love is come to me.

Raise me a dais of silk and down;
   Hang it with vair and purple dyes;
Carve it in doves and pomegranates,
   And peacocks with a hundred eyes;
Work it in gold and silver grapes,
   In leaves and silver fleurs-de-lys;
Because the birthday of my life
   Is come, my love is come to me.

CHRISTINA ROSSETTI

To a Skylark

Hail to thee, blithe Spirit!
   Bird thou never wert,
That from Heaven, or near it,
   Pourest thy full heart
In profuse strains of unpremeditated art.

Higher still and higher
  From the earth thou springest
Like a cloud of fire;
  The blue deep thou wingest,
And singing still dost soar, and soaring ever singest.

In the golden lightning
  Of the sunken sun
O'er which clouds are bright'ning,
  Thou dost float and run,
Like an unbodied joy whose race is just begun.

The pale purple even
  Melts around thy flight;
Like a star of Heaven
  In the broad daylight
Thou art unseen, but yet I hear thy shrill delight:

Keen as are the arrows
  Of that silver sphere,
Whose intense lamp narrows
  In the white dawn clear
Until we hardly see—we feel that it is there.

All the earth and air
  With thy voice is loud,
As when night is bare,
  From one lonely cloud
The moon rains out her beams, and
    Heaven is overflowed.

What thou art we know not;
    What is most like thee?
From rainbow clouds there flow not
    Drops so bright to see
As from thy presence showers a rain of melody.

Like a Poet hidden
    In the light of thought,
Singing hymns unbidden,
    Till the world is wrought
To sympathy with hopes and fears it heeded not:

Like a high-born maiden
    In a palace-tower,
Soothing her love-laden
    Soul in secret hour
With music sweet as love, which overflows her bower:

Like a glow-worm golden
    In a dell of dew,
Scattering unbeholden
    Its aëreal hue
Among the flowers and grass, which screen it from the
    view!

Like a rose embowered
    In its own green leaves,
By warm winds deflowered,
    Till the scent it gives
Makes faint with too much sweet those heavy-winged
    thieves:

Sound of vernal showers
    On the twinkling grass,
Rain-awakened flowers,
    All that ever was
Joyous, and clear, and fresh, thy music doth surpass:

Teach us, Sprite or Bird,
    What sweet thoughts are thine:
I have never heard
    Praise of love or wine
That panted forth a flood of rapture so divine.

Chorus Hymeneal,
    Or triumphal chant,
Matched with thine would be all
    But an empty vaunt,
A thing wherein we feel there is some hidden want.

What objects are the fountains
    Of thy happy strain?
What fields, or waves, or mountains?
    What shapes of sky or plain?
What love of thine own kind? what ignorance of pain?

With thy clear keen joyance
    Languor cannot be:
Shadow of annoyance
    Never came near thee:
Thou lovest—but ne'er knew love's sad satiety.

Waking or asleep,
    Thou of death must deem
Things more true and deep
    Than we mortals dream.
Or how could thy notes flow in such a crystal stream?

We look before and after,
    And pine for what is not:
Our sincerest laughter
    With some pain is fraught;
Our sweetest songs are those that tell of saddest thought.

Yet if we could scorn
    Hate, and pride, and fear;
If we were things born
    Not to shed a tear,
I know not how thy joy we ever should come near.

Better than all measures
    Of delightful sound,
Better than all treasures
    That in books are found,
Thy skill to poet were, thou scorner of the ground!

Teach me half the gladness
    That thy brain must know,
Such harmonious madness
    From my lips would flow
The world should listen then—as I am listening now.

                              PERCY BYSSHE SHELLEY

LIFE

Daybreak

A Wind came up out of the sea,
And said, "O mists, make room for me."

It hailed the ships, and cried, "Sail on,
Ye mariners, the night is gone."

And hurried landward far away,
Crying, "Awake! it is the day."

It said unto the forest, "Shout!
Hang all your leafy banners out!"

It touched the wood-bird's folded wing,
And said, "O bird, awake and sing."

And o'er the farms, "O chanticleer,
Your clarion blow; the day is near."

It whispered to the fields of corn,
"Bow down, and hail the coming morn."

It shouted through the belfry tower,
"Awake, O bell! proclaim the hours."

It crossed the churchyard with a sigh,
And said, "Not yet! in quiet lie."
            HENRY WADSWORTH LONGFELLOW

Commonplace

"A commonplace life," we say, and we sigh,
But why should we sigh as we say?
The commonplace sun in the commonplace sky
Makes up the commonplace day;
The moon and the stars are commonplace things,
And the flower that blooms, and the bird that sings,
But dark were the world, and sad our lot,
If the flowers failed, and the sun shone not;
And God, who studies each separate soul,
Out of commonplace lives makes His beautiful whole.

SUSAN COOLIDGE

He Hears with Gladdened Heart the Thunder

He hears with gladdened heart the thunder
    Peal, and loves the falling dew;
He knows the earth above and under—
    Sits and is content to view.

He sits beside the dying ember,
    God for hope and man for friend,
Content to see, glad to remember,
    Expectant of the certain end.

ROBERT LOUIS STEVENSON

LIVE FOR TODAY

To His Coy Mistress

Had we but world enough, and time,
This coyness, lady, were no crime.
We would sit down, and think which way
To walk, and pass our long love's day.
Thou by the Indian Ganges' side
Shouldst rubies find: I by the tide
Of Humber would complain. I would
Love you ten years before the flood,
And you should, if you please, refuse
Till the conversion of the Jews;
My vegetable love should grow
Vaster than empires and more slow;
An hundred years should go to praise
Thine eyes, and on thy forehead gaze;
Two hundred to adore each breast,
But thirty thousand to the rest;
An age at least to every part,
And the last age should show your heart.
For, lady, you deserve this state;
Nor would I love at lower rate.
But at my back I always hear
Time's winged chariot hurrying near;
And yonder all before us lie
Deserts of vast eternity.
Thy beauty shall no more be found,
Nor in thy marble vault shall sound
My echoing song; then worms shall try
That long preserved virginity;
And your quaint honor turn to dust,
And into ashes all my lust:

The grave's a fine and private place,
But none, I think, do there embrace.

Now therefore, while the youthful hue
Sits on thy skin like morning dew,
And while thy willing soul transpires
At every pore with instant fires,
Now let us sport us while we may,
And now, like amorous birds of prey,
Rather at once our time devour
Than languish in his slow-chapped power,
Let us roll all our strength and all
Our sweetness up into one ball,
And tear our pleasures with rough strife
Thorough the iron gates of life:
Thus, though we cannot make our sun
Stand still, yet we will make him run.

ANDREW MARVELL

O to Be Up and Doing

O to be up and doing,
Unfearing and unashamed to go
In all the uproar and the press
About my human business!
My undissuaded heart I hear
Whisper courage in my ear.
With voiceless calls, the ancient earth
Summons me to a daily birth,
Thou, O my love, ye, O my friends—

The gist of life, the end of ends—
To laugh, to love, to live, to die
Ye call me by the ear and eye!
ROBERT LOUIS STEVENSON

Come Down, O Maid

"Come down, O maid, from yonder mountain height:
What pleasure lives in height (the shepherd sang),
In height and cold, the splendour of the hills?
But cease to move so near the Heavens, and cease
To glide a sunbeam by the blasted Pine,
To sit a star upon the sparkling spire:
And come, for Love is of the valley, come,
For Love is of the valley, come thou down
And find him; by the happy threshold, he,
Or hand in hand with Plenty in the maize,
Or red with spirited purple of the vats,
Or foxlike in the vine; or cares to walk
With Death and Morning on the silver horns,
Nor wilt thou snare him in the white ravine,
Nor find him dropt upon the firths of ice,
That huddling slant in furrow-cloven falls
To roll the torrent out of dusky doors:
But follow: let the torrent dance thee down
To find him in the valley; let the wild
Lean-headed Eagles yelp alone, and leave
The monstrous ledges there to slope, and spill
Their thousand wreaths of dangling watersmoke,
That like a broken purpose waste in air:

311

So waste not thou: but come; for all the vales
Await thee: azure pillars of the hearth
Arise to thee: the children call, and I
Thy shepherd pipe, and sweet is every sound,
Sweeter thy voice, but every sound is sweet;
Myriads of rivulets hurry thro' the lawn,
The moan of doves in immemorial elms,
And murmuring of innumerable bees."

ALFRED, LORD TENNYSON

Away with Funeral Music

Away with funeral music—set
   The pipe to powerful lips—
The cup of life's for him that drinks
   And not for him that sips.

ROBERT LOUIS STEVENSON

What Is to Come

What is to come we know not. But we know
That what has been was good—was good to show,
Better to hide, and best of all to bear.
We are the masters of the days that were;
We have lived, we have loved, we have suffered . . . even so.

Shall we not take the ebb who had the flow?
Life was our friend. Now, if it be our foe—
Dear, though it spoil and break us!—need we care
      What is to come?
Let the great winds their worst and wildest blow,
Or the gold weather round us mellow slow;
We have fulfilled ourselves, and we can dare
And we can conquer, though we may not share
In the rich quiet of the afterglow
      What is to come.
          WILLIAM ERNEST HENLEY

Gather Ye Roses

Gather ye roses while ye may,
   Old time is still a-flying;
A world where beauty fleets away
   Is no world for denying.
Come lads and lasses, fall to play
   Lose no more time in sighing.

The very flowers you pluck to-day
   To-morrow will be dying;
   And all the flowers are crying,
And all the leaves have tongues to say,—
Gather ye roses while ye may.
      ROBERT LOUIS STEVENSON

Glycine's Song

A sunny shaft did I behold,
From sky to earth it slanted:
And poised therein a bird so bold—
Sweet bird, thou wert enchanted!
He sank, he rose, he twinkled, he troll'd
Within that shaft of sunny mist;
His eyes of fire, his beak of gold,
All else of amethyst!

And thus he sang: 'Adieu! adieu!
Love's dreams prove seldom true.
The blossoms, they make no delay:
The sparking dew-drops will not stay.
 Sweet month of May,
  We must away;
  Far, far away!
   To-day! to-day!'
SAMUEL TAYLOR COLERIDGE

LOVE

My Luve

O my luve is like a red, red rose,
   That's newly sprung in June:
O my luve is like the melodie,
   That's sweetly played in tune.

As fair art thou, my bonie lass,
   So deep in luve am I;
And I will luve thee still, my dear,
   Till a' the seas gang dry.

Till a' the seas gang dry, my dear,
   And the rocks melt wi' the sun:
And I will luve thee still, my dear,
   While the sands o' life shall run.

And fare thee weel, my only luve!
   And fare thee weel a while!
And I will come again, my luve,
   Tho' it were ten thousand mile.

ROBERT BURNS

Ruth 1:16–18

And Ruth said, Intreat me not to leave
thee, or to return from following after thee:
for whither thou goest, I will go; and where
thou lodgest, I will lodge: thy people shall be
my people, and thy God my God:

Where thou diest, will I die, and there
will I be buried: the LORD do so to me, and
more also, if ought but death part thee and
me.

Let Me Not to the
Marriage of True Minds

Let me not to the marriage of true minds
Admit impediments. Love is not love
Which alters when it alteration finds,
Or bends with the remover to remove:
O, no! it is an ever-fixed mark,
That looks on tempests and is never shaken;
It is the star to every wandering bark,
Whose worth's unknown, although his height be taken.
Love's not Time's fool, though rosy lips and cheeks
Within his bending sickle's compass come;
Love alters not with his brief hours and weeks,
But bears it out even to the edge of doom.
   If this be error, and upon me prov'd,
   I never writ, nor no man ever lov'd.

WILLIAM SHAKESPEARE

from *Rabbi Ben Ezra*

Grow old along with me!
   The best is yet to be,
The last of life, for which the first was made:
   Our times are in his hand
   Who saith: "A whole I planned,
Youth shows but half; trust God, see all, nor be afraid."

Ah, but a man's reach should exceed his grasp,
Or what's a heaven for?

                       ROBERT BROWNING

The Bargain

My true love hath my heart, and I have his,
   By just exchange one for another given:
I hold his dear, and mine he cannot miss,
   There never was a better bargain driven:
     My true love hath my heart, and I have his.

His heart in me keeps him and me in one,
   My heart in him his thoughts and senses guides:
He loves my heart, for once it was his own,
   I cherish his because in me it bides:
     My true love hath my heart, and I have his.

                       SIR PHILIP SIDNEY

A Welcome

Come in the evening, or come in the morning,
Come when you're looked for, or come without warning,
Kisses and welcomes you'll find here before you,
And the oftener you come here the more I'll adore you.

THOMAS O. DAVIS

Song

Let my voice ring out and over the earth,
    Through all the grief and strife,
With a golden joy in a silver mirth:
    Thank God for life!

Let my voice swell out through the great abyss
    To the azure dome above,
With a chord of faith in the harp of bliss:
    Thank God for Love!

Let my voice ring out beneath and above,
    The whole world through,
O my Love and Life, O my Life and Love,
    Thank God for you!

JAMES THOMSON

Go from Me

Go from me. Yet I feel that I shall stand
Henceforward in thy shadow. Nevermore
Alone upon the threshold of my door
Of individual life, I shall command
The uses of my soul, nor lift my hand
Serenely in the sunshine as before,
Without the sense of that which I forbore—
Thy touch upon the palm. The widest land
Doom takes to part us, leaves thy heart in mine
With pulses that beat double. What I do
And what I dream include thee, as the wine
Must taste of its own grapes. And when I sue
God for myself, He hears that name of thine,
And sees within my eyes the tears of two.

ELIZABETH BARRETT BROWNING

Song

Come, rest in this bosom, my own stricken deer,
Though the herd have fled from thee, thy home is still
   here;
Here still is the smile, that no cloud can o'ercast,
And a heart and a hand all thy own to the last.

Oh! what was love made for, if 'tis not the same
Through joy and through torment, through glory and
   shame?
I know not, I ask not, if guilt's in that heart,
I but know that I love thee, whatever thou art.

Thou hast call'd me thy Angel in moments of bliss,
And thy Angel I'll be, 'mid the horrors of this,—
Through the furnace, unshrinking, thy steps to pursue,
And shield thee, and save thee,—or perish there too!

THOMAS MOORE

To His Lute

My lute, awake! perform the last
Labour that thou and I shall waste,
   And end that I have now begun;
For when this song is said and past,
   My lute, be still, for I have done.

As to be heard where ear is none,
As lead to grave in marble stone,
   My song may pierce her heart as soon:
Should we then sing, or sigh, or moan?
   No, no, my lute! for I have done.

The rocks do not so cruelly
Repulse the waves continually,
   As she my suit and affection:
So that I am past remedy:
   Whereby my lute and I have done.

Proud of the spoil that thou hast got
Of simple hearts thorough Love's shot,
   By whom, unkind, thou hast them won;
Think not he hath his bow forgot,
   Although my lute and I have done.

Vengeance shall fall on thy disdain,
That makest but game of earnest pain:
  Trow not alone under the sun
Unquit to cause thy lover's plain,
  Although my lute and I have done.

May chance thee lie wither'd and old
The winter nights that are so cold,
  Plaining in vain unto the moon:
Thy wishes then dare not be told:
  Care then who list! for I have done.

And then may chance thee to repent
The time that thou has lost and spent
  To cause thy lover's sigh and swoon:
Then shalt thou know beauty but lent,
  And wish and want as I have done.

Now cease, my lute! this is the last
Labour that thou and I shall waste,
  And ended is that we begun:
Now is this song both sung and past—
  My lute, be still, for I have done.
                    SIR THOMAS WYATT

Take Back the Heart

  Take back the heart thou gavest,
  What is my anguish to thee?
  Take back the freedom thou cravest,
  Leaving the letters to me.

Take back the words thou hast spoken.
Fling them aside and be free,
Smile o'er each pitiful token,
Leaving the sorrow to me.
Drink deep of life's fond illusion,
Gaze on the storm cloud and flee,
Swiftly through strife and confusion,
Leaving the burden to me.

Then when at last overtaken,
Time flings its fetters o'er thee,
Come with a trust still unshaken,
Come back a captive to me,
Come back in sadness or sorrow,
Once more my darling to be,
Come as of old, love, to borrow
Glimpses of sunlight from me.
Love shall resume her dominion,
Striving no more to be free,
When on her world-weary pinion,
Flies back my lost love to me.

CHARLOTTE A. BARNARD

Love Not Me for Comely Grace

Love not me for comely grace,
  For my pleasing eyes or face,
Nor for any outward part,
No, nor for a constant heart:
  For these may fail or turn to ill,
  So thou and I shall sever:

Keep, therefore, a true woman's eye,
And love me still but know not why—
So hast thou the same reason still
To dote upon me ever!
AUTHOR UNKNOWN

If Thou Must Love Me

If thou must love me, let it be for naught
Except for love's sake only. Do not say,
"I love her for her smile—her look—her way
Of speaking gently,—for a trick of thought
That falls in well with mine, and certes brought
A sense of pleasant ease on such a day"—
For these things in themselves, Beloved, may
Be changed, or change for thee—and love, so wrought,
May be unwrought so. Neither love me for
Thine own dear pity's wiping my cheeks dry:
A creature might forget to weep, who bore
Thy comfort long, and lose thy love thereby!
But love me for love's sake, that evermore
Thou mayest love on, through love's eternity.
ELIZABETH BARRETT BROWNING

The Canonization

For God's sake hold your tongue, and let me love,
  Or chide my palsy, or my gout,
  My five grey hairs, or ruined fortune flout;
With wealth your state, your mind with arts improve,
    Take you a course, get you a place,
    Observe his Honor, or his Grace;
Or the king's real, or his stamped face
  Contemplate; what you will, approve,
  So you will let me love.

Alas, alas, who's injured by my love?
  What merchant's ships have my sighs drowned?
  Who says my tears have overflowed his ground?
When did my colds a forward spring remove?
    When did the heats which my veins fill
    Add one more to the plaguy bill?
Soldiers find wars, and lawyers find out still
  Litigious men, which quarrels move,
  Though she and I do love.

Call us what you will, we are made such by love;
  Call her one, me another fly,
  We're tapers too, and at our own cost die,
And we in us find the eagle and the dove
    The phoenix riddle hath more wit
    By us; we two being one are it.
So to one neutral thing both sexes fit,
  We die and rise the same, and prove
  Mysterious by this love.

We can die by it, if not live by love,
  And if unfit for tomb or hearse
  Our legend be, it will be fit for verse;
And if no piece of chronicle we prove,
    We'll build in sonnets pretty rooms;
    As well a well-wrought urn becomes
The greatest ashes, as half-acre tombs,
  And by these hymns all shall approve
  Us canonized for love.

And thus invoke us, "You, whom reverend love
  Made one another's hermitage;
  You, to whom love was peace, that now is rage:
Who did the whole world's soul contract, and drove
    Into the glasses of your eyes
    (So made such mirrors, and such spies,
That they did all to you epitomize);
  Countries, towns, courts beg from above
  A pattern of your love."

JOHN DONNE

Love Me Little, Love Me Long

Love me little, love me long,
Is the burden of my song.
Love that is too hot and strong
   Burneth soon to waste.
Still, I would not have thee cold,
Not too backward, nor too bold;
Love that lasteth till 'tis old
Fadeth not in haste.
      Love me little, love me long,
      Is the burden of my song.

If thou lovest me too much,
It will not prove as true as touch;
Love me little, more than such,
   For I fear the end.

I am with little well content,
And a little from thee sent
Is enough, with true intent
   To be steadfast friend.
      Love me little, love me long, etc.

Say thou lov'st me while thou live;
I to thee my love will give,
Never dreaming to deceive
   Whiles that life endures.
Nay, and after death, in sooth,
I to thee will keep my truth,
As now, when in my May of youth;
   This my love assures.
     Love me little, love me long, etc.

Constant love is moderate ever,
And it will through life persever;
Give me that, with true endeavor
   I will it restore.
A suit of durance let it be
For all weathers—that for me,
For the land or for the sea,
   Lasting evermore.
     Love me little, love me long, etc.

Winter's cold, or summer's heat,
Autumn's tempests, on it beat,
It can never know defeat,
   Never can rebel.
Such the love that I would gain,
Such the love, I tell thee plain,
Thou must give, or woo in vain;
   So to thee, farewell!

Love me little, love me long,
Is the burden of my song.
AUTHOR UNKNOWN

Summer Days

In summer, when the days were long,
We walked together in the wood:
   Our heart was light, our step was strong;
Sweet flutterings were there in our blood,
   In summer, when the days were long.

We strayed from morn till evening came;
We gathered flowers, and wove us crowns;
   We walked mid poppies red as flame,
Or sat upon the yellow downs;
   And always wished our life the same.

In summer, when the days were long,
We leaped the hedgerow, crossed the brook;
   And still her voice flowed forth in song,
Or else she read some graceful book,
   In summer, when the days were long.

And then we sat beneath the trees,
With shadows lessening in the noon;
   And in the sunlight and the breeze,
We feasted, many a gorgeous June,
   While larks were singing o'er the leas.

In summer, when the days were long,
On dainty chicken, snow-white bread.
We feasted, with no grace but song;
We plucked wild strawb'rries, ripe and red,
In summer, when the days were long.

We loved, and yet we knew it not,—
For loving seemed like breathing then;
We found a heaven in every spot;
Saw angels, too, in all good men;
And dreamed of God in grove and grot.

In summer, when the days are long,
Alone I wander, muse alone.
I see her not; but that old song
Under the fragrant wind is blown,
In summer, when the days are long.

Alone I wander in the wood:
But one fair spirit hears my sighs;
And half I see, so glad and good,
The honest daylight of her eyes,
That charmed me under earlier skies.

In summer, when the days are long,
I love her as we loved of old.
My heart is light, my step is strong;
For love brings back those hours of gold,
In summer, when the days are long.

ANONYMOUS

The Night Has a
Thousand Eyes

The night has a thousand eyes,
   And the day but one;
Yet the light of the bright world dies
   With the dying sun.

The mind has a thousand eyes,
   And the heart but one;
Yet the light of a whole life dies
   When love is done.
        FRANCIS WILLIAM BOURDILLON

If Love Be Love

In Love, if Love be Love, if Love be ours,
Faith and unfaith can ne'er be equal powers:
Unfaith in aught is want of faith in all.

It is the little rift within the lute,
That by and by will make the music mute,
And ever widening slowly silence all.

The little rift within the lover's lute
Or little pitted speck in garnered fruit,
That rotting inward slowly moulders all.

It is not worth the keeping: let it go:
But shall it? answer, darling, answer, no.
And trust me not at all or all in all.

ALFRED, LORD TENNYSON

Midsummer

You loved me for a little,
   Who could not love me long;
You gave me wings of gladness
   And lent my spirit song.

You loved me for an hour
   But only with your eyes;
Your lips I could not capture
   By storm or by surprise.

Your mouth that I remember
   With rush of sudden pain
As one remembers starlight
   Or roses after rain . . .

Out of a world of laughter
   Suddenly I am sad. . . .
Day and night it haunts me,
   The kiss I never had.

SYDNEY KING RUSSELL

Need of Loving

Folk need a lot of loving in the morning;
    The day is all before, with cares beset—
The cares we know, and they that give no warning;
    For love is God's own antidote for fret.

Folk need a heap of loving at the noontime—
    In the battle lull, the moment snatched from
    strife—
Halfway between the waking and the croon time,
    While bickering and worriment are rife.

Folk hunger so for loving at the nighttime,
    When wearily they take them home to rest—
At slumber song and turning-out-the-light time—
    Of all the times for loving, that's the best.

Folk want a lot of loving every minute—
    The sympathy of others and their smile!
Till life's end, from the moment they begin it,
    Folks need a lot of loving all the while.

                STRICKLAND GILLILAN

On Love

When love beckons to you, follow him,
Though his ways are hard and steep.
And when his wings enfold you yield to him.

Though the sword hidden among his pinions may
    wound you.
And when he speaks to you believe in him,
Though his voice may shatter your dreams as the
    north wind lays waste the garden.

For even as love crowns you so shall he crucify you.
    Even as he is for your growth so is he for your
    pruning.
Even as he ascends to your height and caresses your
    tenderest branches that quiver in the sun,
So shall he descend to your roots and shake them in
    their clinging to the earth.

Like sheaves of corn he gathers you unto himself.
He threshes you to make you naked.
He sifts you to free you from your husks.
He grinds you to whiteness.
He kneads you until you are pliant;
And then he assigns you to his sacred fire, that you
    may become sacred bread for God's sacred
    feast.

Love gives naught but itself and takes naught but
    from itself.
Love possesses not nor would it be possessed;
For love is sufficient unto love.

KAHLIL GIBRAN

Give All to Love

Give all to love;
Obey thy heart;
Friends, kindred, days,
Estate, good-fame,
Plans, credit, and the Muse—
Nothing refuse.

'Tis a brave master;
Let it have scope:
Follow it utterly,
Hope beyond hope:
High and more high
It dives into noon,
With wing unspent,
Untold intent;
But it is a god,
Knows its own path,
And the outlets of the sky.

It was not for the mean;
It requireth courage stout,
Souls above doubt,
Valor unbending;
Such 'twill reward—
They shall return
More than they were,
And ever ascending.

Leave all for love;
Yet, hear me, yet,
One word more thy heart behoved,
One pulse more of firm endeavor—
Keep thee today,
Tomorrow, forever,
Free as an Arab
Of thy beloved.

Cling with life to the maid;
But when the surprise,
First vague shadow of surmise
Flits across her bosom young
Of a joy apart from thee,
Free be she, fancy-free;
Nor thou detain her vesture's hem,
Nor the palest rose she flung
From her summer diadem.

Though thou loved her as thyself,
As a self of purer clay,
Though her parting dims the day,
Stealing grace from all alive;
Heartily know,
When half-gods go,
The gods arrive.

RALPH WALDO EMERSON

Believe Me, If All Those
Endearing Young Charms

Believe me, if all those endearing young charms,
   Which I gaze on so fondly today,
Were to change by tomorrow, and fleet in my arms,
   Like fairy-gifts fading away,
Thou wouldst still be adored, as this moment thou
     art,
   Let thy loveliness fade as it will,
And around the dear ruin each wish of my heart
   Would entwine itself verdantly still.

It is not while beauty and youth are thine own,
   And thy cheeks unprofaned by a tear,
That the fervour and faith of a soul can be known,
   To which time will but make thee more dear;
No, the heart that has truly loved never forgets,
   But as truly loves on to the close,
As the sunflower turns on her god, when he sets,
   The same look which she turned when he rose.

THOMAS MOORE

All Paths Lead to You

All paths lead to you
  Where e'er I stray,
You are the evening star
  At the end of day.

All paths lead to you
  Hill-top or low,
You are the white birch
  In the sun's glow.

All paths lead to you
  Where e'er I roam.
You are the lark-song
  Calling me home!
          BLANCHE SHOEMAKER WAGSTAFF

Forgiven

You left me when the weary weight of sorrow
  Lay, like a stone, upon my bursting heart;
It seemed as if no shimmering tomorrow
  Could dry the tears that you had caused to start.
You left me, never telling why you wandered—
  Without a word, without a last caress;
Left me with but the love that I had squandered,
  The husks of love and a vast loneliness.

And yet if you came back with arms stretched toward me,
  Came back tonight, with carefree, smiling eyes,
And said: "My journeying has somehow bored me,
  And love, though broken, never, never dies!"
I would forget the wounded heart you gave me,
  I would forget the bruises on my soul.
My old-time gods would rise again to save me;
  My dreams would grow supremely new and whole.

What though youth lay, a tattered garment, o'er you?
  Warm words would leap upon my lips, long dumb;
If you came back, with arms stretched out before you,
  And told me, dear, that you were glad to come!

MARGARET E. SANGSTER

When We Two Parted

When we two parted
  In silence and tears,
Half broken-hearted
  To sever for years,
Pale grew thy cheek and cold,
  Colder thy kiss;
Truly that hour foretold
  Sorrow to this.

In secret we met—
  In silence I grieve
That thy heart could forget,
  Thy spirit deceive.
If I should meet thee
  After long years,
How should I greet thee?—
  With silence and tears.

GEORGE GORDON, LORD BYRON

Miss You

Miss you, miss you, miss you;
  Everything I do
Echoes with the laughter
  And the voice of You.

You're on every corner,
    Every turn and twist,
Every old familiar spot
    Whispers how you're missed.

Miss you, miss you, miss you!
    Everywhere I go
There are poignant memories
    Dancing in a row.

Silhouette and shadow
    Of your form and face,
Substance and reality
    Everywhere displace.

Oh, I miss you, miss you!
    God! I miss you, Girl!
There's a strange, sad silence
    'Mid the busy whirl,

Just as tho' the ordinary
    Daily things I do
Wait with me, expectant
    For a word from You.

Miss you, miss you, miss you!
    Nothing now seems true
Only that 'twas heaven
    Just to be with You.

                    DAVID CORY

When in Disgrace with
Fortune and Men's Eyes

When in disgrace with fortune and men's eyes
I all alone beweep my outcast state,
And trouble deaf heaven with my bootless cries,
And look upon myself and curse my fate,
Wishing me like to one more rich in hope,
Featured like him, like him with friends possessed,
Desiring this man's art, and that man's scope,
With what I most enjoy contented least;
Yet in these thoughts myself almost despising,
Haply I think on thee—and then my state,
Like to the lark at break of day arising
From sullen earth, sings hymns at heaven's gate;
   For thy sweet love remembered, such wealth brings
   That then I scorn to change my state with kings.

WILLIAM SHAKESPEARE

At Nightfall

I need so much the quiet of your love
   After the day's loud strife;
I need your calm all other things above
   After the stress of life.

I crave the haven that in your dear heart lies,
    After all toil is done;
I need the starshine of your heavenly eyes,
    After the day's great sun.

CHARLES HANSON TOWNE

Love's Philosophy

The fountains mingle with the river,
    And the rivers with the ocean;
The winds of heaven mix forever,
    With a sweet emotion;
Nothing in the world is single;
    All things by a law divine
In one another's being mingle:—
    Why not I with thine?

See! the mountains kiss high heaven,
    And the waves clasp one another;
No sister flower would be forgiven
    If it disdained its brother;
And the sunlight clasps the earth,
    And the moonbeams kiss the sea:—
What are all these kissings worth,
    If thou kiss not me?

PERCY BYSSHE SHELLEY

The Indian Serenade

I arise from dreams of thee
In the first sweet sleep of night,
When the winds are breathing low,
And the stars are shining bright
I arise from dreams of thee,
And a spirit in my feet
Hath led me—who knows how?
To thy chamber window, Sweet!

The wandering airs they faint
On the dark, the silent stream—
The champak odors fail
Like sweet thoughts in a dream;
The nightingale's complaint,
It dies upon her heart;
As I must on thine,
Oh, beloved as thou art!

O lift me from the grass!
I die! I faint! I fail!
Let thy love in kisses rain
On my lips and eyelids pale.
My cheek is cold and white, alas!
My heart beats loud and fast;—
Oh! press it to thine own again,
Where it will break at last.

PERCY BYSSHE SHELLEY

I Love You

I love your lips when they're wet with wine
    And red with a wild desire;
I love your eyes when the lovelight lies
    Lit with a passionate fire.
I love your arms when the strands enmesh
    Your kisses against my face.

Not for me the cold, calm kiss
    Of a virgin's bloodless love;
Not for me the saint's white bliss,
    Nor the heart of a spotless dove.
But give me the love that so freely gives
    And laughs at the whole world's blame,
With your body so young and warm in my arms,
    It set my poor heart aflame.

So kiss me sweet with your warm wet mouth,
    Still fragrant with ruby wine,
And say with a fervor born of the South
    That your body and soul are mine.
Clasp me close in your warm young arms,
    While the pale stars shine above,
And we'll live our whole young lives away
    In the joys of a living love.

ELLA WHEELER WILCOX

Faithful to Thee, in
My Fashion

Last night, ah, yesternight, betwixt her lips and mine
   There fell thy shadow, Cynara! thy breath was
      shed
Upon my soul between the kisses and the wine;
     And I was desolate and sick of an old passion,
   Yea, I was desolate and bowed my head:
     I have been faithful to thee, Cynara! in my
       fashion.

All night upon mine heart I felt her warm heart beat,
   Night-long within mine arms in love and sleep she
      lay;
Surely the kisses of her bought red mouth were sweet;
     But I was desolate and sick of an old passion,
   When I awoke and found the dawn was gray:
     I have been faithful to thee, Cynara! in my
       fashion.

I have forgot much, Cynara! gone with the wind,
   Flung roses, roses riotously with the throng,
Dancing, to put thy pale, lost lilies out of mind;
     But I was desolate and sick of an old passion,
   Yea, all the time, because the dance was long:
     I have been faithful to thee, Cynara! in my
       fashion.

I cried for madder music and for stronger wine,
But when the feast is finished and the lamps
expire,
Then falls thy shadow, Cynara! the night is thine;
And I am desolate and sick of an old passion,
Yea, hungry for the lips of my desire:
I have been faithful to thee, Cynara! in my
fashion.

ERNEST DOWSON

How Do I Love Thee?

How do I love thee? Let me count the ways.
I love thee to the depth and breadth and height
My soul can reach, when feeling out of sight
For the ends of Being and ideal Grace.
I love thee to the level of everyday's
Most quiet need, by sun and candle-light.
I love thee freely, as men strive for Right;
I love thee purely as they turn from Praise.

I love thee with the passion put to use
In my old griefs, and with my childhood's faith.
I love thee with a love I seemed to lose
With my lost saints,—I love thee with the breath,
Smiles, tears, of all my life!—and, if God choose,
I shall but love thee better after death.

ELIZABETH BARRETT BROWNING

The Legacy

When last I died, and, dear, I die
  As often as from thee I go,
  Though it be but an hour ago
—And lovers' hours be full eternity—
I can remember yet, that I
  Something did say, and something did bestow;
Though I be dead, which sent me, I might be
Mine own executor, and legacy.

I heard me say, "Tell her anon,
  That myself," that is you, not I,
  "Did kill me," and when I felt me die,
I bid me send my heart, when I was gone;
But I alas! could there find none;
  When I had ripp'd, and search'd where hearts should be
It kill'd me again, that I who still was true
In life, in my last will should cozen you.

Yet I found something like a heart,
  But colors it and corners had;
  It was not good, it was not bad,
It was entire to none, and few had part;
As good as could be made by art
  It seemed, and therefore for our loss be sad.
I meant to send that heart instead of mine,
But O! no man could hold it, for 'twas thine.

JOHN DONNE

349

When Our Two Souls Stand Up

When our two souls stand up erect and strong,
Face to face, silent, drawing nigh and nigher,
Until the lengthening wings break into fire
At either curved point,—what bitter wrong
Can the earth do to us, that we should not long
Be here contented? Think. In mounting higher,
The angels would press on us and aspire
To drop some golden orb of perfect song
Into our deep, dear silence. Let us stay
Rather on earth, Belovéd,—where the unfit
Contrarious moods of men recoil away
And isolate pure spirits, and permit
A place to stand and love in for a day,
With darkness and the death-hour rounding it.

ELIZABETH BARRETT BROWNING

To—

One word is too often profaned
  For me to profane it,
One feeling too falsely disdained
  For thee to disdain it;
One hope is too like despair
  For prudence to smother,
And pity from thee more dear
  Than that from another.

I can give not what men call love,
 But wilt thou accept not
The worship the heart lifts above
 And the heavens reject not,—
The desire of the moth for the star,
 Of the night for the morrow,
The devotion to something afar
 From the sphere of our sorrow?
    PERCY BYSSHE SHELLEY

To Celia

Drink to me only with thine eyes,
 And I will pledge with mine;
Or leave a kiss but in the cup
 And I'll not look for wine.
The thirst that from the soul doth rise
 Doth ask a drink divine;
But might I of Jove's nectar sup,
 I would not change for thine.

I sent thee late a rosy wreath,
 Not so much honoring thee
As giving it a hope that there
 It could not withered be;
But thou thereon didst only breathe
 And sent'st it back to me;
Since when it grows, and smells, I swear,
 Not of itself but thee!
    BEN JONSON

The Passionate Shepherd to His Love

Come live with me and be my love,
And we will all the pleasures prove
That hills and valleys, dales and fields,
And all the craggy mountains yields.

And we will sit upon the rocks
Seeing the shepherds feed their flocks,
By shallow rivers, to whose falls
Melodious birds sing madrigals.

And I will make thee beds of roses
And a thousand fragrant posies,
A cap of flowers, and a kirtle
Embroidered all with leaves of myrtle;

A gown made of the finest wool,
Which from our pretty lambs we pull;
Fair linéd slippers for the cold,
With buckles of the purest gold;

A belt of straw and ivy buds
With coral clasps and amber studs:
And if these pleasures may thee move,
Come live with me and be my love.

The shepherd swains shall dance and sing
For thy delight each May morning;
If these delights thy mind may move,
Then live with me and be my love.

CHRISTOPHER MARLOWE

Because

Because you come to me with naught save love,
And hold my hand and lift mine eyes above,
A wider world of hope and joy I see,
Because you come to me.

Because you speak to me in accents sweet,
I find the roses waking round my feet,
And I am led through tears of joy to see,
Because you speak to me.

Because God made thee mine I'll cherish thee
Through light and darkness, through all time to be,
And pray His love may make our lives divine.
Because God made thee mine.

EDWARD TESCHEMACHER

To Althea, from Prison

When Love with unconfinéd wings
    Hovers within my gates,
And my divine Althea brings
    To whisper at the grates;
When I lie tangled in her hair
    And fettered to her eye,
The birds that wanton in the air
    Know no such liberty.

When flowing cups run swiftly round
    With no allaying Thames,
Our careless heads with roses bound,
    Our hearts with loyal flames;
When thirsty grief in wine we steep,
    When healths and draughts go free,
Fishes that tipple in the deep
    Know no such liberty.

When, like committed linnets, I
    With shriller throat will sing
The sweetness, mercy, majesty,
    And glories of my king;
When I shall voice aloud how good
    He is, how great should be,
Enlargéd winds, that curl the flood,
    Know no such liberty.

Stone walls do not a prison make,
    Nor iron bars a cage;
Minds innocent and quiet take
    That for an hermitage;
If I have freedom in my love
    And in my soul am free,
Angels alone, that soar above,
    Enjoy such liberty.

                                        RICHARD LOVELACE

Bedouin Song

From the Desert I come to thee
  On a stallion shod with fire;
And the winds are left behind
  In the speed of my desire.
Under thy window I stand,
  And the midnight hears my cry:
I love thee, I love but thee,
  With a love that shall not die
    Till the sun grows cold,
    And the stars are old,
    And the leaves of the Judgment Book unfold!

Look from thy window and see
  My passion and my pain;
I lie on the sands below,
  And I faint in thy disdain.
Let the night-winds touch thy brow
  With the heat of my burning sigh,
And melt thee to hear the vow
  Of a love that shall not die
    Till the sun grows cold,
    And the stars are old,
    And the leaves of the Judgment Book unfold!

My steps are nightly driven,
    By the fever in my breast,
To hear from thy lattice breathed
    The word that shall give me rest.
Open the door of thy heart,
    And open thy chamber door,
And my kisses shall teach thy lips
    The love that shall fade no more
        Till the sun grows cold,
        And the stars are old,
        And the leaves of the Judgment Book unfold!
                                    BAYARD TAYLOR

The Taxi

When I go away from you
The world beats dead
Like a slackened drum.
I call out for you against the jutted stars
And shout into the ridges of the wind.
Streets coming fast,
One after the other,
Wedge you away from me,
And the lamps of the city prick my eyes
So that I can no longer see your face.
Why should I leave you,
To wound myself upon the sharp edges of the night?
                                    AMY LOWELL

A Match

If love were what the rose is,
    And I were like the leaf,
Our lives would grow together
In sad or singing weather,
Blown fields or flowerful closes,
    Green pleasure or gray grief;
If love were what the rose is,
    And I were like the leaf.

If I were what the words are,
    And love were like the tune,
With double sound and single
Delight our lips would mingle,
With kisses glad as birds are
    That get sweet rain at noon;
If I were what the words are,
    And love were like the tune.

If you were life, my darling,
    And I your love were death,
We'd shine and snow together
Ere March made sweet the weather
With daffodil and starling
    And hours of fruitful breath;
If you were life, my darling,
    And I your love were death.

If you were thrall to sorrow,
   And I were page to joy,
We'd play for lives and seasons
With loving looks and treasons
And tears of night and morrow
   And laughs of maid and boy;
If you were thrall to sorrow,
   And I were page to joy.

If you were April's lady,
   And I were lord in May,
We'd throw with leaves for hours
And draw for days with flowers,
Till day like night were shady
   And night were bright like day;
If you were April's lady,
   And I were lord in May.

If you were queen of pleasure,
   And I were king of pain,
We'd hunt down love together,
Pluck out his flying feather,
And teach his feet a measure,
   And find his mouth a rein;
If you were queen of pleasure,
   And I were king of pain.

ALGERNON CHARLES SWINBURNE

Delight in Disorder

A sweet disorder in the dress
Kindles in clothes a wantonness:
A lawn about the shoulders thrown
Into a fine distraction,
An erring lace, which here and there
Enthralls the crimson stomacher,
A cuff neglectful, and thereby
Ribbands to flow confusedly,
A winning wave (deserving note)
In the tempestuous petticoat,
A careless shoe-string, in whose tie
I see a wild civility,
Do more bewitch me, than when art
Is too precise in every part.

ROBERT HERRICK

What Care I

Shall I, wasting in despair,
Die because a woman's fair?
Or my cheeks make pale with care
'Cause another's rosy are?
Be she fairer than the day
Or the flowery meads in May—
   If she be not so to me,
   What care I how fair she be?

Great or good, or kind or fair,
I will ne'er the more despair;
If she love me, this believe,
I will die ere she shall grieve;

If she slight me when I woo,
I can scorn and let her go.
   For if she be not for me,
   What care I for whom she be?
                GEORGE WITHER

What My Lover Said

By the merest chance, in the twilight gloom,
   In the orchard path he met me;
In the tall, wet grass, with its faint perfume,
And I tried to pass, but he made no room,
   Oh, I tried, but he would not let me.
So I stood and blushed till the grass grew red,
   With my face bent down above it,
While he took my hand as he whispering said—
(How the clover lifted each pink, sweet head,
To listen to all that my lover said;
   Oh, the clover in bloom, I love it!)

In the high, wet grass went the path to hide,
   And the low, wet leaves hung over;
But I could not pass upon either side,
For I found myself, when I vainly tried,
   In the arms of my steadfast lover.
And he held me there and he raised my head,
   While he closed the path before me,
And he looked down into my eyes and said—
(How the leaves bent down from the boughs
     o'er head,
To listen to all that my lover said;
   Oh, the leaves hanging lowly o'er me!)

Had he moved aside but a little way,
   I could surely then have passed him;
And he knew I never could wish to stay,
And would not have heard what he had to say,
   Could I only aside have cast him.
It was almost dark, and the moments sped,
   And the searching night wind found us,
But he drew me nearer and softly said—
(How the pure, sweet wind grew still, instead,
To listen to all that my lover said;
   Oh, the whispering wind around us!)

I know that the grass and the leaves will not tell,
   And I'm sure that the wind, precious rover,
Will carry my secret so safely and well
   That no being shall ever discover

One word of the many that rapidly fell
   From the soul-speaking lips of my lover;
   And from the moon and the stars that looked over
Shall never reveal what a fairy-like spell
They wove round about us that night in the dell,
   In the path through the dew-laden clover,
Nor echo the whispers that made my heart swell
   As they fell from the lips of my lover.

HOMER GREENE

The Highwayman

PART ONE

The wind was a torrent of darkness among the gusty
      trees,
The moon was a ghostly galleon tossed upon cloudy
      seas,
The road was a ribbon of moonlight over the purple
      moor,
And the highwayman came riding—
   Riding—riding—
The highwayman came riding, up to the old inn-door.

He'd a French cocked-hat on his forehead, a bunch of
      lace at his chin,
A coat of claret velvet, and breeches of brown
      doeskin:
They fitted with never a wrinkle; his boots were up to
      the thigh!

And he rode with a jewelled twinkle,
  His pistol butts a-twinkle,
His rapier hilt a-twinkle, under the jewelled sky.

Over the cobbles he clattered and clashed in the dark
    inn-yard,
And he tapped with his whip on the shutters, but all
    was locked and barred:
He whistled a tune to the window, and who should be
    waiting there
But the landlord's black-eyed daughter,
  Bess, the landlord's daughter,
Plaiting a dark red love-knot into her long black hair.

And then in the dark old inn-yard a stable-wicket
    creaked
Where Tim, the ostler, listened; his face was white
    and peaked,
His eyes were hollows of madness, his hair like moldy
    hay;
But he loved the landlord's daughter,
  The landlord's red-lipped daughter:
Dumb as a dog he listened, and he heard the robber
    say—

"One kiss, my bonny sweetheart, I'm after a prize
    tonight,
But I shall be back with the yellow gold before the
    morning light.
Yet if they press me sharply, and harry me through
    the day,
Then look for me by moonlight,
  Watch for me by moonlight:

I'll come to thee by moonlight, though Hell should
    bar the way."

He rose upright in the stirrups, he scarce could reach
    her hand;
But she loosened her hair i' the casement! His face
    burnt like a brand
As the black cascade of perfume came tumbling over
    his breast;
And he kissed its waves in the moonlight,
  (Oh, sweet black waves in the moonlight)
Then he tugged at his reins in the moonlight, and
    galloped away to the West.

PART TWO

He did not come in the dawning; he did not come at
    noon;
And out of the tawny sunset, before the rise o' the
    moon,
When the road was a gypsy's ribbon, looping the pur-
    ple moor,
A red-coat-troop came marching—
    Marching—marching—
King George's men came marching, up to the old inn-
    door.

They said no word to the landlord, they drank his ale
    instead;
But they gagged his daughter and bound her to
    the foot of her narrow bed.
Two of them knelt at her casement, with muskets at
    the side!

There was death at every window;
　　And Hell at one dark window;
For Bess could see, through her casement, the road
　　　that *he* would ride.

They had tied her up to attention, with many a snig-
　　　gering jest:
They had bound a musket beside her, with the barrel
　　　beneath her breast!
"Now keep good watch!" and they kissed her.
　　She heard the dead man say—
Look for me by moonlight;
　　Watch for me by moonlight;
I'll come to thee by moonlight, though Hell should
　　　bar the way!

She twisted her hands behind her; but all the knots
　　　held good!
She writhed her hands till her fingers were wet with
　　　sweat or blood!
They stretched and strained in the darkness, and the
　　　hours crawled by like years;
Till, now, on the stroke of midnight,
　　Cold, on the stroke of midnight,
The tip of one finger touched it! The trigger at least
　　　was hers!

The tip of one finger touched it; she strove no more
　　　for the rest!
Up, she stood up to attention, with the barrel beneath
　　　her breast,

She would not risk their hearing: she would not strive
    again;
For the road lay bare in the moonlight,
    Blank and bare in the moonlight;
And the blood of her veins in the moonlight throbbed
    to her Love's refrain.

Tlot-tlot, tlot-tlot! Had they heard it? The horse-hoofs
    ringing clear—
Tlot-tlot, tlot-tlot, in the distance? Were they deaf
    that they did not hear?
Down the ribbon of moonlight, over the brow of the
    hill,
The highwayman came riding,
    Riding, riding!
The red-coats looked to their priming! She stood up
    straight and still!

Tlot-tlot, in the frosty silence; *Tlot-tlot* in the echoing
    night!
Nearer he came and nearer! Her face was like a light!
Her eyes grew wide for a moment; she drew one last
    deep breath,
Then her finger moved in the moonlight,
    Her musket shattered the moonlight,
Shattered her breast in the moonlight and warned
    him—with her death.

He turned; he spurred him Westward; he did not
    know who stood
Bowed with her head o'er the musket, drenched with
    her own red blood!
Not till the dawn he heard it, and slowly blanched to
    hear
How Bess, the landlord's daughter,
   The landlord's black-eyed daughter,
Had watched for her Love in the moonlight; and died
    in the darkness there.

Back, he spurred like a madman, shrieking a curse to
    the sky,
With the white road smoking behind him, and his
    rapier brandished high!
Blood-red were his spurs i' the golden noon; wine-red
    was his velvet coat;
When they shot him down on the highway,
   Down like a dog on the highway,
And he lay in his blood on the highway, with the
    bunch of lace at his throat.

And still a winter's night, they say, when the wind is
    in the trees,
When the moon is a ghostly galleon tossed upon
    cloudy seas,
When the road is a ribbon of moonlight over the pur-
    ple moor,
A highwayman comes riding—
   Riding—riding—
A highwayman comes riding, up to the old inn-door.

Over the cobbles he clatters and clangs in the dark
    inn-yard;
And he taps with his whip on the shutters, but all is
    locked and barred:
He whistles a tune to the window, and who should be
    waiting there
But the landlord's black-eyed daughter,
    Bess, the landlord's daughter,
Plaiting a dark red love-knot into her long black hair.

ALFRED NOYES

Why So Pale and Wan

Why so pale and wan, fond lover?
    Prithee, why so pale?
Will, when looking well can't move her,
    Looking ill prevail?
    Prithee, why so pale?

Why so dull and mute, young sinner?
    Prithee, why so mute?
Will, when speaking well can't win her,
    Saying nothing do 't?
    Prithee, why so mute?

Quit, quit for shame! This will not move;
    This cannot take her.
If of herself she will not love,
    Nothing can make her.
    The devil take her!

SIR JOHN SUCKLING

LOVE FOR A DOG

The Power of the Dog

There is sorrow enough in the natural way
From men and women to fill our day;
And when we are certain of sorrow in store,
Why do we always arrange for more?
Brothers and Sisters, I bid you beware
Of giving your heart to a dog to tear.

Buy a pup and your money will buy
Love unflinching that cannot lie—
Perfect passion and worship fed
By a kick in the ribs or a pat on the head.
Nevertheless it is hardly fair
To risk your heart for a dog to tear.

When the fourteen years which Nature permits
Are closing in asthma, or tumour, or fits,
And the vet's unspoken prescription runs
To lethal chambers or loaded guns,
Then you will find—it's your own affair—
But . . . you've given your heart to a dog to tear.

When the body that lived at your single will,
With its whimper of welcome, is stilled (how still!);
When the spirit that answered your every mood
Is gone—wherever it goes—for good,
You will discover how much you care,
And will give your heart to a dog to tear.

We've sorrow enough in the natural way,
When it comes to burying Christian clay.
Our loves are not given, but only lent,
At compound interest of cent per cent.
Though it is not always the case, I believe,
That the longer we've kept 'em, the more do we
     grieve:
For, when debts are payable, right or wrong,
A short-time loan is as bad as a long—
So why in—Heaven (before we are there)
Should we give our hearts to a dog to tear?

RUDYARD KIPLING

MARRIAGE

My Beloved Is Mine,
and I Am His

Even like two little bank-dividing brooks
   That wash the pebbles with their wanton streams,
And having ranged and searched a thousand nooks,
   Meet both at length in silver-breasted Thames,
     Where in a greater current they conjoin,
So I my best beloved's am; so he is mine.

Even so we met, and after long pursuit,
   Even so we joined; we both became entire.
No need for either to renew a suit,
   For I was flax, and he was flames of fire,
     Our firm-united souls did more than twine;
So I my best beloved's am; so he is mine.

Nor time, nor place, nor chance, nor death can bow
   My least desires unto the least remove;
He's firmly mine by oath, I his by vow;
   He's mine by faith, and I am his by love;
     He's mine by water, I am his by wine;
Thus I my best beloved's am; thus he is mine.

He is my altar; I, his holy place;
   I am his guest, and he my living food;
I'm his by penitence, he mine by grace;
   I'm his by purchase, he is mine by blood!
     He's my supporting elm, and I his vine;
Thus I my best beloved's am; thus he is mine.

He gives me wealth, I give him all my vows;
  I give him songs, he gives me length of days;
With wreaths of grace he crowns my conquering brows,
    And I his temples with a crown of praise,
      Which he accepts as an everlasting sign
That I my best beloved's am, that he is mine.

FRANCIS QUARLES

To My Dear and Loving Husband

If ever two were one, then surely we.
If ever man were loved by wife, then thee;
If ever wife was happy in a man,
Compare with me ye women if you can.
I prize thy love more than whole mines of gold,
Or all the riches that the East doth hold.
My love is such that rivers cannot quench,
Nor ought but love from thee give recompense.
Thy love is such I can no way repay;
The heavens reward thee manifold, I pray.
Then while we live, in love let's so persever,
That when we live no more we may live ever.

ANNE BRADSTREET

A Woman's Last Word

Let's contend no more, Love,
   Strive nor weep;
All be as before, Love,
   —Only sleep!

What so wild as words are?
   I and thou
In debate, as birds are,
   Hawk on bough!

See the creature stalking
   While we speak!
Hush and hide the talking,
   Cheek on cheek!

What so false as truth is,
   False to thee?
Where the serpent's tooth is
   Shun the tree—

Where the apple reddens
   Never pry—
Lest we lose our Edens,
   Eve and I.

Be a god and hold me
   With a charm!
Be a man and fold me
   With thine arm!

Teach me, only teach, Love!
    As I ought
I will speak thy speech, Love,
    Think thy thought—

Meet, if thou require it,
    Both demands,
Laying flesh and spirit
    In thy hands.

That shall be tomorrow
    Not tonight:
I must bury sorrow
    Out of sight:

—Must a little weep, Love,
    (Foolish me!)
And so fall asleep, Love,
    Loved by thee.
                    ROBERT BROWNING

A Bridge Instead of a Wall

They say a wife and husband, bit by bit,
    Can rear between their lives a mighty wall,
So thick they can not talk with ease through it,
    Nor can they see across, it stands so tall!
Its nearness frightens them but each alone
    Is powerless to tear its bulk away,
And each, dejected, wishes he had known
    For such a wall, some magic thing to say.

378

So let us build with master art, my dear,
    A bridge of faith between your life and mine,
A bridge of tenderness and very near
    A bridge of understanding, strong and fine—
        Till we have formed so many lovely ties
        There never will be room for walls to rise!

AUTHOR UNKNOWN

On Marriage

You were born together, and together you shall be
    forevermore.
You shall be together when the white wings of death
    scatter your days.
Ay, you shall be together even in the silent memory
    of God.
But let there be spaces in your togetherness,
And let the winds of the heavens dance between you.

Love one another, but make not a bond of love:
Let it rather be a moving sea between the shores of
    your souls.
Fill each other's cup but drink not from one cup.

Give one another of your bread but eat not from the
    same loaf.
Sing and dance together and be joyous, but let each
    one of you be alone,
Even as the strings of a lute are alone though they
    quiver with the same music.

Give your hearts, but not into each other's keeping.
For only the hand of Life can contain your hearts.
And stand together yet not too near together:
For the pillars of the temple stand apart,
And the oak tree and the cypress grow not in each
    other's shadow.

KAHLIL GIBRAN

Prayer of Any Husband

Lord, may there be no moment in her life
When she regrets that she became my wife,
And keep her dear eyes just a trifle blind
To my defects, and to my failings kind!

Help me to do the utmost that I can
To prove myself her measure of a man,
But, if I often fail as mortals may,
Grant that she never sees my feet of clay!

And let her make allowance—now and then—
That we are only grown-up boys, we men,
So, loving all our children, she will see,
Sometimes, a remnant of the child in me!

Since years must bring to all their load of care,
Let us together every burden bear,
And when Death beckons one its path along,
May not the two of us be parted long!

MAZIE V. CARUTHERS

Together

You and I by this lamp with these
Few books shut out the world. Our knees
Touch almost in this little space.
But I am glad. I see your face.
The silences are long, but each
Hears the other without speech.
And in this simple scene there is
The essence of all subtleties,
The freedom from all fret and smart,
The one sure sabbath of the heart.

The world—we cannot conquer it,
Nor change the minds of fools one whit.
Here, here alone do we create
Beauty and peace inviolate;
Here night by night and hour by hour
We build a high impregnable tower
Whence may shine, now and again,
A light to light the feet of men
When they see the rays thereof:
And this is marriage, this is love.

LUDWIG LEWISOHN

MEMORY

Music, When Soft Voices Die

Music, when soft voices die,
Vibrates in the memory—
Odors, when sweet violets sicken,
Live within the sense they quicken.

Rose leaves, when the rose is dead,
Are heaped for the beloved's bed;
And so thy thoughts, when thou art gone,
Love itself shall slumber on.

PERCY BYSSHE SHELLEY

Home-Thoughts, from Abroad

Oh, to be in England
Now that April's there,
And whoever wakes in England
Sees, some morning, unaware,
That the lowest boughs and the brush-wood sheaf
Round the elm-tree bole are in tiny leaf,
While the chaffinch sings on the orchard bough
In England—now!

And after April, when May follows,
And the whitethroat builds, and all the swallows!
Hark, where my blossomed pear-tree in the hedge
Leans to the field and scatters on the clover
Blossoms and dewdrops—at the bent-spray's edge—

That's the wise thrush; he sings each song twice over
Lest you should think he never could recapture
The first fine careless rapture!
And though the fields look rough with hoary dew,
All will be gay when noontide wakes anew
The buttercups, the little children's dower,
—Far brighter than this gaudy melon-flower!

ROBERT BROWNING

When to the Sessions of Sweet Silent Thought

When to the sessions of sweet silent thought
I summon up remembrance of things past,
I sigh the lack of many a thing I sought,
And with old woes new wail my dear times' waste:
Then can I drown an eye, unus'd to flow,
For precious friends hid in death's dateless night,
And weep afresh love's long since cancell'd woe,
And moan the expense of many a vanish'd sight:
Then can I grieve at grievances foregone,
And heavily from woe to woe tell o'er
The sad account of fore-bemoaned moan,
Which I new pay as if not paid before.
But if the while I think on thee, dear friend,
All losses are restor'd and sorrows end.

WILLIAM SHAKESPEARE

My Lost Youth

Often I think of the beautiful town
   That is seated by the sea;
Often in thought go up and down
The pleasant streets of that dear old town,
   And my youth comes back to me.
      And a verse of a Lapland song
      Is haunting my memory still:
      "A boy's will is the wind's will,
And the thoughts of youth are long, long thoughts."

I can see the shadowy lines of its trees,
   And catch, in sudden gleams,
The sheen of the far-surrounding seas,
And islands that were the Hesperides
   Of all my boyish dreams.
      And the burden of that old song,
      It murmurs and whispers still:
      "A boy's will is the wind's will,
And the thoughts of youth are long, long thoughts."

I remember the black wharves and the slips,
   And the sea-tides tossing free;
And Spanish sailors with bearded lips,
And the beauty and mystery of the ships,
   And the magic of the sea.
      And the voice of that wayward song
      Is singing and saying still:
      "A boy's will is the wind's will,
And the thoughts of youth are long, long thoughts."

I remember the bulwarks by the shore,
    And the fort upon the hill;
The sunrise gun, with its hollow roar,
The drum-beat repeated o'er and o'er,
    And the bugle wild and shrill.
        And the music of that old song
        Throbs in my memory still:
        "A boy's will is the wind's will,
And the thoughts of youth are long, long thoughts."

I remember the sea-fight far away,
    How it thundered o'er the tide!
And the dead captains, as they lay
In their graves, o'erlooking the tranquil bay
    Where they in battle died.
        And the sound of that mournful song
        Goes through me with a thrill:
        "A boy's will is the wind's will,
And the thoughts of youth are long, long thoughts."

I can see the breezy dome of groves,
    The shadows of Deering's Woods;
And the friendships old and the early loves
Come back with a Sabbath sound, as of doves
    In quiet neighborhoods.
        And the verse of that sweet old song,
        It flutters and murmurs still:
        "A boy's will is the wind's will,
And the thoughts of youth are long, long thoughts."

I remember the gleams and glooms that dart
   Across the school-boy's brain;
The song and the silence in the heart,
That in part are prophecies, and in part
   Are longings wild and vain.
     And the voice of that fitful song
     Sings on, and is never still:
     "A boy's will is the wind's will,
And the thoughts of youth are long, long thoughts."

There are things of which I may not speak;
   There are dreams that cannot die;
There are thoughts that make the strong heart weak,
And bring a pallor into the cheek,
   And a mist before the eye.
     And the words of that fatal song
     Come over me like a chill:
     "A boy's will is the wind's will,
And the thoughts of youth are long, long thoughts."

Strange to me now are the forms I meet
   When I visit the dear old town;
But the native air is pure and sweet,
And the trees that o'ershadow each well-known street,
   As they balance up and down,
     Are singing the beautiful song,
     Are sighing and whispering still:
     "A boy's will is the wind's will,
And the thoughts of youth are long, long thoughts."

And Deering's Woods are fresh and fair,
    And with joy that is almost pain
My heart goes back to wander there,
And among the dreams of the days that were,
    I find my lost youth again.
        And the strange and beautiful song,
        The groves are repeating it still:
        "A boy's will is the wind's will,
And the thoughts of youth are long, long thoughts."
                    HENRY WADSWORTH LONGFELLOW

The Coliseum

Type of the antique Rome! Rich reliquary
Of lofty contemplation left to Time
By buried centuries of pomp and power!
At length—at length—after so many days
Of weary pilgrimage and burning thirst
(Thirst for the springs of lore that in thee lie),
I kneel, an altered and an humble man,
Amid thy shadows, and so drink within
My very soul thy grandeur, gloom, and glory!
Vastness! and Age! and Memories of Eld!
Silence! and Desolation! and dim Night!
 I feel ye now—I feel ye in your strength—
O spells more sure than e'er Judaean king
Taught in the gardens of Gethsemane!
O charms more potent than the rapt Chaldee
Ever drew down from out the quiet stars!

Here, where a hero fell, a column falls!
Here, where a mimic eagle glared in gold,
A midnight vigil holds the swarthy bat!
Here, where the dames of Rome their gilded hair
Waved to the wind, now wave the reed and thistle!
Here, where on golden throne the monarch lolled,
Glides, spectre-like, unto his marble home,
Lit by the wan light of the hornèd moon,
The swift and silent lizard of the stones!

But stay! these walls—these ivy-clad arcades—
These mouldering plinths—these sad and blackened
    shafts—
These vague entablatures—this crumbling frieze—
These shattered cornices—this wreck—this ruin—
These stones—alas! these gray stones—are they all—
All of the famed, and the colossal left
By the corrosive Hours to Fate and me?

"Not all"—the Echoes answer me—"not all!
Prophetic sounds and loud arise forever
From us, and from all Ruin, unto the wise,
As melody from Memnon to the Sun.
We rule the hearts of mightiest men—we rule
With a despotic sway all giant minds.
We are not impotent—we pallid stones.
Not all our power is gone—not all our fame—
Not all the magic of our high renown—
Not all the wonder that encircles us—
Not all the mysteries that in us lie—
Not all the memories that hang upon
And cling around about us as a garment,
Clothing us in a robe of more than glory."

EDGAR ALLAN POE

The Past

Thou unrelenting Past!
Strong are the barriers round thy dark domain,
  And fetters, sure and fast,
Hold all that enter thy unbreathing reign.

  Far in thy realm withdrawn,
Old empires sit in sullenness and gloom,
  And glorious ages gone
Lie deep within the shadow of thy womb.

  Childhood, with all its mirth,
Youth, Manhood, Age that draws us to the ground,
  And last, Man's Life on earth,
Glide to thy dim dominions, and are bound.

  Thou hast my better years;
Thou hast my earlier friends, the good, the kind,
  Yielded to thee with tears—
The venerable form, the exalted mind.

  My spirit yearns to bring
The lost ones back—yearns with desire intense,
  And struggles hard to wring
Thy bolts apart, and pluck thy captives thence.

  In vain; thy gates deny
All passage save to those who hence depart;
  Nor to the streaming eye
Thou giv'st them back—nor to the broken heart.

In the abysses hide
Beauty and excellence unknown; to thee
   Earth's wonder and her pride
Are gathered, as the waters to the sea;

   Labors of good to man,
Unpublished charity, unbroken faith,
   Love, that midst grief began,
And grew with years, and faltered not in death.

   Full many a mighty name
Lurks in thy depths, unuttered, unrevered;
   With thee are silent fame,
Forgotten arts, and wisdom disappeared.

   Thine for a space are they—
Yet shalt thou yield thy treasures up at last:
   Thy gates shall yet give way,
Thy bolts shall fall, inexorable Past!

   All that of good and fair
Has gone into thy womb from earliest time,
   Shall then come forth to wear
The glory and the beauty of its prime.

   They have not perished—no!
Kind words, remembered voices once so sweet,
   Smiles, radiant long ago,
And features, the great soul's apparent seat.

   All shall come back; each tie
Of pure affection shall be knit again;
   Alone shall Evil die,
And Sorrow dwell a prisoner in thy reign.

And then shall I behold
Him, by whose kind paternal side I sprung,
   And her, who, still and cold,
Fills the next grave—the beautiful and young.
             WILLIAM CULLEN BRYANT

Jenny Kiss'd Me

Jenny kiss'd me when we met,
   Jumping from the chair she sat in;
Time, you thief, who love to get
   Sweets into your list, put that in!
Say I'm weary, say I'm sad,
   Say that health and wealth have miss'd me,
Say I'm growing old, but add,
   Jenny kiss'd me.
               LEIGH HUNT

Break, Break, Break

Break, break, break,
   On thy cold gray stones, O Sea!
And I would that my tongue could utter
   The thoughts that arise in me.

O well for the fisherman's boy,
   That he shouts with his sister at play!
O well for the sailor lad,
   That he sings in his boat on the bay!

And the stately ships go on
   To their haven under the hill;
But O for the touch of a vanished hand,
   And the sound of a voice that is still!

Break, break, break,
   At the foot of thy crags, O Sea!
But the tender grace of a day that is dead
   Will never come back to me.
ALFRED, LORD TENNYSON

Remembrance

This memory of my mother stays with me
   Throughout the years: the way she used to stand
   Framed in the door when any of her band
Of children left . . . as long as she could see
Their forms, she gazed, as if she seemed to be
   Trying to guard—to meet some far demand;
   And then before she turned to tasks at hand,
She breathed a little prayer inaudibly.

And now, I think, in some far heavenly place,
   She watches still, and yet is not distressed,
But rather as one who, after life's long race,
   Has found contentment in a well-earned rest,
There, in a peaceful, dreamlike reverie,
She waits, from earthly cares forever free.
MARGARET E. BRUNER

Tears, Idle Tears

Tears, idle tears, I know not what they mean,
Tears from the depth of some divine despair
Rise in the heart, and gather to the eyes,
In looking on the happy autumn-fields,
   And thinking of the days that are no more.

Fresh as the first beam glittering on a sail,
That brings our friends up from the underworld,
Sad as the last which reddens over one
That sinks with all we love below the verge;
   So sad, so fresh, the days that are no more.

Ah, sad and strange as in dark summer dawns
The earliest pipe of half-awakened birds
To dying ears, when unto dying eyes
The casement slowly grows a glimmering square;
   So sad, so strange, the days that are no more.

Dear as remembered kisses after death,
And sweet as those by hopeless fancy feigned
On lips that are for others; deep as love,
Deep as first love, and wild with all regret;
O Death in Life, the days that are no more!

ALFRED, LORD TENNYSON

My Heart Leaps Up

My heart leaps up when I behold
   A rainbow in the sky:
So was it when my life began;
So is it now I am a man;
So be it when I shall grow old,
   Or let me die!
The Child is father of the Man;
And I could wish my days to be
Bound each to each by natural piety.
                    WILLIAM WORDSWORTH

People Liked Him

People liked him, not because
   He was rich or known to fame;
He had never won applause
   As a star in any game.
His was not a brilliant style,
   His was not a forceful way,
But he had a gentle smile
   And a kindly word to say.

Never arrogant or proud,
   On he went with manner mild;
Never quarrelsome or loud,
   Just as simple as a child;
Honest, patient, brave and true:
   Thus he lived from day to day,
Doing what he found to do
   In a cheerful sort of way.

Wasn't one to boast of gold
    Or belittle it with sneers,
Didn't change from hot to cold,
    Kept his friends throughout the years,

Sort of man you like to meet
    Any time or any place.
There was always something sweet
    And refreshing in his face.

Sort of man you'd like to be:
    Balanced well and truly square;
Patient in adversity,
    Generous when his skies were fair.
Never lied to friend or foe,
    Never rash in word or deed,
Quick to come and slow to go
    In a neighbor's time of need.

Never rose to wealth or fame,
    Simply lived, and simply died,
But the passing of his name
    Left a sorrow, far and wide.
Not for glory he'd attained,
    Nor for what he had of pelf,
Were the friends that he had gained,
    But for what he was himself.

EDGAR GUEST

MORTALITY

The House on the Hill

They are all gone away,
  The House is shut and still,
There is nothing more to say.

Through broken walls and gray
  The winds blow bleak and shrill;
They are all gone away.

Nor is there one today
  To speak them good or ill:
There is nothing more to say.

Why is it then we stray
  Around that sunken sill?
They are all gone away,

And our poor fancy-play
  For them is wasted skill:
There is nothing more to say.

There is ruin and decay
  In the House on the Hill:
They are all gone away,
There is nothing more to say.
      EDWIN ARLINGTON ROBINSON

When the Lamp Is Shattered

When the lamp is shattered,
The light in the dust lies dead;
When the cloud is scattered,
The rainbow's glory is shed;
When the lute is broken,
Sweet tones are remembered not;
When the lips have spoken,
Loved accents are soon forgot.

As music and splendor
Survive not the lamp and the lute,
The heart's echoes render
No song when the spirit is mute:—
No song but sad dirges,
Like the wind through a ruined cell,
Or the mournful surges
That ring the dead seaman's knell.

When hearts have once mingled,
Love first leaves the well-built nest;
The weak one is singled
To endure what it once possessed.
O Love! who bewailest
The frailty of all things here,
Why choose you the frailest
For your cradle, your home, and your bier?

Its passions will rock thee,
As the storms rock the ravens on high;
Bright reason will mock thee,
Like the sun from a wintry sky.

From thy nest every rafter
Will rot, and thine eagle home
Leave the naked to laughter,
When leaves fall and cold winds come.
PERCY BYSSHE SHELLEY

To the Virgins to Make Much of Time

Gather ye rose-buds while ye may,
  Old Time is still a-flying:
And this same flower that smiles today,
  Tomorrow will be dying.

The glorious lamp of heaven, the Sun,
  The higher he's a-getting
The sooner will his race be run,
  And nearer he's to setting.

That age is best which is the first,
  When youth and blood are warmer;
But being spent, the worse, and worst
  Times, still succeed the former.

Then be not coy, but use your time;
  And while ye may, go marry:
For having lost but once your prime,
  You may for ever tarry.
ROBERT HERRICK

MOTHER

A Wonderful Mother

God made a wonderful mother,
A mother who never grows old;
He made her smile of the sunshine,
And He molded her heart of pure gold;
In her eyes He placed bright shining stars,
In her cheeks, fair roses you see;
God made a wonderful mother,
And He gave that dear mother to me.

PAT O'REILLY

Rock Me to Sleep

Backward, turn backward, O Time, in your flight,
Make me a child again just for to-night!
Mother, come back from the echoless shore,
Take me again to your heart as of yore;
Kiss from my forehead the furrows of care,
Smooth the few silver threads out of my hair;
Over my slumbers your loving watch keep—
Rock me to sleep, mother—rock me to sleep!

Backward, flow backward, O tide of the years!
I am so weary of toil and of tears—
Toil without recompense, tears all in vain—
Take them and give me my childhood again!

I have grown weary of dust and decay,
Weary of flinging my soul-wealth away,
Weary of sowing for others to reap—
Rock me to sleep, mother—rock me to sleep!

Tired of the hollow, the base, the untrue,
Mother, O mother, my heart calls for you!
Many a summer the grass has grown green,
Blossomed and faded, our faces between;
Yet, with strong yearning and passionate pain,
Long I to-night for your presence again;
Come from the silence so long and so deep—
Rock me to sleep, mother—rock me to sleep!

Over my heart in the days that are flown,
No love like mother-love ever has shone;
No other worship abides and endures,
Faithful, unselfish, and patient, like yours;
None like a mother can charm away pain
From the sick soul and the world-weary brain;
Slumber's soft calms o'er my heavy lids creep—
Rock me to sleep, mother—rock me to sleep!

Come, let your brown hair, just lighted with gold,
Fall on your shoulders again as of old;
Let it drop over my forehead to-night,
Shading my faint eyes away from the light;
For with its sunny-edge shadows once more,
Haply will throng the sweet visions of yore;
Lovingly, softly, its bright billows sweep—
Rock me to sleep, mother—rock me to sleep!

Mother, dear mother, the years have been long
Since I last listened your lullaby song;
Sing, then, and unto my soul it shall seem
Womanhood's years have been only a dream.
Clasped to your heart in a loving embrace,
With your light lashes just sweeping my face,
Never hereafter to wake or to weep—
Rock me to sleep, mother—rock me to sleep!

ELIZABETH AKERS

Mother

As long ago we carried to your knees
    The tales and treasures of eventful days,
    Knowing no deed too humble for your praise,
Nor any gift too trivial to please,

So still we bring with older smiles and tears,
    What gifts we may to claim the old, dear right;
    Your faith beyond the silence and the night;
Your love still close and watching through the years.

AUTHOR UNKNOWN

The Old Mother

Poor old lady, set her aside—
    Her children are grown, and her work is done;
True, in their service, her locks turned gray,
    But shove her away, unsought, alone.

Give her a home, for decency's sake,
  In some back room, far out of the way,
Where her tremulous voice cannot be heard—
  It might check your mirth when you would be
      gay.

Strive to forget how she toiled for you
  And cradled you oft on her loving breast—
Told you stories and joined your play,
  Many an hour when she needed rest.

No matter for that—huddle her off;
  Your friends might wince at her unwitty jest;
She is too old-fashioned, and speaks so plain—
  Get her out of the way of the coming guest.

Once you valued her cheerful voice,
  Her hearty laugh and her merry song;
But to ears polite they are quite too loud—
  Her jokes too flat, her tales too long.

So, poor old lady, hustle her off—
  In her cheerless room let her sit alone;
She must not meet with your guests tonight,
  For her children are grown and her work is done.

                                    AUTHOR UNKNOWN

Mother's Hands

Dear gentle hands have stroked my hair
   And cooled my brow,
Soft hands that pressed me close
   And seemed to know somehow
Those fleeting moods and erring thoughts
   That cloud my day,
Which quickly melt beneath their suffrage
   And pass away.

No other balm for earthly pain
   Is half so sure,
No sweet caress so filled with love
   Nor half so pure,
No other soul so close akin that understands,
No touch that brings such perfect peace as Mother's
     hands.

W. DAYTON WEDGEFARTH

NATURE

Inscription for the Entrance
to a Wood

Stranger, if thou hast learned a truth which needs
No school of long experience, that the world
Is full of guilt and misery, and hast seen
Enough of all its sorrows, crimes, and cares,
To tire thee of it, enter this wild wood
And view the haunts of Nature. The calm shade
Shall bring a kindred calm, and the sweet breeze
That makes the green leaves dance, shall waft a balm
To thy sick heart. Thou wilt find nothing here
Of all that pained thee in the haunts of men,
And made thee loathe thy life. The primal curse
Fell, it is true, upon the unsinning earth,
But not in vengeance. God hath yoked to guilt
Her pale tormentor, misery. Hence, these shades
Are still the abodes of gladness; the thick roof
Of green and stirring branches is alive
And musical with birds, that sing and sport
In wantonness of spirit; while below
The squirrel, with raised paws and form erect,
Chirps merrily. Throngs of insects in the shade
Try their thin wings and dance in the warm beam
That waked them into life. Even the green trees
Partake the deep contentment; as they bend
To the soft winds, the sun from the blue sky
Looks in and sheds a blessing on the scene.

Scarce less the cleft-born wild-flower seems to enjoy
Existence than the wingèd plunderer
That sucks its sweets. The mossy rocks themselves,
And the old and ponderous trunks of prostrate trees
That lead from knoll to knoll a causey rude
Or bridge the sunken brook, and their dark roots,
With all their earth upon them, twisting high,
Breathe fixed tranquillity. The rivulet
Sends forth glad sounds, and tripping o'er its bed
Of pebbly sands, or leaping down the rocks,
Seems, with continuous laughter, to rejoice
In its own being. Softly tread the marge,
Lest from her midway perch thou scare the wren
That dips her bill in water. The cool wind,
That stirs the stream in play, shall come to thee,
Like one that loves thee nor will let thee pass
Ungreeted, and shall give its light embrace.

WILLIAM CULLEN BRYANT

Song from *Pippa Passes*

The year's at the spring,
And day's at the morn;
Morning's at seven;
The hill-side's dew-pearled;
Th lark's on the wing;
The snail's on the thorn;
God's in His Heaven—
All's right with the world!

ROBERT BROWNING

The Snowstorm

Announced by all the trumpets of the sky,
Arrives the snow, and, driving o'er the fields,
Seems nowhere to alight: the whited air
Hides hills and woods, the river, and the heaven,
And veils the farm-house at the garden's end.
The sled and traveller stopped, the courier's feet
Delayed, all friends shut out, the housemates sit
Around the radiant fireplace, enclosed
In a tumultuous privacy of storm.

Come see the north wind's masonry.
Out of an unseen quarry evermore
Furnished with tile, the fierce artificer
Curves his white bastions with projected roof
Round every windward stake, or tree, or door.
Speeding, the myriad-handed, his wild work
So fanciful, so savage, nought cares he
For number or proportion. Mockingly,
On coop or kennel he hangs Parian wreaths;
A swan-like form invests the hidden thorn;
Fills up the farmer's lane from wall to wall,
Maugre the farmer's sighs; and, at the gate,
A tapering turret overtops the work.
And when his hours are numbered, and the world
Is all his own, retiring, as he were not,
Leaves, when the sun appears, astonished Art
To mimic in slow structures, stone by stone,
Built in an age, the mad wind's night-work,
The frolic architecture of the snow.

RALPH WALDO EMERSON

On the Grasshopper and Cricket

The poetry of earth is never dead:
    When all the birds are faint with the hot sun.
    And hide in cooling trees, a voice will run
From hedge to hedge about the new-mown mead;
That is the grasshopper's—he takes the lead
    In summer luxury,—he has never done
    With his delights, for when tired out with fun
He rests at ease beneath some pleasant weed.
The poetry of earth is ceasing never:
    On a lone winter evening, when the frost
Has wrought a silence, from the stove there shrills
The cricket's song, in warmth increasing ever,
    And seems to one, in drowsiness half-lost,
The grasshopper's among some grassy hills.

JOHN KEATS

The Lamb

Little Lamb, who made thee?
Dost thou know who made thee,
Gave thee life, and bade thee feed
By the stream and o'er the mead;
Gave thee clothing of delight,
Softest clothing, woolly, bright;
Gave thee such a tender voice,
Making all the vales rejoice?
    Little Lamb, who made thee?
    Dost thou know who made thee?

Little Lamb, I'll tell thee,
Little Lamb, I'll tell thee;
He is called by thy name,
For He calls Himself a Lamb.
He is meek, and He is mild;
He became a little child.
I a child, and thou a lamb,
We are called by His name.
    Little Lamb, God bless thee!
    Little Lamb, God bless thee.
WILLIAM BLAKE

The Tiger

Tiger! Tiger! burning bright
In the forests of the night,
What immortal hand or eye
Could frame thy fearful symmetry?

In what distant deeps or skies
Burnt the fire of thine eyes?
On what wings dare he aspire?
What the hand dare seize the fire?

And what shoulder, and what art,
Could twist the sinews of thy heart?
And when thy heart began to beat,
What dread hand? and what dread feet?

What the hammer? what the chain?
In what furnace was thy brain?

What the anvil? what dread grasp
Dare its deadly terrors clasp?

When the stars threw down their spears,
And watered heaven with their tears,
Did he smile his work to see?
Did he who made the Lamb make thee?

Tiger! Tiger! burning bright
In the forests of the night,
What immortal hand or eye,
Dare frame thy fearful symmetry?

WILLIAM BLAKE

Who Has Seen the Wind?

Who has seen the wind?
  Neither I nor you:
But when the leaves hang trembling,
  The wind is passing through.

Who has seen the wind?
  Neither you nor I:
But when the trees bow down their heads,

CHRISTINA ROSSETTI

O sweet spontaneous

O sweet spontaneous
earth how often have
the
doting

      fingers of
prurient philosophers pinched
and
poked

thee
,has the naughty thumb
of science prodded
thy
    beauty, how
often have religions taken
thee upon their scraggy knees
squeezing and

buffeting thee that thou mightest
conceive gods
    (but
true

to the incomparable
couch of death thy
rhythmic
lover

                thou answerest

them only with

                    spring)

e. e. cummings

PATRIOTISM

Native Land

Breathes there the man with soul so dead,
Who never to himself hath said,
   'This is my own, my native land!'
Whose heart hath ne'er within him burn'd
As home his footsteps he hath turn'd
   From wandering on a foreign strand?
If such there breathe, go, mark him well;
For him no minstrel raptures swell;
High though his titles, proud his name,
Boundless his wealth as wish can claim;
Despite those titles, power, and pelf,
The wretch, concentred all in self,
Living, shall forfeit fair renown,
And, doubly dying, shall go down
To the vile dust from whence he sprung,
Unwept, unhonour'd, and unsung.

                    SIR WALTER SCOTT

For You O Democracy

Come, I will make the continent indissoluble,
I will make the most splendid race the sun ever shone upon,
I will make divine magnetic lands,
   With the love of comrades,
   With the life-long love of comrades.

I will plant companionship thick as trees along all the rivers
    of America, and along the shores of the great lakes, and
    all over the prairies,
I will make inseparable cities with their arms about each
    other's necks,
      By the love of comrades,
      By the manly love of comrades.

For you these from me, O Democracy, to serve you ma
    femme!
For you, for you I am trilling these songs.

WALT WHITMAN

Concord Hymn

By the rude bridge that arched the flood,
   Their flag to April's breeze unfurled,
Here once the embattled farmers stood,
   And fired the shot heard round the world.

The foe long since in silence slept;
   Alike the conqueror silent sleeps;
And Time the ruined bridge has swept
   Down the dark stream that seaward creeps.

Spirit, that made those heroes dare
   To die, and leave their children free,
Bid Time and Nature gently spare
   The shaft we raise to them and thee.

RALPH WALDO EMERSON

In Flanders Fields

In Flanders fields the poppies blow
Between the crosses, row on row,
   That mark our place; and in the sky
   The larks, still bravely singing, fly
Scarce heard amid the guns below.

We are the Dead. Short days ago
We lived, felt dawn, saw sunset glow,
   Loved and were loved, and now we lie
   In Flanders fields.

Take up our quarrel with the foe:
To you from failing hands we throw
   The torch; be yours to hold it high.
   If ye break faith with us who die
We shall not sleep, though poppies grow
   In Flanders fields.

JOHN McCRAE

The Soldier

If I should die, think only this of me;
   That there's some corner of a foreign field
That is forever England. There shall be
   In that rich earth a richer dust concealed;
A dust whom England bore, shaped, made aware,

Gave, once, her flowers to love, her ways to
      roam,
A body of England's breathing English air,
   Washed by the rivers, blest by suns of home.

And think, this heart, all evil shed away,
   A pulse in the eternal mind, no less
      Gives somewhere back the thoughts by
         England given;
Her sights and sounds; dreams happy as her day;
   And laughter, learnt of friends; and gentleness,
      In hearts at peace, under an English heaven.

RUPERT BROOKE

America the Beautiful

O beautiful for spacious skies,
   For amber waves of grain,
For purple mountain majesties
   Above the fruited plain!
America! America!
   God shed His grace on thee
And crown thy good with brotherhood
   From sea to shining sea!

O beautiful for pilgrim feet,
   Whose stern, impassioned stress
A thoroughfare for freedom beat
   Across the wilderness!

America! America!
  God mend thine every flaw,
Confirm thy soul in self-control,
  Thy liberty in law!

O beautiful for heroes proved
  In liberating strife,
Who more than self their country loved,
  And mercy more than life!
America! America!
  May God thy gold refine,
Till all success be nobleness
  And every gain divine!

O beautiful for patriot dream
  That sees beyond the years
Thine alabaster cities gleam
  Undimmed by human tears!
America! America!
  God shed His grace on thee,
And crown thy good with brotherhood
  From sea to shining sea!

KATHARINE LEE BATES

The Charge of the Light Brigade

Half a league, half a league,
  Half a league onward,
All in the valley of Death
Rode the six hundred.

"Forward, the Light Brigade!
Charge for the guns," he said:
Into the valley of Death
    Rode the six hundred.

"Forward, the Light Brigade!"
Was there a man dismay'd?
Not tho' the soldier knew
    Someone had blunder'd:
Theirs not to make reply,
Theirs not to reason why,
Theirs but to do and die:
Into the valley of Death
    Rode the six hundred.

Cannon to right of them,
Cannon to left of them,
Cannon in front of them
    Volley'd and thunder'd;
Storm'd at with shot and shell,
Boldly they rode and well,
Into the jaws of Death,
Into the mouth of Hell
    Rode the six hundred.

Flash'd all their sabers bare,
Flash'd as they turn'd in air
Sabring the gunners there,
Charging an army, while
    All the world wonder'd:
Plung'd in the battery-smoke
Right thro' the line they broke;
Cossack and Russian

Reel'd from the saber-stroke
Shatter'd and sunder'd.
Then they rode back, but not,
Not the six hundred.

When can their glory fade?
O the wild charge they made!
All the world wonder'd.
Honor the charge they made!
Honor the Light Brigade,
Noble six hundred!
ALFRED, LORD TENNYSON

The Isles of Greece

The isles of Greece! the isles of Greece
Where burning Sappho loved and sung,
Where grew the arts of war and peace,
Where Delos rose, and Phoebus sprung!
Eternal summer gilds them yet,
But all, except their sun, is set.

The mountains look on Marathon—
And Marathon looks on the sea;
And musing there an hour alone,
I dream'd that Greece might still be free;
For standing on the Persians' grave,
I could not deem myself a slave.
GEORGE GORDON, LORD BYRON

PEACE

The Epitaph

Here rests his head upon the lap of Earth
   A youth, to Fortune and to Fame unknown;
Fair Science frown'd not on his humble birth
   And Melancholy mark'd him for her own.

Large was his bounty, and his soul sincere;
   Heaven did a recompense as largely send:
He gave to Misery (all he had) a tear,
   He gain'd from Heaven ('twas all he wish'd) a friend.

No farther seek his merits to disclose,
   Or draw his frailties from their dread abode
(There they alike in trembling hope repose)
   The bosom of his Father and his God.

THOMAS GRAY

Sleeping at Last

Sleeping at last, the struggle and horror past,
Sleeping at last, the trouble and tumult over,
Cold and white, out of sight of friend and of lover,
     Sleeping at last.

No more a tired heart downcast or overcast,
No more pangs that wring or shifting fears that hover,
Sleeping at last in a dreamless sleep locked fast.

Fast asleep. Singing birds in their leafy cover
  Cannot wake her, nor shake her the gusty blast.
Under the purple thyme and the purple clover
      Sleeping at last.

CHRISTINA ROSSETTI

PHILOSOPHY

from *Evangeline*

Talk not of wasted affection! affection never was
    wasted;
If it enrich not the heart of another, its waters,
    returning
Back to their springs, like the rain, shall fill them full
    of refreshment:
That which the fountain sends forth returns again to
    the fountain.

HENRY WADSWORTH LONGFELLOW

Brahma

If the red slayer think he slays,
   Or if the slain think he is slain,
They know not well the subtle ways
   I keep, and pass, and turn again.

Far or forgot to me is near;
   Shadow and sunlight are the same;
The vanished gods to me appear;
   And one to me are shame and fame.

They reckon ill who leave me out;
   When me they fly, I am the wings;
I am the doubter and the doubt,
   And I the hymn the Brahmin sings.

The strong gods pine for my abode,
 And pine in vain the sacred Seven;
But thou, meek lover of the good!
 Find me, and turn thy back on heaven.
 RALPH WALDO EMERSON

Happiness

Happiness is like a crystal,
Fair and exquisite and clear,
Broken in a million pieces,
Shattered, scattered far and near.
Now and then along life's pathway,
Lo! some shining fragments fall;
But there are so many pieces
No one ever finds them all.

You may find a bit of beauty,
Or an honest share of wealth,
While another just beside you
Fathers honor, love or health.
Vain to choose or grasp unduly,
Broken is the perfect ball;
And there are so many pieces
No one ever finds them all.

Yet the wise as on they journey
Treasure every fragment clear,
Fit them as they may together,
Imaging the shattered sphere,
Learning ever to be thankful,
Though their share of it is small;
For it has so many pieces
No one ever finds them all.

PRISCILLA LEONARD

Cool Tombs

When Abraham Lincoln was shoveled into the tombs,
    he forgot the copperheads and the assassin . . .
    in the dust, in the cool tombs.

And Ulysses Grant lost all thought of con men and
    Wall Street, cash and collateral turned ashes
    . . . in the dust, in the cool tombs.

Pocahontas' body, lovely as a poplar, sweet as a red
    haw in November or a pawpaw in May, did
    she wonder? does she remember? . . . in the
    dust, in the cool tombs?

Take any streetful of people buying clothes and
    groceries, cheering a hero or throwing confetti
    and blowing tin horns . . . tell me if the lovers
    are losers . . . tell me if any get more than the
    lovers . . . in the dust . . . in the cool tombs.

CARL SANDBURG

Don't Give Up

'Twixt failure and success the point's so fine
Men sometimes know not when they touch the line,
Just when the pearl was waiting one more plunge,
How many a struggler has thrown up the sponge!
Then take this honey from the bitterest cup:
"There is no failure save in giving up!"

AUTHOR UNKNOWN

Stanzas from the Kasidah

Friends of my youth, a last adieu!
   Haply some day we meet again;
Yet ne'er the self same men shall meet;
   The years shall make us other men:

Fie, fie! you visionary things,
   Ye motes that dance in sunny glow,
Who base and build Eternities
   On briefest moment here below;

Who pass through Life like caged birds,
   The captives of a despot will;
Still wond'ring How and When and Why,
   And Whence and Whither, wond'ring still;

Who knows not Whence he came nor Why,
   Who kens not Whither bound and When,
Yet such is Allah's choicest gift,
   The blessing dreamt by foolish men;

Hardly we learn to wield the blade
    Before the wrist grows stiff and old;
Hardly we learn to ply the pen
    Ere Thought and Pancy faint with cold.

When swift the Camel-rider spans
    The howling waste, by Kismet sped,
And of his Magic Wand a wave
    Hurries the quick to join the dead.

How Thought is impotent to divine
    The secret which the gods defend,
The Why of birth and life and death,
    That Isis-veil no hand may rend.

O the dread pathos of our lives!
    How durst thou, Allah, thus to play
With Love, Affection, Friendship,
    All that shows the god in mortal clay.

Cease, Man, to mourn, to weep, to wail;
    Enjoy thy shining hour of sun;
We dance along Death's icy brink,
    But is the dance less full of fun?

How shall the Shown pretend to ken
    Aught of the Showman or the Show?
Why meanly bargain to believe,
    Which only means thou ne'er canst know?

There is no Good, there is no Bad;
    These be the whims of mortal will:
What works me weal that call I "good,"
    What harms and hurts I hold as "ill:"

They change with place, they shift with race;
   And, in the veriest span of Time,
Each Vice has won a Virtue's crown;
   All good was banned as Sin or Crime:

All Faith is false, all Faith is true:
   Truth is the shattered mirror strown
In myriad bits; while each believes
   His little bit the whole to own.

What is the Truth? was askt of yore.
   Reply all object Truth is one
As twain of halves aye makes as whole;
   The moral Truth for all is none.

With God's foreknowledge man's free will!
   What monster-growth of human brain,
What powers of light shall ever pierce
   This puzzle dense with words inane?

There is no Heaven, there is no Hell;
   These be the dreams of baby minds;
Tools of the wily Fetisheer,
   To 'fright the fools his cunning blinds.

Who drinks one bowl hath scant delight;
   To poorest passion he was born;
Who drains the score must e'er expect
   To rue the headache of the morn.

From self-approval seek applause:
   What ken not men thou kennest, thou!
Spurn ev'ry idol others raise:
   Before thine own Ideal bow:

444

Be thine own Deus: Make self free,
   Liberal as the circling air:
Thy Thought to thee an Empire be;
   Break every prisoning lock and bar:
SIR RICHARD F. BURTON

Ozymandias

I met a traveler from an antique land,
Who said: Two vast and trunkless legs of stone
Stand in the desert. Near them, on the sand,
Half sunk, a shattered visage lies, whose frown,
And wrinkled lip, and sneer of cold command,
Tell that its sculptor well those passions read,
Which yet survive, stamped on these lifeless things,
The hand that mocked them, and the heart that fed:
And on the pedestal these words appear:
"My name is Ozymandias, King of Kings:
Look on my works, ye Mighty, and despair!"
Nothing beside remains. Round the decay
Of that colossal wreck, boundless and bare
The lone and level sands stretch far away.
PERCY BYSSHE SHELLEY

The World Is Too Much
With Us

The world is too much with us; late and soon,
Getting and spending, we lay waste our powers:
Little we see in Nature that is ours;
We have given our hearts away, a sordid boon!
The sea that bares her bosom to the moon;
The winds that will be howling at all hours,
And are up-gathered now like sleeping flowers;
For this, for everything, we are out of tune;
It moves us not.—Great Godl I'd rather be
A pagan suckled in a creed outworn.
So might I, standing on this pleasant lea,
Have glimpses that would make me less forlorn;
Have sight of Proteus rising from the sea;
Or hear old Triton blow his wreathed horn.

WILLLAM WORDSWORTH

Vitae Summa Brevis

They are not long, the weeping and the laughter,
　Love and desire and hate;
I think they have no portion in us after
　　We pass the gate.

They are not long, the days of wine and roses:
　Out of a misty dream
Our path emerges for a while, then closes
　　Within a dream.

ERNEST DOWSON

Ulysses

It little profits that an idle king,
By this still hearth, among these barren crags,
Matched with an aged wife, I mete and dole
Unequal laws unto a savage race,
That hoard, and sleep, and feed, and know not me.
I cannot rest from travel: I will drink
Life to the lees: all times I have enjoyed
Greatly, have suffered greatly, both with those
That loved me, and alone; on shore, and when
Through scudding drifts the rainy Hyades
Vext the dim sea. I am become a name;
For always roaming with a hungry heart
Much have I seen and known: cities of men
And manners, climates, councils, governments,
Myself not least, but honored of them all,—
And drunk delight of battle with my peers,
Far on the ringing plains of windy Troy.
I am a part of all that I have met;
Yet all experience is an arch wherethrough
Gleams that untraveled world, whose margin fades
For ever and for ever when I move.
How dull it is to pause, to make an end,
To rust unburnished, not to shine in use!
As though to breathe were life. Life piled on life
Were all too little, and of one to me
Little remains: but every hour is saved
From that eternal silence, something more,
A bringer of new things; and vile it were

For some three suns to store and hoard myself,
And this gray spirit yearning in desire
To follow knowledge, like a sinking star,
Beyond the utmost bound of human thought.

    This is my son, mine own Telemachus,
To whom I leave the scepter and the isle—
Well-loved of me, discerning to fulfill
This labor, by slow prudence to make mild
A rugged people, and through soft degrees
Subdue them to the useful and the good.
Most blameless is he, centered in the sphere
Of common duties, decent not to fail
In offices of tenderness, and pay
Meet adoration to my household gods,
When I am gone. He works his work, I mine.

    There lies the port: the vessel puffs her sail:
There gloom the dark broad seas. My mariners,
Souls that have toiled, and wrought, and thought
      with me—
That ever with a frolic welcome took
The thunder and the sunshine, and opposed
Free hearts, free foreheads—you and I are old;
Old age hath yet his honor and his toil;
Death closes all: but something ere the end,
Some work of noble note, may yet be done,
Not unbecoming men that strove with Gods.
The lights begin to twinkle from the rocks:
The long day wanes: the slow moon climbs: the deep
Moans round with many voices. Come, my friends,
'Tis not too late to seek a newer world.
Push off, and sitting well in order smite
The sounding furrows; for my purpose holds
To sail beyond the sunset, and the baths
Of all the western stars, until I die.

It may be that the gulfs will wash us down:
It may be we shall touch the Happy Isles,
And see the great Achilles, whom we knew.
Though much is taken, much abides; and though
We are not now that strength which in old days
Moved earth and heaven, that which we are, we
  are,—
One equal temper of heroic hearts,
Made weak by time and fate, but strong in will
To strive, to seek, to find, and not to yield.

      ALFRED, LORD TENNYSON

Ode

We are the music-makers,
 And we are the dreamers of dreams,
Wandering by lone sea-breakers,
 And sitting by desolate streams;
World-losers and world-forsakers,
 On whom the pale moon gleams:
Yet we are the movers and shakers
 Of the world for ever, it seems.

With wonderful deathless ditties
We build up the world's cities,
 And out of a fabulous story
 We fashion an empire's glory:
One man with a dream, at pleasure,
 Shall go forth and conquer a crown;
And three with a new song's measure
 Can trample an empire down.

We, in the ages lying
   In the buried past of the earth,
Built Nineveh with our sighing,
   And Babel itself with our mirth;
And o'erthrew them with prophesying
   To the old of the new world's worth;
For each age is a dream that is dying,
   Or one that is coming to birth.

ARTHUR O'SHAUGHNESSY

POETRY

The Author to Her Book

Thou ill-formed offspring of my feeble brain,
Who after birth didst by my side remain,
Till snatched from thence by fri ends, less wise than
true, Who thee abroad, exposed to public view,
Made thee in rags, halting to th' press to trudge, Where
errors were not lessened (all may judge).
At thy return my blushing was not small,
My rambling brat (in print) should mother call,
I cast thee by as one unfit for light,
Thy visage was so irksome in my sight;
Yet being mine own, at length affection would
Thy blemishes amend, if so I could:

I washed thy face, but more defects I saw,
And rubbing off a spot still made a flaw.
I stretched thy joints to make thee even feet,
Yet still thou run'st more hobbling than is meet;
In better dress to trim thee was my mind,
But nought save homespun cloth i' th' house I find.
In this array 'mongst vulgars may'st thou roam.
In critic's hands beware thou dost not come,
And take thy way where yet thou art not known;
If for thy father asked, say thou hadst none;
And for thy mother, she alas is poor,
Which caused her thus to send thee out of door.

ANNE BRADSTREET

The Apology

Think me not unkind and rude
   That I walk alone in grove and glen;
I go to the god of the wood
   To fetch his word to men.

Tax not my sloth that I
   Fold my arms beside the brook;
Each cloud that floated in the sky
   Writes a letter in my book.

Chide me not, laborious band,
   For the idle flowers I brought;
Every aster in my hand
   Goes home loaded with a thought.

There was never mystery
   But 't is figured in the flowers;
Was never secret history
   But birds tell it in the bowers.

One harvest from thy field
   Homeward brought the oxen strong;
A second crop thine acres yield,
   Which I gather in a song.

RALPH WALDO EMERSON

The Poet

Thou, who wouldst wear the name
  Of poet mid thy brethren of mankind,
And clothe in words of flame
  Thoughts that shall live within the general mind!
Deem not the framing of a deathless lay
The pastime of a drowsy summer day.

But gather all thy powers,
  And wreak them on the verse that thou dost weave,
And in thy lonely hours,
  At silent morning or at wakeful eve,
While the warm current tingles through thy veins,
Set forth the burning words in fluent strains.

No smooth array of phrase,
  Artfully sought and ordered though it be,
Which the cold rhymer lays
  Upon his page with languid industry,
Can wake the listless pulse to livelier speed,
Or fill with sudden tears the eyes that read.

The secret wouldst thou know
  To touch the heart or fire the blood at will?
Let thine own eyes o'erflow;
  Let thy lips quiver with the passionate thrill; Seize
the great thought, ere yet its power be past, And
bind, in words, the fleet emotion fast.

Then, should thy verse appear
    Halting and harsh, and all unaptly wrought,
Touch the crude line with fear,
    Save in the moment of impassioned thought;
  Then summon back the original glow, and mend
  The strain with rapture that with fire was penned.

Yet let no empty gust
    Of passion find an utterance in thy lay,
A blast that whirls the dust
    Along the howling street and dies away;
But feelings of calm power and mighty sweep, Like
currents journeying through the windless deep.

Seek'st thou, in living lays,
    To limn the beauty of the earth and sky?
Before thine inner gaze
    Let all that beauty in clear vision lie;
Look on it with exceeding love, and write
The words inspired by wonder and delight.

Of tempests wouldst thou sing,
    Or tell of battles—make thyself a part
Of the great tumult; cling
    To the tossed wreck with terror in thy heart;
Scale, with the assaulting host, the rampart's height,
And strike and struggle in the thickest fight.

So shalt thou frame a lay
    That haply may endure from age to age,
And they who read shall say:
"What witchery hangs upon this poet's page!
What art is his the written spells to find
That sway from mood to mood the willing mind!"

WILLIAM CULLEN BRYANT

God of Visions

Oh, thy bright eyes must answer now,
When Reason, with a scornful brow,
Is mocking at my overthrow;
Oh, thy sweet tongue must plead for me
And tell why I have chosen thee!

Stern Reason is to judgment come,
Arrayed in all her forms of gloom:
Wilt thou, my advocate, be dumb?
No, radiant angel, speak and say
Why I did cast the world away.

Why I have persevered to shun
The common paths that others run;
And on a strange road journeyed on,
Heedless alike of wealth and power—
Of glory's wreath and pleasure's flower.

These, once, indeed, seemed Beings divine;
And they, perchance, heard vows of mine,
And saw my offerings on their shrine;
But careless gifts are seldom prized,
And mine were worthily despised.

So, with a ready heart. I swore
To seek their altar-stone no more;
And gave my spirit to adore
Thee, ever-present, phantom thing—
My slave, my comrade, and my king.

A slave, because I rule thee still;
Incline thee to my changeful will,
And make thy influence good or ill:
A comrade, for by day and night
Thou art my intimate delight—

My darling pain that wounds and sears,
And wrings a blessing out from tears
By deadening me to real cares;
And yet, a king, though prudence well
Have taught thy subject to rebel.

And am I wrong to worship where
Faith cannot doubt, nor hope despair,
Since my own soul can grant my prayer?

Speak, God of visions, plead for me,
And tell why I have chosen thee!

EMILY BRONTË

PORTRAITS

My Last Duchess

That's my last Duchess painted on the wall,
Looking as if she were alive. I call
That piece a wonder, now: Frà Pandolf's hands
Worked busily a day, and there she stands.
Will't please you sit and look at her? I said
"Frà Pandolf" by design, for never read
Strangers like you that pictured countenance,
The depth and passion of its earnest glance,
But to myself they turned (since none puts by
The curtain I have drawn for you, but I)
And seemed as they would ask me, if they durst,
How such a glance came there; so, not the first
Are you to turn and ask thus. Sir, 'twas not
Her husband's presence only, called that spot
Of joy into the Duchess' cheek: perhaps
Frà Pandolf chanced to say, "Her mantle laps
Over my Lady's wrist too much," or "Paint
Must never hope to reproduce the faint
Half-flush that dies along her throat"; such stuff
Was courtesy, she thought, and cause enough
For calling up that spot of joy. She had
A heart—how shall I say?—too soon made glad,
Too easily impressed; she liked whate'er
She looked on, and her looks went everywhere.
Sir, 'twas all one! My favor at her breast,
The dropping of the daylight in the West,
The bough of cherries some officious fool
Broke in the orchard for her, the white mule
She rode with round the terrace—all and each
Would draw from her alike the approving speech,

Or blush, at least. She thanked men,—good; but thanked
Somehow—I know not how—as if she ranked
My gift of a nine-hundred-years'-old name
With anybody's gift. Who'd stoop to blame
This sort of trifling? Even had you skill
In speech—(which I have not)—to make your will
Quite clear to such an one, and say, "Just this
Or that in you disgusts me; here you miss,
Or there exceed the mark"—and if she let
Herself be lessoned so, nor plainly set
Her wits to yours, forsooth, and made excuse,
—E'en then would be some stooping, and I choose
Never to stoop. Oh, sir, she smiled, no doubt,
Whene'er I passed her; but who passed without
Much the same smile? This grew; I gave commands;
Then all smiles stopped together. There she stands
As if alive. Will't please you rise? We'll meet
The company below, then. I repeat,
The Count your master's known munificence
Is ample warrant that no just pretence
Of mine for dowry will be disallowed;
Though his fair daughter's self, as I avowed
At starting, is my object. Nay, we'll go
Together down, sir! Notice Neptune, though,
Taming a sea-horse, thought a rarity,
Which Claus of Innsbruck cast in bronze for me!

ROBERT BROWNING

Gunga Din

You may talk o' gin and beer
When you're quartered safe out 'ere,
An' you're sent to penny-fights an' Aldershot it;
But when it comes to slaughter
You will do your work on water,
An' you'll lick the bloomin' boots of 'im that's got it.
Now in Injia's sunny clime,
Where I used to spend my time
A-servin' of 'Er Majesty the Queen,
Of all them blackfaced crew
The finest man I knew
Was our regimental bhisti, Gunga Din.
    He was "Din! Din! Din!
  "You limpin' lump o' brick-dust, Gunga Din!
    "Hi! Slippy *hitherao*!
    "Water, get it! *Panee lao*,
  "You squidgy-nosed old idol Gunga Din."

The uniform 'e wore
Was nothin' much before,
An' rather less than 'arf o' that be'ind,
For a piece o' twisty rag
An' a goatskin water-bag
Was all the field-equipment 'e could find.
When the sweatin' troop-train lay
In a sidin' through the day,
Where the 'eat would make your bloomin' eyebrows crawl,
We shouted "Harry By!"
Till our throats were bricky-dry,
Then we wopped 'im 'cause 'e couldn't serve us all.

It was "Din! Din! Din!
"You 'eathen, where the mischief 'ave you been?
"You put some *juldee* in it
"Or I'll *marrow* you this minute
"If you don't fill up my helmet, Gunga Din!"

'E would dot an' carry one
Till the longest day was done;
An' 'e didn't seem to know the use o' fear.
If we charged or broke or cut,
You could bet your bloomin' nut,
'E'd be waitin' fifty paces right flank rear.
With 'is mussick on 'is back,
'E would skip with our attack,
An' watch us till the bugles made "Retire,"
An' for all 'is dirty 'ide
'E was white, clear white, inside
When 'e went to tend the wounded under fire!
It was "Din! Din! Din!"
With the bullets kickin' dust-spots on the green.
When the cartridges ran out,
You could hear the front-ranks shout,
"Hi! ammunition-mules an' Gunga Din!"

I shan't forgit the night
When I dropped be'ind the fight
With a bullet where my belt-plate should 'a' been.
I was chokin' mad with thirst,
An' the man that spied me first
Was our good old grinnin', gruntin' Gunga Din.
'E lifted up my 'ead,
An' he plugged me where I bled,
An' 'e guv me 'arf-a-pint o' water green.

It was crawlin' and it stunk,
But of all the drinks I've drunk,
I'm gratefullest to one from Gunga Din.
    It was "Din! Din! Din!
  "'Ere's a beggar with a bullet through 'is spleen;
    "'E's chawin' up the ground,
    "An' 'e's kickin' all around:
  "For Gawd's sake git the water, Gunga Din!"

'E carried me away
To where a dooli lay,
An' a bullet come an' drilled the beggar clean.
'E put me safe inside,
An' just before 'e died,
"I 'ope you liked your drink," sez Gunga Din.
So I'll meet 'im later on
At the place where 'e is gone—
Where it's always double drill and no canteen.
'E'll be squattin' on the coals
Givin' drink to poor damned souls,
An' I'll get a swig in hell from Gunga Din!
    Yes, Din! Din! Din!
  You Lazarushian-leather Gunga Din!
    Though I've belted you and flayed you,
    By the livin' Gawd that made you,
  You're a better man than I am, Gunga Din!

RUDYARD KIPLING

Porphyria's Lover

The rain set early in to-night,
    The sullen wind was soon awake,
It tore the elm-tops down for spite,
    And did its worst to vex the lake:
    I listened with heart fit to break.
When glided in Porphyria: straight
    She shut the cold out and the storm,
And kneeled and made the cheerless grate
    Blaze up, and all the cottage warm;
    Which done, she rose and from her form
Withdrew the dripping cloak and shawl,
    And laid her soiled gloves by, untied
Her hat and let the damp hair fall,
    And, last, she sat down by my side
    And called me. When no voice replied,
She put my arm about her waist,
    And made her smooth white shoulder bare,
    And, stooping, made my cheek lie there,
    And spread o'er all her yellow hair,
Murmuring how she loved me—she
    Too weak, for all her heart's endeavor,
To set its struggling passion free
    From pride, and vainer ties dissever,
    And give herself to me for ever.
But passion sometimes would prevail,
    Nor could to-night's gay feast restrain
A sudden thought of one so pale
    For love of her, and all in vain:
    So, she was come through wind and rain.

Be sure I looked up at her eyes
    Happy and proud: at last I knew
Porphyria worshipped me: surprise
    Made my heart swell, and still it grew
    While I debated what to do.
That moment she was mine, mine, fair,
    Perfectly pure and good: I found
A thing to do, and all her hair
    In one long yellow string I wound
    Three times her little throat around,
And strangled her. No pain felt she;
    I am quite sure she felt no pain.
As a shut bud that holds a bee,
    I warily oped her lids: again
    Laughed the blue eyes without a stain.
And I untightened next the tress
    About her neck: her cheeks once more
Blushed bright beneath my burning kiss:
    I propped her head up as before,
    Only, this time my shoulder bore
Her head, which droops upon it still:
    The smiling rosy little head,
So glad it has its utmost will,
    That all it scorned at once is fled,
    And I, its love, am gained instead!
Porphyria's love: she guessed not how
    Her darling one wish would be heard
And thus we sit together now,
    And all night long we have not stirred,
    And yet God has not said a word!
ROBERT BROWNING

La Belle Dame Sans Merci

O what can ail thee, knight-at-arms,
   Alone and palely loitering?
The sedge has wither'd from the lake,
   And no birds sing.

O what can ail thee, knight-at-arms,
   So haggard and so woe-begone?
The squirrel's granary is full,
   And the harvest's done.

I see a lily on thy brow
   With anguish moist and fever dew;
And on thy cheeks a fading rose
   Fast withereth too.

I met a lady in the meads,
   Full beautiful—a faëry's child,
Her hair was long, her foot was light,
   And her eyes were wild.

I made a garland for her head,
   And bracelets too, and fragrant zone;
She look'd at me as she did love,
   And made sweet moan.

I set her on my pacing steed,
   And nothing else saw all day long,
For sidelong would she bend, and sing
   A faëry's song.

She found me roots of relish sweet,
  And honey wild, and manna dew,
And sure in language strange she said,
  "I love thee true!"

She took me to her elfin grot,
  And there she wept and sigh'd full sore,
And there I shut her wild, wild eyes
  With kisses four.

And there she lulled me asleep,
  And there I dream'd,—ah! woe betide!
The latest dream I ever dream'd
  On the cold hill's side.

I saw pale kings and princes too,
  Pale warriors, death-pale were they all;
They cried—"La Belle Dame sans Merci
  Hath thee in thrall!"

I saw their starved lips in the gloam,
  With horrid warning gaped wide,
And I awoke and found me here,
  On the cold hill's side.

And this is why I sojourn here,
  Alone and palely loitering,
Though the sedge is wither'd from the lake,
  And no birds sing.

JOHN KEATS

Mr. Flood's Party

Old Eben Flood, climbing alone one night
Over the hill between the town below
And the forsaken upland hermitage
That held as much as he should ever know
On earth again of home, paused warily.
The road was his with not a native near;
And Eben, having leisure, said aloud,
For no man else in Tilbury Town to hear:

"Well, Mr. Flood, we have the harvest moon
Again, and we may not have many more;
The bird is on the wing, the poet says,
And you and I have said it here before.
Drink to the bird." He raised up to the light
The jug that he had gone so far to fill,
And answered huskily: "Well, Mr. Flood,
Since you propose it, I believe I will."

Alone, as if enduring to the end
A valiant armor of scarred hopes outworn,
He stood there in the middle of the road
Like Roland's ghost winding a silent horn.
Below him, in the town among the trees,
Where friends of other days had honored him,
A phantom salutation of the dead
Rang thinly till old Eben's eyes were dim.

Then, as a mother lays her sleeping child
Down tenderly, fearing it may awake,
He set the jug down slowly at his feet
With trembling care, knowing that most things break:
And only when assured that on firm earth
It stood, as the uncertain lives of men
Assuredly did not, he paced away,
And with his hand extended paused again:

"Well, Mr. Flood, we have not met like this
In a long time; and many a change has come
To both of us, I fear, since last it was
We had a drop together. Welcome home!"
Convivially returning with himself,
Again he raised the jug up to the light;
And with an acquiescent quaver said,
"Well, Mr. Flood, if you insist, I might.

"Only a very little, Mr. Flood—
For auld lang syne. No more, sir; that will do."
So, for the time, apparently it did,
And Eben evidently thought so too:
For soon amid the silver loneliness
Of night he lifted up his voice and sang,
Secure, with only two moons listening,
Until the whole harmonious landscape range—

"For auld lang syne." The eary throat gave out,
The last word wavered, and the song was done.
He raised again the jug regretfully
And shook his head, and was again alone.
There was not much that was ahead of him,
And there was nothing in the town below—
Where strangers would have shut the many doors
That many friends had opened long ago.

EDWIN ARLINGTON ROBINSON

PRAYER

Mihi Adhaerere Deo Bonum Est
(My Good Consists in Cleaving
to God)

God be in my hede
And in my understandyng.
God be in myne eyes
And in my lokyng.
God be in my mouth
And in my speakyng.
God be in my harte
And in my thynkyng.
God be at mine ende
And at my departyng.

AUTHOR UNKNOWN

Psalm 23

The Lord is my shepherd; I shall not want.

He maketh me to lie down in green pastures: he leadeth me beside the still waters.

He restoreth my soul: he leadeth me in the paths of righteousness for his name's sake.

Yea, though I walk through the valley of the shadow of death, I will fear no evil: for thou art with me; thy rod and thy staff they comfort me.

Thou preparest a table before me in the presence of mine enemies: thou anointest my head with oil; my cup runneth over.

Surely goodness and mercy shall follow me all the days of my life: and I will dwell in the house of the Lord for ever.

Hanukkah Hymn

Rock of Ages, let our song,
Praise Thy saving power;
Thou, amidst the raging foes,
Wast our sheltering tower.
Furious, they assailed us,
But Thine arm availed us,
And Thy word
Broke their sword
When our own strength failed us.

Kindling new the holy lamps,
Priest approved in suffering,
Purified the nation's shrine,
Brought to God their offering.
And His courts surrounding,
Hear, in joy abounding,
Happy throngs
Singing songs
With a mighty sounding.

Children of the martyr race,
Whether free or fettered,
Wake the echoes of the songs
Where ye may be scattered.
Yours the message cheering
That the time is nearing
Which will see
All men free,
Tyrants disappearing.

AUTHOR UNKNOWN

Prayer of St. Francis of Assisi

Lord, make me an instrument of your peace.
Where there is hatred, let me sow love;
Where there is injury, pardon;
Where there is doubt, faith;
Where there is despair, hope;
Where there is darkness, light;
And where there is sadness, joy.
O, Divine Master, grant that I may not so much seek to be
    consoled as to console;
To be understood as to understand;
To be loved as to love;
For it is in giving that we receive;
It is in pardoning that we are pardoned;
It is in dying that we are born to eternal life.

Prayer of an Unknown
Confederate Soldier

I asked God for strength, that I might achieve,
I was made weak, that I might learn humbly to obey . . .
I asked for health, that I might do greater things,
I was given infirmity, that I might do better things . . .
I asked for riches, that I might be happy,
I was given poverty that I might be wise . . .
I asked for power, that I might have the praise of men,
I was given weakness, that I might feel the need of God . . .
I asked for all things, that I might enjoy life,
I was given life, that I might enjoy all things . . .

I got nothing that I asked for—but everything that I had
     hoped for.
Almost despite myself, my unspoiled prayers were ans-
     wered.
I am among all men, most richly blessed.

Bless This House

Bless this house, O Lord, we pray
Make it safe by night and day:
Bless these walls so firm and stout
Keeping want and trouble out;

Bless the roof and chimneys tall,
Let Thy peace lie over all:
Bless this door, that it may prove
Ever open to joy and love.

Bless these windows shining bright,
Letting in God's heavenly light:
Bless the hearth ablazing there,
With smoke ascending like a prayer:

Bless the people here within,
Keep them pure and free from sin;
Bless us all that we may be
Fit, O Lord, to dwell with thee.

                    MARY H. BRAHE AND HELEN TAYLOR

An Irish Wish

May the road rise to meet you.
May the wind be ever at your back.
May the Good Lord keep you in the hollow of His hand.
May your heart be as warm as your hearthstone.
And when you come to die may the wail of the poor be the
   only sorrow you'll leave behind.
May God bless you always.

AUTHOR UNKNOWN

My Prayer

Great God, I ask thee for no meaner pelf
Than that I may not disappoint myself;
That in my action I may soar as high
As I can now discern with this clear eye.

And next in value, which thy kindness lends,
That I may greatly disappoint my friends,
Howe'er they think or hope that it may be,
They may not dream how thou'st distinguished me;

That my weak hand may equal my firm faith,
And my life practice more than my tongue saith;
   That my low conduct may not show,
      Nor my relenting lines,
   That I thy purpose did not know,
      Or overrated thy designs.

HENRY DAVID THOREAU

For a New Home

Oh, love this house, and make of it a Home—
A cherished, hallowed place.
Root roses at its base, and freely paint
The glow of welcome on its smiling face!
For after friends are gone, and children marry,
And you are left alone . . .
The house you loved will clasp you to its heart,
Within its arms of lumber and of stone.

ROSA ZAGNONI MARINONI

Recessional

God of our fathers, known of old—
    Lord of our far-flung battle-line—
Beneath whose awful Hand we hold
    Dominion over palm and pine—
Lord God of Hosts, be with us yet,
Lest we forget, lest we forget!

The tumult and the shouting dies—
    The captains and the kings depart—
Still stands Thine ancient sacrifice,
    An humble and a contrite heart.
Lord God of Hosts, be with us yet,
Lest we forget, lest we forget!

Far-call'd our navies melt away—
    On dune and headland sinks the fire—

480

Lo, all our pomp of yesterday
    Is one with Nineveh and Tyre!
Judge of the Nations, spare us yet,
Lest we forget, lest we forget!

If, drunk with sight of power, we loose
    Wild tongues that have not Thee in awe—
Such boasting as the Gentiles use
    Or lesser breeds without the Law—
Lord God of Hosts, be with us yet,
Lest we forget, lest we forget!

For heathen heart that puts her trust
    In reeking tube and iron shard—
All valiant dust that builds on dust,
    And guarding calls not Thee to guard—
For frantic boast and foolish word,
Thy Mercy on Thy People, Lord!

                    RUDYARD KIPLING

My Evening Prayer

If I have wounded any soul to-day,
If I have caused one foot to go astray,
If I have walked in my own wilful way—
    Good Lord, forgive!

If I have uttered idle words or vain,
If I have turned aside from want or pain,
Lest I myself should suffer through the strain—
    Good Lord, forgive!

If I have craved for joys that are not mine,
If I have let my wayward heart repine,
Dwelling on things of earth, not things divine—
    Good Lord, forgive!

If I have been perverse, or hard, or cold,
If I have longed for shelter in Thy fold,
When Thou hast given me some part to hold—
    Good Lord, forgive.

Forgive the sins I have confessed to Thee,
Forgive the secret sins I do not see,
That which I know not, Father, teach Thou me—
    Help me to live.

CHARLES H. GABRIEL

A Prayer

Let me do my work each day;
And if the darkened hours of despair overcome me,
May I not forget the strength that comforted me
In the desolation of other times.
May I still remember the bright hours that found me
Walking over the silent hills of my childhood,
Or dreaming on the margin of the quiet river,
When a light glowed within me,
And I promised my early God to have courage
Amid the tempests of the changing years.
Spare me from bitterness
And from the sharp passions of unguarded moments.
May I not forget that poverty and riches are of the
    spirit.

Though the world know me not,
May my thoughts and actions be such
As shall keep me friendly with myself.
Lift my eyes from the earth,
And let me not forget the uses of the stars.
Forbid that I should judge others,
Lest I condemn myself.
Let me not follow the clamor of the world,
But walk calmly in my path.
Give me a few friends who will love me for what I
    am;
And keep ever burning before my vagrant steps
The kindly light of hope.
And though age and infirmity overtake me,
And I come not within sight of the castle of my
    dreams,
Teach me still to be thankful for life,
And for time's olden memories that are good and
    sweet;
And may the evening's twilight find me gentle still.

MAX EHRMANN

A Prayer for Every Day

Make me too brave to lie or be unkind.
Make me too understanding, too, to mind
The little hurts companions give, and friends,
The careless hurts that no one quite intends.
Make me too thoughtful to hurt others so.
Help me to know
The inmost hearts of those for whom I care,
Their secret wishes, all the loads they bear,
That I may add my courage to their own.

May I make lonely folks feel less alone,
And happier ones a little happier yet.
May I forget
What ought to be forgotten; and recall,
Unfailing, all
That ought to be recalled, each kindly thing,
Forgetting what might sting.
To all upon my way,
Day after day,
Let me be joy, be hope! Let my life sing!

MARY CAROLYN DAVIES

A Prayer Found in Chester Cathedral

Give me a good digestion, Lord
    And also something to digest;
Give me a healthy body, Lord,
    With sense to keep it at its best.

Give me a healthy mind, good Lord,
    To keep the good and pure in sight;
Which, seeing sin, is not appalled,
    But finds a way to set it right.

Give me a mind that is not bored,
    That does not whimper, whine or sigh;
Don't let me worry overmuch
    About the fussy thing called "I."

Give me a sense of humor, Lord,
    Give me the grace to see a joke;
To get some happiness from life,
    And pass it on to other folk.
                    AUTHOR UNKNOWN

A Morning Prayer

Let me today do something that will take
    A little sadness from the world's vast store,
And may I be so favored as to make
    Of joy's too scanty sum a little more.

Let me not hurt, by any selfish deed
    Or thoughtless word, the heart of foe or friend,
Nor would I pass unseeing worthy need,
    Or sin by silence when I should defend.

However meager by my worldly wealth,
    Let me give something that shall aid my kind—
A word of courage, or a thought of health
    Dropped as I pass for troubled hearts to find.

Let me tonight look back across the span
    Twixt dawn and dark, and to my conscience
        say—
Because of some good act to beast or man—
    "The world is better that I lived today."

ELLA WHEELER WILCOX

Morning Prayer

When little things would irk me, and I grow
Impatient with my dear one, make me know
How in a moment joy can take its flight
And happiness be quenched in endless night.
Keep this thought with me all the livelong day
That I may guard the harsh words I might say
When I would fret and grumble, fiery hot,
At trifles that tomorrow are forgot—
Let me remember, Lord, how it would be
If these, my loved ones, were not here with me.

ELLA WHEELER WILCOX

REBELLION

Dirge Without Music

I am not resigned to the shutting away of loving hearts in
   the hard ground.
So it is, and so it will be, for so it has been, time out of mind:
Into the darkness they go, the wise and the lovely.
   Crowned with lilies and with laurel they go; but I am
     not resigned.

Lovers and thinkers, into the earth with you.
Be one with the dull, the indiscriminate dust.
A fragment of what you felt, of what you knew,
A formula, a phrase remains,—but the best is lost.

The answers quick and keen, the honest look, the laughter,
   the love,—
They are gone. They are gone to feed the roses. Elegant and
   curled
Is the blossom. Fragrant is the blossom. I know. But I do not
   approve.
More precious was the light in your eyes than all the roses
   of the world.

Down, down, down into the darkness of the grave
Gently they go, the beautiful, the tender, the kind;
Quietly they go, the intelligent, the witty, the brave.
I know. But I do not approve. And I am not resigned.

EDNA ST. VINCENT MILLAY

REFLECTIONS

A Wise Old Owl

A wise old owl lived in an oak;
The more he saw the less he spoke;
The less he spoke the more he heard:
Why can't we all be like that bird?
AUTHOR UNKNOWN

To a Fat Lady Seen from the Train

O why do you walk through the fields in gloves,
  Missing so much and so much?
O fat white woman, whom nobody loves,
Why do you walk through the fields in gloves,
When the grass is soft as the breast of doves
  And shivering-sweet to the touch?
O why do you walk through the fields in gloves,
  Missing so much and so much?
FRANCES CORNFORD

Get a Transfer

If you are on the Gloomy Line,
  Get a transfer.
If you're inclined to fret and pine,
  Get a transfer.

Get off the track of doubt and gloom,
Get on the Sunshine Track—there's room—
    Get a transfer.

If you're on the Worry Train,
    Get a transfer.
You must not stay there and complain,
    Get a transfer.
The Cheerful Cars are passing through,
And there's lots of room for you—
    Get a transfer.
If you're on the Grouchy Track,
    Get a transfer.
Just take a Happy Special back,
    Get a transfer.
Jump on the train and pull the rope,
That lands you at the station Hope—
    Get a transfer.

AUTHOR UNKNOWN

The Good Great Man

How seldom, friend, a good great man inherits
    Honor and wealth, with all his worth and pains!
It seems a story from the world of spirits
When any man obtains that which he merits,
    Or any merits that which he obtains.

For shame, my friend! renounce this idle strain!
What wouldst thou have a good great man obtain?
Wealth, title, dignity, a golden chain,
Or heap of corpses which his sword hath slain?
Goodness and greatness are not means, but ends.

Hath he not always treasures, always friends,
The great good man? Three treasures,—love, and light,
    And calm thoughts, equable as infant's breath;
And three fast friends, more sure than day or night,—
    Himself, his Maker, and the angel Death.

SAMUEL TAYLOR COLERIDGE

Grass

Pile the bodies high at Austerlitz and Waterloo.
Shovel them under and let me work—
    I am the grass; I cover all.

And pile them high at Gettysburg
And pile them high at Ypres and Verdun.
Shovel them under and let me work.
Two years, ten years, and passengers ask the
    conductor:
    What place is this?
    Where are we now?

    I am the grass.
    Let me work.

CARL SANDBURG

from *The Rubaiyat*
of Omar Khayyam

Come, fill the Cup, and in the fire of Spring
Your Winter-garment of Repentance fling:
    The Bird of Time has but a little way
To flutter—and the Bird is on the Wing.

Whether at Naishapur or Babylon,
Whether the Cup with sweet or bitter run,
    The Wine of Life keeps oozing drop by drop,
The Leaves of Life keep falling one by one.

A Book of Verses underneath the Bough,
A Jug of Wine, a Loaf of Bread—and Thou
    Beside me singing in the Wilderness—
O, Wilderness were Paradise enow!

Some for the Glories of This World; and some
Sigh for the Prophet's Paradise to come;
    Ah, take he Cash, and let the Credit go,
Nor heed the rumble of a distant Drum!

Ah, my Beloved, fill the Cup that clears
To-day of past Regrets and future Fears;
    To-morrow!—Why, To-morrow I may be
Myself with Yesterday's Sev'n thousand Years.

For some we loved, the loveliest and the best
That from his Vintage rolling Time hath prest,
    Have drunk their Cup a Round or two before.
And one by one crept silently to rest.

Ah, make the most of what we yet may spend,
Before we too into the Dust descend;
    Dust into Dust, and under Dust to lie,
Sans Wine, sans Song, sans Singer, and—sans End!

And if the Wine you drink, the Lip you press,
End in what All begins and ends in—Yes;
    Think then you are To-day what Yesterday
You were—To-morrow you shall not be less.

When You and I behind the Veil are past,
Oh, but the long, long while the World shall last
    Which of our Coming and Departure heeds
As the Sea's self should heed a pebble cast.

The Moving Finger writes; and, having writ,
Moves on: nor all your Piety nor Wit
    Shall lure it back to cancel half a Line,
Nor all your Tears wash out a Word of it.

And that inverted Bowl they call the Sky,
Whereunder crawling coop'd we live and die,
    Lift not your hands to *It* for help—for It
As impotently moves as you or I.

Oh Thou, who didst with pitfall and with gin
Beset the Road I was to wander in,
    Thou wilt not with Predestined Evil round
Enmesh, and then impute my Fall to Sin!

Oh Thou, who Man of baser Earth didst make,
And ev'n with paradise devise the Snake;
    For all the Sin wherewith the Face of Man
    Is blacken'd—Man's forgiveness give—and take!

Indeed, indeed, Repentance oft before
I swore—but was I sober when I swore!
   And then and then came Spring, and Rose-in-hand
My thread-bare Penitence apieces tore.

Ah Love! could you and I with Him conspire
To grasp this sorry Scheme of Things Entire,
   Would not we shatter it to bits—and then
Re-mould it nearer to the Heart's desire! . . .

EDWARD FITZGERALD

Who Hath a Book

Who hath a book
   Has friends at hand,
And gold and gear
   At his command;

And rich estates,
   If he but look,
Are held by him
   Who hath a book.

Who hath a book
   Has but to read
And he may be
   A king indeed;

His Kingdom is
   His inglenook;
All this is his
   Who hath a book.

WILBUR D. NESBIT

Elegy Written in a
Country Churchyard

The curfew tolls the knell of parting day,
   The lowing herd winds slowly o'er the lea,
The plowman homeward plods his weary way,
   And leaves the world to darkness and to me.

Now fades the glimmering landscape on the sight,
   And all the air a solemn stillness holds,
Save where the beetle wheels his droning flight,
   And drowsy tinklings lull the distant folds;

Save that from yonder ivy-mantled tow'r
   The moping owl does to the moon complain
Of such, as wand'ring near her secret bow'r,
   Molest her ancient solitary reign.

Beneath those rugged elms, that yew-tree's shade,
   Where leaves the turf in many a mould'ring heap,
Each in his narrow cell for ever laid,
   The rude Forefathers of the hamlet sleep.

The breezy call of incense-breathing Morn,
   The swallow twittering from the straw-built shed,
The cock's shrill clarion, or the echoing horn,
   No more shall rouse them from their lowly bed.

For them no more the blazing hearth shall burn,
   Or busy housewife ply her evening care:
No children run to lisp their sire's return,
   Or climb his knees the envied kiss to share.

Oft did the harvest to their sickle yield,
    Their furrow oft the stubborn glebe has broke:
How jocund did they drive their team afield!
    How bow'd the woods beneath their sturdy
        stroke!

Let not Ambition mock their useful toil,
    Their homely joys, and destiny obscure;
Nor Grandeur hear with a disdainful smile,
    The short and simple annals of the poor.

The boast of heraldry, the pomp of pow'r,
    And all that beauty, all that wealth e'er gave,
Awaits alike th' inevitable hour:
    The paths of glory lead but to the grave.

Nor you, ye proud, impute to these the fault,
    If Memory o'er their tomb no trophies raise.
Where through the long-drawn aisle and fretted
        vault
    The pealing anthem swells the note of praise.

Can storied urn or animated bust
    Back to its mansion call the fleeting breath?
Can Honour's voice provoke the silent dust,
    Or Flatt'ry soothe the dull cold ear of death?

Perhaps in this neglected spot is laid
    Some heart once pregnant with celestial fire;
Hands that the rod of empire might have sway'd
    Or waked to ecstasy the living lyre.

But Knowledge to their eyes her ample page
   Rich with the spoils of time did ne'er unroll;
Chill Penury repress'd their noble rage,
   And froze the genial current of the soul.

Full many a gem of purest ray serene,
   The dark unfathom'd caves of ocean bear:
Full many a flower is born to blush unseen,
   And waste its sweetness on the desert air.

Some village Hampden that with dauntless breast
   The little tyrant of his fields withstood;
Some mute inglorious Milton here may rest,
   Some Cromwell guiltless of his country's blood.

Th' applause of list'ning senates to command,
   The threats of pain and ruin to despise,
To scatter plenty o'er a smiling land,
   And read their history in a nation's eyes,

Their lot forbade: nor circumscribed alone
   Their growing virtues, but their crimes confined;
Forbade to wade through slaughter to a throne,
   And shut the gates of mercy on mankind.

The struggling pangs of conscious truth to hide,
   To quench the blushes of ingenuous shame,
Or heap the shrine of Luxury and Pride
   With incense kindled at the Muse's flame.

Far from the madding crowd's ignoble strife,
   Their sober wishes never learn'd to stray;
Along the cool sequester'd vale of life
   They kept the noiseless tenor of their way.

Yet ev'n these bones from insult to protect,
  Some frail memorial still erected nigh,
With uncouth rhymes and shapeless sculpture deck't,
  Implores the passing tribute of a sigh.

Their name, their years, spelt by th' unletter'd Muse,
  The place of fame and elegy supply:
And many a holy text around she strews,
  That teach the rustic moralist to die.

For who, to dumb Forgetfulness a prey,
  This pleasing anxious being e'er resign'd,
Left the warm precincts of the cheerful day,
  Nor cast one longing lingering look behind?

On some fond breast the parting soul relies,
  Some pious drops the closing eye requires;
E'en from the tomb the voice of Nature cries,
  E'en in our ashes live their wonted fires.

For thee, who, mindful of th' unhonour'd dead,
  Dost in these lines their artless tale relate;
If chance, by lonely contemplation led,
  Some kindred spirit shall inquire thy fate,

Haply some hoary-headed swain may say,
  "Oft have we seen him at the peep of dawn
Brushing with hasty steps the dews away
  To meet the sun upon the upland lawn.

"There at the foot of yonder nodding beech
  That wreathes its old fantastic roots so high,
His listless length at noontide would he stretch,
  And pore upon the brook that babbles by.

"Hard by yon wood, now smiling as in scorn,
    Muttering his wayward fancies he would rove;
Now drooping, woeful-wan, like one forlorn,
    Or crazed with care, or cross'd in hopeless love.

"One morn I miss'd him on the custom'd hill,
    Along the heath, and near his fav'rite tree;
Another came, nor yet beside the rill,
    Nor up the lawn, nor at the wood was he;

"The next, with dirges due in sad array
    Slow through the church-way path we saw him borne,
Approach and read (for thou canst read) the lay
    Graved on the stone beneath yon aged thorn."

The Epitaph

Here rests his head upon the lap of earth
    A youth to Fortune and to Fame unknown.
Fair Science frown'd not on his humble birth
    And Melancholy mark'd him for her own.

Large was his bounty, and his soul sincere;
    Heav'n did a recompense as largely send:
He gave to Mis'ry all he had, a tear,
    He gain'd from Heav'n ('twas all he wish'd) a
        friend.

No farther seek his merits to disclose,
    Or draw his frailties from their dread abode.
(There they alike in trembling hope repose,)
    The bosom of his Father and his God.

THOMAS GRAY

503

Richard Cory

Whenever Richard Cory went down town,
  We people on the pavement looked at him;
He was a gentleman from sole to crown,
  Clean favored, and imperially slim.

And he was always quietly arrayed,
  And he was always human when he talked;
But still he fluttered pulses when he said,
  "Good-morning," and he glittered when he
    walked.

And he was rich—yes, richer than a king—
  And admirably schooled in every grace:
In fine, we thought that he was everything
  To make us wish that we were in his place.

So on we worked, and waited for the light,
  And went without the meat, and cursed the bread;
And Richard Cory, one calm summer night,
  Went home and put a bullet through his head.

EDWIN ARLINGTON ROBINSON

The Garden of Proserpine

Here, where the world is quiet;
　　Here, where all trouble seems
Dead winds' and spent waves' riot
　　In doubtful dreams of dreams
I watch the green field growing
For reaping folk and sowing,
For harvest-time and mowing,
　　A sleepy world of streams.

I am tired of tears and laughter,
　　And men that laugh and weep;
Of what may come hereafter
　　For men that sow to reap:
I am weary of days and hours,
Blown buds of barren flowers,
Desires and dreams and powers
　　And everything but sleep.

Here life has death for neighbor,
　　And far from eye or ear
Wan waves and wet winds labor,
　　Weak ships and spirits steer;
They drive adrift, and whither
They wot not who make thither;
But no such winds blow hither,
　　And no such things grow here.

No growth of moor or coppice,
    No heather-flower or vine,
But bloomless buds of poppies,
    Green grapes of Proserpine,
Pale beds of blowing rushes,
Where no leaf blooms or blushes
Save this whereout she crushes
    For dead men deadly wine.

Pale, without name or number,
    In fruitless fields of corn,
They bow themselves and slumber
    All night till light is born;
And like a soul belated,
In hell and haven unmated,
By cloud and mist abated
    Comes out of darkness morn.

Though one were strong as seven,
    He too with death shall dwell,
Nor wake with wings in heaven,
    Nor weep for pains in hell;
Though one were fair as roses,
His beauty clouds and closes;
And well though love reposes,
    In the end it is not well.

Pale, beyond porch and portal,
    Crowned with calm leaves, she stands
Who gathers all things mortal
    With cold immortal hands;
Her languid lips are sweeter
Than love's who fears to greet her,
To men that mix and meet her
    From many times and lands.

She waits for each and other,
　　She waits for all men born;
Forgets the earth her mother,
　　The life of fruits and corn;
And spring and seed and swallow
Take wing for her and follow
Where summer song rings hollow
　　And flowers are put to scorn.

There go the loves that wither,
　　The old loves with wearier wings;
And all dead years draw thither,
　　And all disastrous things;
Dead dreams of days forsaken,
Blind buds that snows have shaken,
Wild leaves that winds have taken,
　　Red strays of ruined springs.

We are not sure of sorrow;
　　And joy was never sure;
To-day will die to-morrow;
　　Time stoops to no man's lure,
And love, grown faint and fretful,
With lips but half regretful
Sighs, and with eyes forgetful
　　Weeps that no loves endure.

From too much love of living,
　　From hope and fear set free,
We thank with brief thanksgiving
　　Whatever gods may be
That no life lives for ever;
That dead men rise up never;
That even the weariest river
　　Winds somewhere safe to sea.

Then star nor sun shall waken,
  Nor any change of light:
Nor sound of waters shaken,
  Nor any sound or sight:
Nor wintry leaves nor vernal,
Nor days nor things diurnal;
Only the sleep eternal
  In an eternal night.
                    ALGERNON CHARLES SWINBURNE

On File

If an unkind word appears,
  File the thing away.
If some novelty in jeers,
  File the thing away.
If some clever little bit
Of a sharp and pointed wit,
Carrying a sting with it—
  File the thing away.

If some bit of gossip come,
  File the thing away.
Scandalously spicy crumb,
  File the thing away.
If suspicion comes to you
That your neighbor isn't true
Let me tell you what to do—
  File the thing away.

Do this for a little while,
Then go out and burn the file.
JOHN KENDRICK BANGS

Dover Beach

The sea is calm to-night.
The tide is full, the moon lies fair
Upon the straits;—on the French coast the light
Gleams and is gone; the cliffs of England stand
Glimmering and vast, out in the tranquil bay.

Come to the window, sweet is the night-air!
Only, from the long line of spray
Where the sea meets the moon-blanch'd land,
Listen! you hear the grating roar
Of pebbles which the waves draw back, and fling,
At their return, up the high strand,
Begin, and cease, and then again begin,
With tremulous cadence slow, and bring
The eternal note of sadness in.

Sophocles long ago
Heard it on the Aegean, and it brought
Into his mind the turbid ebb and flow,
Of human misery; we
Find also in the sound a thought,
Hearing it by this distant northern sea.

The Sea of Faith
Was once, too, at the full, and round earth's shore
Lay like the folds of a bright girdle furl'd.
But now I only hear
Its melancholy, long, withdrawing roar,
Retreating, to the breath
Of the night-wind, down the vast edges drear
And naked shingles of the world.

Ah, love, let us be true
To one another! for the world, which seems
To lie before us like a land of dreams,
So various, so beautiful, so new,
Hath really neither joy, nor love, nor light,
Nor certitude, nor peace, nor help for pain;
And we are here as on a darkling plain
Swept with confused alarms of struggle and flight,
Where ignorant armies clash by night.

MATTHEW ARNOLD

REGRET

A Superscription

Look in my face; my name is Might-have-been;
I am also called No-more, Too-late, Farewell;
Unto thine ear I hold the dead-sea-shell
Cast up thy Life's foam-fretted feet between;
Unto thine eyes the glass where that is seen
Which had Life's form and Love's, but by my spell
Is now a shaken shadow intolerable,
Of ultimate things unuttered the frail screen.
Mark me, how still I am! But should there dart
One moment through thy soul the soft surprise
Of that winged Peace which lulls the breath of sighs,—
Then shalt thou see me smile, and turn apart
Thy visage to mine ambush at thy heart
Sleepless with cold commemorative eyes.

DANTE GABRIEL ROSSETTI

Ah, Fading Joy

Ah, fading joy, how quickly art thou past!
    Yet we thy ruine haste:
As if the cares of Humane Life were few,
    We seek out new,
And follow Fate that does too fast pursue.

See how on ev'ry Bough the Birds express
    In their sweet notes their happiness.

They all enjoy and nothing spare;
But on their Mother Nature lay their care;
Why then should Man, the Lord of all below,
   Such troubles chuse to know,
As none of all his Subjects undergo?

JOHN DRYDEN

Broken Friendship

Alas! they had been friends in youth,
But whispering tongues can poison truth!
And constancy lives in realms above!
And life is thorny, and Youth is vain!
And to be wroth with one we love,
Doth work like madness in the brain!
They parted—ne'er to meet again!
But never either found another
To free the hollow heart from paining!
They stood aloof, the scars remaining;
Like cliffs which had been rent asunder!
A dreary sea now flows between;
But neither heat, nor frost, nor thunder,
Shall wholly do away, I ween,
The marks of that which once had been.

SAMUEL TAYLOR COLERIDGE

My Playmate

The pines were dark on Ramoth hill,
  Their song was soft and low;
The blossoms in the sweet May wind
  Were falling like the snow.

The blossoms drifted at our feet,
  The orchard birds sang clear;
The sweetest and the saddest day
  It seemed of all the year.

For, more to me than birds or flowers,
  My playmate left her home.
And took with her the laughing spring,
  The music and the bloom.

She kissed the lips of kith and kin,
  She laid her hand in mine:
What more could ask the bashful boy
  Who fed her father's kine?

She left us in the bloom of May:
  The constant years told o'er
Their seasons with as sweet May morns,
  But she came back no more.

I walk, with noiseless feet, the round
  Of uneventful years;
Still o'er and o'er I sow the spring
  And reap the autumn ears.

She lives where all the golden year
    Her summer roses blow;
The dusky children of the sun
    Before her come and go.

There haply with her jewelled hands
    She smooths her silken gown,—
No more the homespun lap wherein
    I shook the walnuts down.

The wild grapes wait us by the brook,
    The brown nuts on the hill,
And still the May-day flowers make sweet
    The woods of Follymill.

The lilies blossom in the pond,
    The bird builds in the tree,
The dark pines sing on Ramoth hill
    The slow song of the sea.

I wonder if she thinks of them,
    And how the old time seems,—
If ever the pines of Ramoth wood
    Are sounding in her dreams.

I see her face, I hear her voice;
    Does she remember mine?
And what to her is now the boy
    Who fed her father's kine?

What cares she that the orioles build
    For other eyes than ours,—
That other hands with nuts are filled,
    And other laps with flowers?

O playmate in the golden time!
    Our mossy seat is green,
Its fringing violets blossom yet,
    The old trees o'er it lean.

The winds so sweet with birch and fern
    A sweeter memory blow;
And there in spring the veeries sing
    The song of long ago.

And still the pines of Ramoth wood
    Are moaning like the sea,—
The moaning of the sea of change
    Between myself and thee!
        JOHN GREENLEAF WHITTIER

Lost Days

The lost days of my life until to-day,
    What were they, could I see them on the street
    Lie as they fell? Would they be ears of wheat
Sown once for food but trodden into clay?
Or golden coins squandered and still to pay?
    Or drops of blood dabbling the guilty feet?
    Or such spilt water as in dreams must cheat
The undying throats of Hell, athirst alway?

I do not see them here; but after death
    God knows I know the faces I shall see
Each one a murdered self, with low last breath.
    'I am thyself,—what hast thou done to me?'

'And I—and I—thyself,' (lo! each one saith,)
'And thou thyself to all eternity!'

DANTE GABRIEL ROSSETTI

Maud Muller

Maud Muller on a summer's day
Raked the meadow sweet with hay.

Beneath her torn hat glowed the wealth
Of simple beauty and rustic health.

Singing, she wrought, and her merry glee
The mock-bird echoed from his tree.

But when she glanced to the far-off town,
White from its hill-slope looking down,

The sweet song died, and a vague unrest
And a nameless longing filled her breast,—

A wish that she hardly dared to own,
For something better than she had known.

The Judge rode slowly down the lane,
Smoothing his horse's chestnut mane.

He drew his bridle in the shade
Of the apple-trees, to greet the maid,

And asked a draught from the spring that flowed
Through the meadow across the road.

She stooped where the cool spring bubbled up,
And filled for him her small tin cup,

And blushed as she gave it, looking down
On her feet so bare, and her tattered gown.

"Thanks!" said the Judge, "a sweeter draught
From a fairer hand was never quaffed."

He spoke of the grass and flowers and trees,
Of the singing birds and the humming bees;

Then talked of the haying, and wondered whether
The cloud in the west would bring foul weather.

And Maud forgot her brier-torn gown,
And her graceful ankles bare and brown;

And listened, while a pleased surprise
Looked from her long-lashed hazel eyes.

At last, like one who for delay
Seeks a vain excuse, he rode away.

Maud Muller looked and sighed: "Ah me!
That I the Judge's bride might be!

"He would dress me up in silks so fine,
And praise and toast me at his wine.

"My father should wear a broadcloth coat,
My brother should sail a painted boat.

"I'd dress my mother so grand and gay,
And the baby should have a new toy each day.

"And I'd feed the hungry and clothe the poor,
And all should bless me who left our door."

The Judge looked back as he climbed the hill,
And saw Maud Muller standing still.

"A form more fair, a face more sweet,
Ne'er hath it been my lot to meet.

"And her modest answer and graceful air
Show her wise and good as she is fair.

"Would she were mine, and I to-day,
Like her, a harvester of hay;

"No doubtful balance of rights and wrongs,
Nor weary lawyers with endless tongues,

"But low of cattle and song of birds,
And health and quiet and loving words."

But he thought of his sisters, proud and cold,
And his mother, vain of her rank and gold.

So, closing his heart, the Judge rode on,
And Maud was left in the field alone.

But the lawyers smiled that afternoon,
When he hummed in court an old love-tune;

And the young girl mused beside the well
Till the rain on the unraked clover fell.

He wedded a wife of richest dower,
Who lived for fashion, as he for power.

Yet oft, in his marble hearth's bright glow,
He watched a picture come and go;

And sweet Maud Muller's hazel eyes
Looked out in their innocent surprise.

Oft, when the wine in his glass was red,
He longed for the wayside well instead;

And closed his eyes on his garnished rooms
To dream of meadows and clover-blooms.

And the proud man sighed, with a secret pain,
"Ah, that I were free again!

"Free as when I rode that day,
Where the barefoot maiden raked her hay."

She wedded a man unlearned and poor,
And many children played round her door.

But care and sorrow, and childbirth pain,
Left their traces on heart and brain.

And oft, when the summer sun shone hot
On the new-mown hay in the meadow lot,

And she heard the little spring brook fall
Over the roadside, through the wall,

In the shade of the apple-tree again
She saw a rider draw his rein;

And, gazing down with timid grace,
She felt his pleased eyes read her face.

Sometimes her narrow kitchen walls
Stretched away into stately halls;

The weary wheel to a spinet turned,
The tallow candle an astral burned,

And for him who sat by the chimney lug,
Dozing and grumbling o'er pipe and mug,

A manly form at her side she saw,
And joy was duty and love was law.

Then she took up her burden of life again
Saying only, "It might have been."

Alas for maiden, alas for Judge,
For rich repiner and household drudge!

God pity them both! and pity us all,
Who vainly the dreams of youth recall.

For of all sad words of tongue or pen,
The saddest are these: "It might have been!"

Ah, well! for us all some sweet hope lies
Deeply buried from human eyes;

And, in the hereafter, angels may
Roll the stone from its grave away!

JOHN GREENLEAF WHITTIER

REMEMBRANCE

With Rue My Heart Is Laden

With rue my heart is laden
   For golden friends I had,
For many a rose-lipt maiden
   And many a lightfoot lad.

By brooks too broad for leaping
   The lightfoot boys are laid;
The rose-lipt girls are sleeping
   In fields where roses fade.
               A.E. HOUSMAN

John Anderson, My Jo

John Anderson, my jo, John,
   When we were first acquent;
Your locks were like the raven,
   Your bonnie brow was brent;[1]
But now your brow is bald, John,
   Your locks are like the snow;
But blessings on your frosty pow,[2]
   John Anderson, my jo.

John Anderson, my jo, John,
   We clamb the hill thegither;
And mony a cantie[3] day, John,
   We've had wi' ane anither:

1. *bright*
2. *head*
3. *merry*

Now we maun totter down, John,
  And hand in hand we'll go,
And sleep thegither at the foot,
  John Anderson, my jo.

ROBERT BURNS

Daisy

Where the thistle lifts a purple crown
  Six foot out of the turf,
And the harebell shakes on the windy hill—
  O the breath of the distant surf!—

The hills look over on the South,
  And southward dreams the sea;
And, with the sea-breeze hand in hand,
  Came innocence and she.

Where 'mid the gorse the raspberry
  Red for the gatherer springs,
Two children did we stray and talk
  Wise, idle, childish things.

She listen'd with big-lipp'd surprise,
  Breast-deep 'mid flower and spine:
Her skin was like a grape, whose veins
  Run snow instead of wine.

She knew not those sweet words she spake,
  Nor knew her own sweet way;
But there's never a bird, so sweet a song
  Throng'd in whose throat that day!

O, there were flowers in Storrington
    On the turf and on the spray;
But the sweetest flower on Sussex hills
    Was the Daisy-flower that day!

Her beauty smooth'd earth's furrow'd face!
    She gave me tokens three:—
A look, a word of her winsome mouth,
    And a wild raspberry.

A berry red, a guileless look,
    A still word,—strings of sand!
And yet they made my wild, wild heart
    Fly down to her little hand.

For, standing artless as the air,
    And candid as the skies,
She took the berries with her hand,
    And the love with her sweet eyes.

The fairest things have fleetest end:
    Their scent survives their close,
But the rose's scent is bitterness
    To him that loved the rose!

She looked a little wistfully,
    Then went her sunshine way:—
The sea's eye had a mist on it,
    And the leaves fell from the day.

She went her unremembering way,
    She went, and left in me
The pang of all the partings gone,
    And partings yet to be.

She left me marvelling why my soul
  Was sad that she was glad;
At all the sadness in the sweet,
  The sweetness in the sad.

Still, still I seem'd to see her, still
  Look up with soft replies,
And take the berries with her hand,
  And the love with her lovely eyes.

Nothing begins, and nothing ends,
  That is not paid with moan;
For we are born in other's pain,
  And perish in our own.

FRANCIS THOMPSON

I Remember, I Remember

I remember, I remember,
  The house where I was born,
The little window where the sun
  Came peeping in at morn:
He never came a wink too soon,
  Nor brought too long a day;
But now, I often wish the night
  Had borne my breath away.

I remember, I remember,
  The roses, red and white;
The violets and the lily-cups,
  Those flowers made of light!

The lilacs where the robin built,
   And where my brother set
The laburnum on his birthday,—
   The tree is living yet!

I remember, I remember,
   Where I was used to swing;
And thought the air must rush as fresh
   To swallows on the wing:
My spirit flew in feathers then,
   That is so heavy now,
And summer pools could hardly cool
   The fever on my brow!

I remember, I remember,
   The fir trees dark and high;
I used to think their slender tops
   Were close against the sky:
It was a childish ignorance,
   But now 'tis little joy
To know I'm farther off from heaven
   Than when I was a boy.
             THOMAS HOOD

Ben Bolt

Don't you remember sweet Alice, Ben Bolt,—
   Sweet Alice whose hair was so brown,
Who wept with delight when you gave her a smile,
   And trembled with fear at your frown?

In the old churchyard in the valley, Ben Bolt,
  In a corner obscure and alone,
They have fitted a slab of the granite so gray,
  And Alice lies under the stone.
And don't you remember the school, Ben Bolt,
  With the master so cruel and grim,
And the shaded nook in the running brook
  Where the children went to swim?
Grass grows on the master's grave, Ben Bolt,
  The spring of the brook is dry,
And of all the boys who were schoolmates then
  There are only you and I.

THOMAS DUNN ENGLISH

RENEWAL

Who Would Have Thought?

Who would have thought my shrivelled heart
Could have recovered greenness? It was gone
   Quite under ground, as flowers depart
To feed their mother-root when they have blown;
    Where they together
    All the hard weather,
Dead to the world, keep house unknown.

Dead are thy wonders, Lord of Power,
Killing and quickening, bringing down to hell
   And up to heaven in an hour;
Making a chiming of a passing bell.
    We say amiss,
    This or that is:
Thy word is all, if we could spell.

And now in age I bud again;
After so many deaths I live and write;
   I once more smell the dew and rain,
And relish versing: O my only Light,
    It cannot be
    That I am he
On whom thy tempest fell all night.

GEORGE HERBERT

Evolution

Out of the dusk a shadow,
Then, a spark;
Out of the cloud a silence,
Then, a lark;
Out of the heart a rapture,
Then, a pain;
Out of the dead, cold ashes,
Life again.

JOHN BANISTER TABB

I Am a Parcel of Vain Strivings Tied

I am a parcel of vain strivings tied
By a chance bond together,
Dangling this way and that, their links
Were made so loose and wide,
Methinks,
For milder weather.

A bunch of violets without their roots,
And sorrel intermixed,
Encircled by a wisp of straw
Once coiled about their shoots,
The law
By which I'm fixed.

A nosegay which Time clutched from out
    Those fair Elysian fields,
With weeds and broken stems, in haste,
    Doth make the rabble rout
      That waste
    The day he yields.

And here I bloom for a short hour unseen,
    Drinking my juices up,
With no root in the land
    To keep my branches green,
      But stand
    In a bare cup.

Some tender buds were left upon my stem
    In mimicry of life,
But ah! the children will not know.
    Till time has withered them,
      The woe
    With which they're rife.

But now I see I was not plucked for naught,
    And after in life's vase
Of glass set while I might survive,
    But by a kind hand brought
      Alive
    To a strange place.

That stock thus thinned will soon redeem its hours,
    And by another year,
Such as God knows, with freer air,
    More fruits and fairer flowers
      Will bear,
    While I droop here.

HENRY DAVID THOREAU

Hertha

I am that which began;
　　Out of me the years roll;
Out of me God and man;
　　I am equal and whole;
God changes, and man, and the form of them bodily; I am
　　the soul.

Before ever land was,
　　Before ever the sea,
Or soft hair of the grass,
　　Or fair limbs of the tree,
Or the flesh-coloured fruit of my branches, I was, and thy
　　soul was in me.

First life on my sources
　　First drifted and swam;
Out of me are the forces
　　That save it or damn;
Out of me man and woman, and wild-beast and bird; before
　　God was, I am.

Beside or above me
　　Nought is there to go;
Love or unlove me,
　　Unknow me or know,
I am that which unloves me and loves; I am stricken, and I
　　am the blow.

I the mark that is missed
　And the arrows that miss,
I the mouth that is kissed
　And the breath in the kiss,
The search, and the sought, and the seeker, the soul and
　the body that is.

I am that thing which blesses
　My spirit elate;
That which caresses
　With hands uncreate.
My limbs unbegotten that measure the length of the meas-
　ure of fate.

But what thing dost thou now,
　Looking Godward, to cry
'I am I, thou art thou,
　I am low, thou art high'?
I am thou, whom thou seekest to find him; find thou but
　thyself, thou art I.

I the grain and the furrow,
　The plough-cloven clod
And the ploughshare drawn thorough,
Hast thou known how I fashioned thee,
　Child, underground?
Fire that impassioned thee,
　Iron that bound,
Dim changes of water, what thing of all these hast thou
　known of or found?

Canst thou say in thine heart
 Thou hast seen with thine eyes
With what cunning of art
 Thou wast wrought in what wise,
By what force of what stuff thou wast shapen, and shown
 on my breast to the skies?

Who hath given, who hath sold it thee,
 Knowledge of me?
Hath the wilderness told it thee?
 Hast thou learnt of the sea?
Hast thou communed in spirit with night? have the winds
 taken counsel with thee?

Have I set such a star
 To show light on thy brow
That thou sawest from afar
 What I show to thee now?
Have ye spoken as brethren together, the sun and the
 mountains and thou?

What is here, dost thou know it?
 What was, hast thou known?

Prophet nor poet
 Nor tripod nor throne
Nor spirit nor flesh can make answer, but only thy mother
 alone.

Mother, not maker,
 Born, and not made;
Though her children forsake her,
 Allured or afraid,
Praying prayers to the God of their fashion, she stirs not
 for all that have prayed.

A creed is a rod,
To grow straight in the strength of thy spirit, and live out
    thy life as the light.
    I am in thee to save thee,
        As my soul in thee saith;
    Give thou as I gave thee,
        Thy life-blood and breath,
Green leaves of thy labour, white flowers of thy thought,
    and red fruit of thy death.

    Be the ways of thy giving
        As mine were to thee;
    The free life of thy living,
        Be the gift of it free;
Not as servant to lord, nor as master to slave, shalt thou
    give thee to me.

    O children of banishment,
        Souls overcast,
    Were the lights ye see vanish meant
        Alway to last,
Ye would know not the sun overshining the shadows and
    stars overpast.

    I that saw where ye trod
        The dim paths of the night
    Set the shadow called God
        In your skies to give light;
But the morning of manhood is risen, and the shadowless
    soul is in sight.

The tree many-rooted
     That swells to the sky
With frondage red-fruited,
     The life-tree am I;
In the buds of your lives is the sap of my leaves: ye shall live
     and not die.

But the Gods of your fashion
     That take and that give,
In their pity and passion
     That scourge and forgive,
That are worms that are bred in the bark that falls off; they
     shall die and not live.

My own blood is what stanches
     The wounds in my bark;
Stars caught in my branches
     Make day of the dark,
And are worshiped as suns till the sunrise shall tread out
     their fires as a spark.

Where dead ages hide under
     The live roots of the tree,
In my darkness the thunder
     Makes utterance of me;
In the clash of my boughs with each other ye hear the
     waves sound of the sea.

That noise is of Time,
     As his feathers are spread
And his feet set to climb
     Through the boughs overhead,
And my foliage rings round him and rustles, and branches
     are bent with his tread.

The storm-winds of ages
   Blow through me and cease,
The war-wind that rages,
   The spring-wind of peace,
Ere the breath of them roughens my tresses, ere one of my
   blossoms increase.

All sounds of all changes,
   All shadows and lights
On the world's mountain-ranges
   And stream-riven heights,
Whose tongue is the wind's tongue and language of storm-
   clouds or earth-shaking nights;

All forms of all faces,
   All works of all hands
In unsearchable places
   Of time-stricken lands,
All death and all life, and all reigns and all ruins, drop
   through me as sands

Though sore be my burden
   And more than ye know,
And my growth have no guerdon
   But only to grow,
Yet I fail not of growing for lightnings above me or death-
   worms below.

These too have their part in me,
   As I too in these;
Such fire is at heart in me,
   Such sap is this tree's,
Which hath in it all sounds and all secrets of infinite lands
   and of seas.

In the spring-coloured hours
    When my mind was as May's,
There brake forth of me flowers
    By centuries of days,
Strong blossoms with perfume of manhood, shot out from
    my spirit as rays.

And the sound of them springing
    And smell of their shoots
Were as warmth and sweet singing
    And strength to my roots;
And the lives of my children made perfect with freedom of
    soul were my fruits.

I bid you but be;
    I have need not of prayer;
I have need of you free
    As your mouths of mine air;
That my heart may be greater within me, beholding the
    fruits of me fair.

More fair than strange fruit is
    Of faiths ye espouse;
In me only the root is
    That blooms in your boughs;
Behold now your God that ye made you, to feed him
    with faith of your vows.

In the darkening and whitening
    Abysses adored,
With dayspring and lightning
    For lamp and for sword,
God thunders in heaven, and his angels are red with the
    wrath of the Lord.

O my sons, O too dutiful
   Toward Gods not of me,
Was not I enough beautiful?
   Was it hard to be free?
For behold, I am with you, am in you and of you; look forth
  now and see.

Lo, winged with world's wonders,
   With miracles shod,
With the fires of his thunders
   For raiment and rod,
God trembles in heaven, and his angels are white with the
  terror of God.

For his twilight is come on him,
   His anguish is here;
And his spirits gaze dumb on him,
   Grown grey from his fear;
And his hour taketh hold on him striken, the last of his
  infinite year.

Thought made him and breaks him,
   Truth slays and forgives;
But to you, as time takes him,
   This new thing it gives,
Even love, the beloved Republic, that feeds upon freedom
  and lives.

For truth only is living,
   Truth only is whole,
And the love of his giving
   Man's polestar and pole;
Man, pulse of my centre, and fruit of my body, and seed of
  my soul.

One birth of my bosom;
   One beam of mine eye;
One topmost blossom
   That scales the sky;
Man, equal and one with me, man that is made of me, man
   that is I.

ALGERNON CHARLES SWINBURNE

REVERENCE FOR LIFE

Woodman, Spare That Tree

Woodman, spare that tree!
   Touch not a single bough!
In youth it sheltered me,
   And I'll protect it now.
'Twas my forefather's hand
   That placed it near his cot;
There, woodman, let it stand,
   Thy axe shall harm it not!

That old familiar tree,
   Whose glory and renown
Are spread o'er land and sea,
   And wouldst thou hew it down?
Woodman, forbear thy stroke!
   Cut not its earth-bound ties;
O, spare that aged oak,
   Now towering to the skies!

When but an idle boy
   I sought its grateful shade;
In all their gushing joy
   Here too my sisters played.
My mother kissed me here;
   My father pressed my hand—
Forgive this foolish tear,
   But let that old oak stand!

My heart-strings round thee cling,
   Close as thy bark, old friend!
Here shall the wild-bird sing,
   And still thy branches bend.

Old tree! the storm still brave!
  And, woodman, leave the spot;
While I've a hand to save,
  Thy axe shall hurt it not.
GEORGE PERKINS MORRIS

The Fly

Little Fly,
Thy summer's play
My thoughtless hand
Has brushed away.

Am not I
A fly like thee?
Or art not thou
A man like me?

For I dance
And drink and sing,
Till some blind hand
Shall brush my wing.

If thought is life
And strength and breath,
And the want
Of thought is death,

Then am I
A happy fly
If I live
Or if I die.
WILLIAM BLAKE

Auguries of Innocence

To see a world in a grain of sand
And a Heaven in a wild flower,
Hold Infinity in the palm of your hand
And Eternity in an hour.

A robin redbreast in a cage
Puts all Heaven in a rage.
A dove-house filled with doves and pigeons
Shudders Hell through all its regions.
A dog starved at his master's gate
Predicts the ruin of the state.
A horse misused upon the road
Calls to Heaven for human blood.

Each outcry of the hunted hare
A fibre from the brain does tear.
A skylark wounded in the wing,
A cherubim does cease to sing.
The game cock clipped and armed for fight
Does the rising sun affright.
Every wolf's and lion's howl
Raises from Hell a human soul.

The wild deer wandering here and there
Keeps the human soul from care.
The lamb misused breeds public strife
And yet forgives the butcher's knife.
The bat that flits at close of eve
Has left the brain that won't believe.
The owl that calls upon the night
   Speaks the unbeliever's fright.

He who shall hurt the little wren
Shall never be beloved by men.
He who the ox to wrath had moved
Shall never be by woman loved.

The wanton boy that kills the fly
Shall feel the spider's enmity.
He who torments the chafer's sprite
Weaves a bower in endless night.

The caterpillar on the leaf
Repeats to thee thy mother's grief.
Kill not the moth nor butterfly
For the Last Judgment draweth nigh.

WILLIAM BLAKE

SACRIFICES

To Primroses
Filled with Morning Dew

Why do ye weep, sweet babes? Can tears
Speak grief in you,
Who were but born
Just as the modest morn
Teemed her refreshing dew?
Alas! ye have not known that shower
That mars a flower:

Nor felt the unkind
Breath of a blasting wind;
Nor are ye worn with years;
Or warped as we,
Who think it strange to see
Such pretty flowers, like to orphans young.
Speaking by tears before ye have a tongue.

Speak, whimpering younglings, and make known
The reason why
Ye droop and weep.
Is it for want of sleep,
Or childish lullaby?
Or that ye have not seen as yet
The violet?
Or brought a kiss
From that sweetheart to this?
No, no; this sorrow shown
By your tears shed,
Would have this lecture read:
That things of greatest, so of meanest worth,
Conceived with grief are, and with tears brought forth.

ROBERT HERRICK

Eros Turannos

She fears him, and will always ask
    What fated her to choose him;
She meets in his engaging mask
    All reasons to refuse him;

But what she meets and what she fears
Are less than are the downward years,
Drawn slowly to the foamless weirs
    Of age, were she to lose him.

Between a blurred sagacity
    That once had power to sound him,
And Love, that will not let him be
    The Judas that she found him,
Her pride assuages her almost,
As if it were alone the cost,—
He sees that he will not be lost,
    And waits and looks around him.

A sense of ocean and old trees
    Envelops and allures him;
Tradition, touching all he sees,
    Beguiles and reassures him;
And all her doubts of what he says
Are dimmed with what she knows of days—
Till even prejudice delays
    And fades, and she secures him.

The falling leaf inaugurates
    The reign of her confusion;
The pounding wave reverberates
    The dirge of her illusion;
And home, where passion lived and died,
Becomes a place where she can hide,
While all the town and harbor side
    Vibrate with her seclusion.

We tell you, tapping on our brows,
    The story as it should be,—

As if the story of a house
    Were told, or ever could be;
We'll have no kindly veil between
Her visions and those we have seen,—
As if we guessed what hers have been,
        Or what they are or would be.

Meanwhile we do no harm; for they
    That with a god have striven,
Not hearing much of what we say,
    Take what the god has given;
Though like waves breaking it may be
Or like a changed familiar tree,
Or like a stairway to the sea
    Where down the blind are driven.
                EDWIN ARLINGTON ROBINSON

SOUL

Darest Thou Now O Soul

Darest thou now O soul,
Walk out with me toward the unknown region,
Where neither ground is for the feet nor any path to
    follow?

No map there, nor guide,
Nor voice sounding, nor touch of human hand,
Nor face with blooming flesh, nor lips, nor eyes, are in that
    land.

I know it not O soul,
Nor dost thou, all is a blank before us,
All waits undream'd of in that region, that inaccessible land.

Till when the ties loosen,
All but the ties eternal, Time and Space,
Nor darkness, gravitation sense, nor any bounds
    bounding us.

Then we burst forth, we float,
In Time and Space O soul, prepared for them,
Equal, equipt at last (O joy! O fruit of all!) them to fulfill
    O soul.

WALT WHITMAN

I Sought My Soul

I sought my soul,
But my soul I could not see.
I sought my God,
But my God eluded me.
I sought my brother,
And I found all three.
AUTHOR UNKNOWN

The Old Stoic

Riches I hold in light esteem,
And love I laugh to scorn;
And lust of fame was but a dream,
That vanished with the morn:

And if I pray, the only prayer
That moves my lips for me
Is, "Leave the heart that now I bear,
And give me liberty!"

Yes, as my swift days near the goal,
'Tis all that I implore;
In life and death a chainless soul,
With courage to endure.
EMILY BRONTË

To the Soul

Dull soul aspire;
Thou art not earth. Mount higher!
Heaven gave the spark; to it return the fire.

Let sin ne'er quench
Thy high-flamed spirit hence;
To earth the heat, to heaven the flame dispense!

Rejoice! Rejoice!
Turn, turn, each part a voice;
While to the heart-strings' tune ye all rejoice.

The house is swept
Which sin so long foul kept;
The penny's found for which the loser wept.

And, purged with tears,
God's image reappears.
The penny truly shows whose stamp it bears.

The sheep long lost,
Sin's wilderness oft crossed,
Is found, regained, returned. Spare, spare no cost!

'Tis heaven's own suit;
Hark how it woos you to't.
When angels needs must speak, shall man be mute?

JOHN COLLOP

Valediction Forbidding Mourning

As virtuous men pass mildly away,
   And whisper to their souls to go,
Whilst some of their sad friends do say,
   "The breath goes now," and some say "No";

So let us melt and make no noise,
   No tear-floods nor sigh-tempests move;
'Twere profanation of our joys
   To tell the laity our love.

Moving of th' earth brings harms and fears;
   Men reckon what it did and meant;
But trepidation of the spheres,
   Though greater far, is innocent.

Dull sublunary lovers' love
   (Whose soul is sense) cannot admit
Absence, because it doth remove
   Those things which elemented it.

But we by a love so much refined
   That ourselves know not what it is,
Inter-assurèd of the mind,
   Careless eyes, lips, and hands to miss.

Our two souls, therefore, which are one,
   Though I must go, endure not yet
A breach, but an expansion,
   Like gold to airy thinness beat.

If they be two, they are two so
    As stiff twin compasses are two:
Thy soul, the fixt foot, makes no show
    To move, but both do if the other do.

And though it in the center sit,
    Yet when the other far doth roam,
It leans and harkens after it,
    And grows erect as that comes home.

Such wilt thou be to me, who must
    Like th' other foot, obliquely run;
Thy firmness makes my circle just,
    And makes me end, where I begun.

                    JOHN DONNE

A Noiseless Patient Spider

A noiseless patient spider,
I mark'd where on a little promontory it stood isolated,
Mark'd how to explore the vacant vast surrounding,
It launch'd forth filament, filament, filament, out of itself,
Ever unreeling them, ever tirelessly speeding them.

And you O my soul where you stand,
Surrounded, detached, in measureless oceans of space,
Ceaselessly musing, venturing, throwing, seeking the
   spheres to connect them,
Till the bridge you will need be form'd, till the ductile
   anchor hold,
Till the gossamer thread you fling catch somewhere, O my
   soul.

                    WALT WHITMAN

The Silken Tent

She is as in a field a silken tent
At midday when a sunny summer breeze
Has dried the dew and all its ropes relent,
So that in guys it gently sways at ease,
And its supporting central cedar pole,
That is its pinnacle to heavenward
And signifies the sureness of the soul,
Seems to owe naught to any single cord,
But strictly held by none, is loosely bound
By countless silken ties of love and thought
To everything on earth the compass round,
And only by one's going slightly taut
In the capriciousness of summer air
Is of the slightest bondage made aware.

ROBERT FROST

No Coward Soul Is Mine

No coward soul is mine,
No trembler in the world's storm-troubled sphere;
I see Heaven's glories shine,
And faith shines equal, arming me from fear.

O God within my breast,
Almighty, ever-present Deity!
Life—that in me has rest,
As I—undying Life—have power in Thee!

Vain are the thousand creeds
That move men's hearts—unutterably vain;
Worthless as withered weeds,
Or idlest froth amid the boundless main,

To waken doubt in one
Holding so fast by Thine infinity;
So surely anchored on
The steadfast rock of immortality.

With wide-embracing love
Thy spirit animates eternal years
Pervades and broods above,
Changes, sustains, dissolves, creates, and rears.

Though earth and man were gone,
And suns and universes ceased to be,
And Thou were left alone,
Every existence would exist in Thee.

There is not room for Death,
Nor atom that his might could render void;
Thou—Thou art Being and Breath,
And what Thou art may never be destroyed.

EMILY BRONTË

TALES

Casey at the Bat

The outlook wasn't brilliant for the Mudville nine that day;
The score stood four to two, with but one inning more to
    play;
And so, when Cooney died at first, and Barrows did the
    same,
A sickly silence fell upon the patrons of the game.

A straggling few got up to go in deep despair. The rest
Clung to the hope which springs eternal in the human
    breast;
They thought, if only Casey could but get a whack, at that,
They'd put up even money now, with Casey at the bat.

But Flynn preceded Casey, as did also Jimmy Blake,
And the former was a pudding and the latter was a fake;
So upon that stricken multitude grim melancholy sat,
For there seemed but little chance of Casey's getting to the
    bat.

But Flynn let drive a single, to the wonderment of all,
And Blake, the much despised, tore the cover off the ball;
And when the dust had lifted, and they saw what had
    occurred,
There was Jimmy safe on second, and Flynn a-hugging
    third.

Then from the gladdened multitude went up a joyous yell,
It bounded from the mountain-top, and rattled in the dell;
It struck upon the hillside, and recoiled upon the flat;
For Casey, mighty Casey, was advancing to the bat.

There was ease in Casey's manner as he stepped into his
   place,
There was pride in Casey's bearing, and a smile on Casey's
   face;
And when, responding to the cheers, he lightly doffed his
   hat,
No stranger in the crowd could doubt 'twas Casey at the
   bat.

Ten thousand eyes were on him as he rubbed his hands
   with dirt,
Five thousand tongues applauded when he wiped them on
   his shirt;
Then while the writhing pitcher ground the ball into his
   hip,
Defiance gleamed in Casey's eye, a sneer curled Casey's lip.

And now the leather-covered sphere came hurtling
   through the air,
And Casey stood a-watching it in haughty grandeur there;
Close by the sturdy batsman the ball unheeded sped.
"That ain't my style," said Casey. "Strike one," the umpire
   said.

From the benches, black with people, there went a muffled
   roar,
Like the beating of the storm-waves on a stern and distant
   shore;
"Kill him! kill the umpire!" shouted someone on the stand.
And it's likely they'd have killed him had not Casey raised
   his hand.

With a smile of Christian charity great Casey's visage
   shone;
He stilled the rising tumult; he bade the game go on;
He signalled to the pitcher, and once more the spheroid
   flew,
But Casey still ignored it, and the umpire said, "Strike two."
"Fraud!" cried the maddened thousands, and the echo
   answered, "Fraud!"
But a scornful look from Casey, and the audience was awed;
They saw his face grow stern and cold, they saw his
   muscles strain,
And they knew that Casey wouldn't let that ball go by
   again.

The sneer is gone from Casey's lips, his teeth are clenched
   in hate,
He pounds with cruel violence his bat upon the plate;
And now the pitcher holds the ball, and now he lets it go,
And now the air is shattered by the force of Casey's blow.

Oh! somewhere in this favored land the sun is shining
   bright,
The band is playing somewhere, and somewhere hearts are
   light;
And somewhere men are laughing, and somewhere
   children shout,
But there is no joy in Mudville—mighty Casey has struck
   out.

ERNEST LAWRENCE THAYER

Paul Revere's Ride

Listen, my children, and you shall hear
Of the midnight ride of Paul Revere,
On the eighteenth of April, in Seventy-five;
Hardly a man is now alive
Who remembers that famous day and year.

He said to his friend, "If the British march
By land or sea from the town tonight,
Hang a lantern aloft in the belfry arch
Of the North Church tower as a signal light—
One, if by land, and two, if by sea;
And I on the opposite shore will be,
Ready to ride and spread the alarm
Through every Middlesex village and farm,
For the country folk to be up and to arm."

Then he said, "Good night!" and with muffled oar
Silently rowed to the Charlestown shore,
Just as the moon rose over the bay,
Where swinging wide at her moorings lay
The Somerset, British man-of-war;
A phantom ship, with each mast and spar
Across the moon like a prison bar,
And a huge black hulk, that was magnified
By its own reflection in the tide.

Meanwhile, his friend, through alley and street,
Wanders and watches with eager ears,
Till in the silence around him he hears
The muster of men at the barrack door,

The sound of arms, and the tramp of feet,
And the measured tread of the grenadiers,
Marching down to their boats on the shore.

Then he climbed the tower of the Old North Church,
By the wooden stairs, with stealthy tread,
To the belfry-chamber overhead,
And startled the pigeons from their perch
On the somber rafters, that round him made
Masses and moving shapes of shade—
By the trembling ladder, steep and tall,
To the highest window in the wall,
Where he paused to listen and look down
A moment on the roofs of the town,
And the moonlight flowing over all.

Beneath, in the churchyard, lay the dead,
In their night-encampment on the hill,
Wrapped in silence so deep and still
That he could hear, like a sentinel's tread,
The watchful night-wind, as it went
Creeping along from tent to tent,
And seeming to whisper, "All is well!"

A moment only he feels the spell
Of the place and the hour, and the secret dread
Of the lonely belfry and the dead;
For suddenly all his thoughts are bent
On a shadowy something far away,
Where the river widens to meet the bay—
A line of black that bends and floats
On the rising tide, like a bridge of boats.

Meanwhile, impatient to mount and ride,
Booted and spurred, with a heavy stride
On the opposite shore walked Paul Revere.
Now he patted his horse's side,
Now gazed at the landscape far and near,
Then, impetuous, stamped the earth,
And turned and tightened his saddle-girth;
But mostly he watched with eager search
The belfry-tower of the Old North Church,
As it rose above the graves on the hill,
Lonely and spectral and somber and still.
And lo! as he looks, on the belfry's height
A glimmer, and then a gleam of light!
He springs to the saddle, the bridle he turns,
But lingers and gazes, till full on his sight
A second lamp in the belfry burns!

A hurry of hoofs in a village street,
A shape in the moonlight, a bulk in the dark,
And beneath, from the pebbles, in passing, a spark
Struck out by a steed flying fearless and fleet;
That was all! And yet, through the gloom and the light,
The fate of a nation was riding that night;
And the spark struck out by that steed in his flight,
Kindled the land into flame with its heat.

He has left the village and mounted the steep,
And beneath him, tranquil and broad and deep,
Is the Mystic, meeting the ocean tides;
And under the alders that skirt its edge,
Now soft on the sand, now loud on the ledge,
Is heard the tramp of his steed as he rides.

It was twelve by the village clock
When he crossed the bridge into Medford town.
He heard the crowing of the cock,
And the barking of the farmer's dog,
And felt the damp of the river fog,
That rises after the sun goes down.

It was one by the village clock,
When he galloped into Lexington.
He saw the gilded weathercock
Swim in the moonlight as he passed,
And the meeting-house windows, blank and bare,
Gaze at him with a spectral glare,
As if they already stood aghast
At the bloody work they would look upon.

It was two by the village clock,
When he came to the bridge in Concord town.
He heard the bleating of the flock,
And the twitter of birds among the trees,
And felt the breath of the morning breeze
Blowing over the meadows brown.
And one was safe and asleep in his bed
Who at the bridge would be first to fall,
Who that day would be lying dead,
Pierced by a British musket-ball.

You know the rest. In the books you have read,
How the British Regulars fired and fled—
How the farmers gave them ball for ball,
From behind each fence and farmyard wall,
Chasing the redcoats down the lane,
Then crossing the fields to emerge again
Under the trees at the turn of the road,
And only pausing to fire and load.

So through the night rode Paul Revere;
And so through the night went his cry of alarm
To every Middlesex village and farm—
A cry of defiance, and not of fear,
A voice in the darkness, a knock at the door,
And a word that shall echo forevermore!
For, borne on the night-wind of the Past,
Through all our history, to the last,
In the hour of darkness and peril and need,
The people will waken and listen to hear
The hurrying hoofbeats of that steed,
And the midnight message of Paul Revere.

HENRY WADSWORTH LONGFELLOW

Fable

The mountain and the squirrel
Had a quarrel,
And the former called the latter "Little Prig;"
Bun replied,
"You are doubtless very big;
But all sorts of things and weather
Must be taken in together,
To make up a year
And a sphere.
And I think it no disgrace
To occupy my place.
If I'm not so large as you,
You are not so small as I,
And not half so spry.

I'll not deny you make
A very pretty squirrel track;
Talents differ; all is well and wisely put;
If I cannot carry forests on my back,
Neither can you crack a nut."
RALPH WALDO EMERSON

The Raven

Once upon a midnight dreary, while I pondered, weak and
    weary,
Over many a quaint and curious volume of forgotten
    lore,—
While I nodded, nearly napping, suddenly there came a
    tapping,
As of some one gently rapping, rapping at my chamber
    door.
"'Tis some visitor," I muttered, "tapping at my chamber door:
    Only this and nothing more."

Ah, distinctly I remember it was in the bleak December,
And each separate dying ember wrought its ghost upon the
    floor.
Eagerly I wished the morrow;—vainly I had sought to
    borrow
From my books surcease of sorrow—sorrow for the lost
    Lenore,
For the rare and radiant maiden whom the angels name
    Lenore:
    Nameless here for evermore.

And the silken sad uncertain rustling of each purple curtain
Thrilled me—filled me with fantastic terrors never felt
   before;
So that now, to still the beating of my heart, I stood
   repeating
"'Tis some visitor entreating entrance at my chamber door,
Some late visitor entreating entrance at my chamber door:
     This it is and nothing more."

Presently my soul grew stronger; hesitating then no
   longer,
"Sir," said I, "or Madam, truly your forgiveness I implore;
But the fact is I was napping, and so gently you came
   rapping,
And so faintly you came tapping, tapping at my chamber
   door,
That I scarce was sure I heard you"—here I opened wide the
door:—
     Darkness there and nothing more.

Deep into that darkness peering, long I stood there
   wondering, fearing,
Doubting, dreaming dreams no mortal ever dared to dream
   before;
But the silence was unbroken, and the stillness gave no
   token,
And the only word there spoken was the whispered word,
   "Lenore?"
This I whispered, and an echo murmured back the word,
   "Lenore:"
     Merely this and nothing more.

Back into the chamber turning, all my soul within me
    burning,
Soon again I heard a tapping somewhat louder than before.
"Surely," said I, "surely that is something at my window
    lattice;
Let me see, then, what thereat is, and this mystery explore;
Let my heart be still a moment and this mystery explore:
      'Tis the wind and nothing more."

Open here I flung the shutter, when, with many a flirt and
    flutter,
In there stepped a stately Raven of the saintly days of yore.
Not the least obeisance made he; not a minute stopped or
    stayed he;
But, with mien of lord or lady, perched above my chamber
    door,
Perched upon a bust of Pallas just above my chamber door:
      Perched, and sat, and nothing more.

Then this ebony bird beguiling my sad fancy into smiling
By the grave and stern decorum of the countenance it
    wore,—
"Though thy crest be shorn and shaven, thou," I said, "art
    sure no craven,
Ghastly grim and ancient Raven wandering from the
    Nightly shore:
Tell me what thy lordly name is on the Night's Plutonian
    shore!"
      Quoth the Raven, "Nevermore."

Much I marvelled this ungainly fowl to hear discourse so
    plainly,
Though its answer little meaning—little relevancy bore;
For we cannot help agreeing that no living human being
Ever yet was blessed with seeing bird above his chamber
    door,
Bird or beast upon the sculptured bust above his chamber
    door,
    With such name as "Nevermore."

But the Raven, sitting lonely on the placid bust, spoke only
That one word, as if his soul in that one word he did
    outpour.
Nothing further then he uttered, not a feather then he
    fluttered,
Till I scarcely more than muttered,—"Other friends have
    flown before;
On the morrow *he* will leave me, as my Hopes have flown
    before."
    Then the bird said, "Nevermore."

Startled at the stillness broken by reply so aptly spoken,
"Doubtless," said I, "what it utters is its only stock and
    store,
Caught from some unhappy master whom unmerciful
    Disaster
Followed fast and followed faster till his songs one burden
    bore:
Till the dirges of his Hope that melancholy burden bore
    Of 'Never—nevermore.'"

But the Raven still beguiling my sad fancy into smiling,
Straight I wheeled a cushioned seat in front of bird and bust
    and door;
Then, upon the velvet sinking, I betook myself to linking
Fancy unto fancy, thinking what this ominous bird of yore,
What this grim, ungainly, ghastly, gaunt, and ominous bird
    of yore
        Meant in croaking "Nevermore."

This I sat engaged in guessing, but no syllable expressing
To the fowl whose fiery eyes now burned into my
    core;
This and more I sat divining, with my head at ease reclining
On the cushion's velvet lining that the lamp-light gloated
    o'er,
But whose velvet violet lining with the lamp-light gloating
    o'er
        She shall press, ah, nevermore!

Then, methought, the air grew denser, perfumed from an
    unseen censer
Swung by seraphim whose foot-falls tinkled on the tufted
    floor.
"Wretch," I cried, "thy God hath lent thee—by these angels
    he hath sent thee
Respite—respite and nepenthe from thy memories of
    Lenore!
Quaff, oh quaff this kind nepenthe, and forget this lost
    Lenore!"
        Quoth the Raven, "Nevermore."

"Prophet!" said I, "thing of evil! prophet still, if bird or devil!
Whether Tempter sent, or whether tempest tossed thee
here ashore,
Desolate yet all undaunted, on this desert land enchanted—
On this home by Horror haunted—tell me truly, I implore:
Is there—*is* there balm in Gilead?—tell me—tell me,
I implore!"
Quoth the Raven, "Nevermore."

"Prophet!" said I, "thing of evil—prophet still, if bird or
devil!
By that Heaven that bends above us, by that God we both
adore,
Tell this soul with sorrow laden if, within the distant
Aidenn,
It shall clasp a sainted maiden whom the angels name
Lenore:
Clasp a rare and radiant maiden whom the angels name
Lenore!"
Quoth the Raven, "Nevermore."

"Be that word our sign of parting, bird or fiend!" I shrieked,
upstarting:
"Get thee back into the tempest and the Night's Plutonian
shore!
Leave no black plume as a token of that lie thy soul hath
spoken!
Leave my loneliness unbroken! quit the bust above my
door!
Take thy beak from out my heart, and take thy form from
off my door!"
Quoth the Raven, "Nevermore."

And the Raven, never flitting, still is sitting, still is sitting
On the pallid bust of Pallas just above my chamber door;
And his eyes have all the seeming of a demon's that is
    dreaming,
And the lamp-light o'er him streaming throws his shadow
    on the floor:
And my soul from out that shadow that lies floating on the
    floor
       Shall be lifted—nevermore!

EDGAR ALLAN POE

A Visit from St. Nicholas

'Twas the night before Christmas, when all through the
    house
Not a creature was stirring, not even a mouse;
The stockings were hung by the chimney with care,
In hopes that St. Nicholas soon would be there;
The children were nestled all snug in their beds,
While visions of sugar-plums danced in their heads;
And mamma in her 'kerchief, and I in my cap,
Had just settled our brains for a long winter's nap,
When out on the lawn there arose such a clatter,
I sprang from the bed to see what was the matter.
Away to the window I flew like a flash,
Tore open the shutters and threw up the sash.
The moon on the breast of the new-fallen snow
Gave the lustre of mid-day to objects below,
When, what to my wondering eyes should appear,
But a miniature sleigh, and eight tiny reindeer,
With a little old driver, so lively and quick,
I knew in a moment it must be St. Nick.

More rapid than eagles his coursers they came,
And he whistled, and shouted, and called them by name;
'Now, Dasher! now, Dancer! now, Prancer and Vixen!
On, Comet! on Cupid! on, Donder and Blitzen!
To the top of the porch! to the top of the wall!
Now dash away! dash away! dash away all!"
As dry leaves that before the wild hurricane fly,
When they meet with an obstacle, mount to the sky,
So up to the house-top the coursers they flew,
With the sleigh full of toys, and St. Nicholas too.
And then, in a twinkling, I heard on the roof
The prancing and pawing of each little hoof.
As I drew in my head, and was turning around,
Down the chimney St. Nicholas came with a bound.
He was dressed all in fur, from his head to his foot,
And his clothes were all tarnished with ashes and soot;
A bundle of toys he had flung on his back,
And he looked like a peddler just opening his pack.
His eyes—how they twinkled—his dimples how merry!
His cheeks were like roses, his nose like a cherry!
His droll little mouth was drawn up like a bow,
And the beard of his chin was as white as the snow;
The stump of a pipe he held tight in his teeth,
And the smoke it encircled his head like a wreath;
He had a broad face and a little round belly,
That shook, when he laughed, like a bowlful of jelly.
He was chubby and plump, a right jolly old elf,
And I laughed when I saw him, in spite of myself;
A wink of his eye and a twist of his head,
Soon gave me to know I had nothing to dread;
He spoke not a word, but went straight to his work,
And filled all the stockings; then turned with a jerk,
And laying his finger aside of his nose,
And giving a nod, up the chimney he rose;

He sprang to his sleigh, to his team gave a whistle,
And away they all flew like the down of a thistle.
But I heard him exclaim, ere he drove out of sight,
"Happy Christmas to all, and to all a good-night."
CLEMENT CLARKE MOORE

THOUGHTFULNESS

Tell Her So

Amid the cares of married strife
   In spite of toil and business life
If you value your dear wife—
   Tell her so!

When days are dark and deeply blue
   She has her troubles, same as you
Show her that your love is true
   Tell her so!

Whether you mean or care,
Gentleness, kindness, love, and hate,
Envy, anger, are there.
Then, would you quarrels avoid
And peace and love rejoice?
Keep anger not only out of your words—
Keep it out of your voice.

AUTHOR UNKNOWN

If We Knew

If we knew the woe and heartache
   Waiting for us down the road,
If our lips could taste the wormwood,
   If our backs could feel the load,
Would we waste the day in wishing
   For a time that ne'er can be?

Would we wait in such impatience
   For our ships to come from sea?

If we knew the baby fingers
   Pressed against the windowpane
Would be cold and stiff tomorrow—
   Never trouble us again—
Would the bright eyes of our darling
   Catch the frown upon our brow?
Would the print of rosy fingers
   Vex us then as they do now?

Ah! these little ice-cold fingers—
   How they point our memories back
To the hasty words and actions
   Strewn along our backward track!
How these little hands remind us,
   As in snowy grace they lie,
Not to scatter thorns—but roses—
   For our reaping by and by.

Strange we never prize the music
   Till the sweet-voiced bird has flown;
Strange that we should slight the violets
   Till the lovely flowers are gone;
Strange that summer skies and sunshine
   Never seem one half so fair
As when winter's snowy pinions
   Shake their white down in the air!

Lips from which the seal of silence
  None but God can roll away,
Never blossomed in such beauty
  As adorns the mouth today;
And sweet words that freight our memory
  With their beautiful perfume,
Come to us in sweeter accents
  Through the portals of the tomb.

Let us gather up the sunbeams
  Lying all around our path;
Let us keep the wheat and roses,
  Casting out the thorns and chaff;
Let us find our sweetest comfort
  In the blessings of today,
With a patient hand removing
  All the briars from the way.

MAY RILEY SMITH

Those We Love the Best

One great truth in life I've found,
  While journeying to the West—
The only folks we really wound
  Are those we love the best.

The man you thoroughly despise
  Can rouse your wrath, 'tis true;
Annoyance in your heart will rise
  At things mere strangers do.

But those are only passing ills;
  This rule all lives will prove;
The rankling wound which aches and thrills
  Is dealt by hands we love.

The choicest garb, the sweetest grace,
  Are oft to strangers shown;
The careless mien, the frowning face,
  Are given to our own.

We flatter those we scarcely know,
  We please the fleeting guest,
And deal full many a thoughtless blow
  To those we love the best. . . .

ELLA WHEELER WILCOX

The Sin of Omission

It isn't the thing you do;
  It's the thing you leave undone,
Which gives you a bit of heartache
  At the setting of the sun.

The tender word forgotten,
  The letter you did not write,
The flower you might have sent,
  Are your haunting ghosts tonight.

The stone you might have lifted
  Out of a brother's way,
The bit of heartsome counsel
  You were hurried too much to say.

The loving touch of the hand,
  The gentle and winsome tone,
That you had no time or thought for
  With troubles enough of your own.

The little acts of kindness,
  So easily out of mind;
Those chances to be helpful
  Which everyone may find—

No, it's not the thing you do,
  It's the thing you leave undone,
Which gives you the bit of heartache
  At the setting of the sun.
                MARGARET E. SANGSTER

Our Own

If I had known in the morning
  How wearily all the day
The words unkind would trouble my mind
  That I said when you went away,
I had been more careful, darling,
  Nor given you needless pain;
But we vex our own with look and tone
  We may never take back again.

For though in the quiet evening
  You may give me the kiss of peace,
Yet it well might be that never for me
  The pain of the heart should cease!

How many go forth at morning
   Who never come home at night!
And hearts have broken for harsh words spoken
   That sorrow can ne'er set right.

We have careful thought for the stranger,
   And smiles for the sometime guest;
But oft for "our own" the bitter tone,
   Though we love our own the best.
Ah! lips with the curve impatient,
   Ah! brow with the shade of scorn,
'Twere a cruel fate, were the night too late
   To undo the work of the morn!

MARGARET E. SANGSTER

If I Had Known

If I had known what trouble you were bearing;
What griefs were in the silence of your face;
I would have been more gentle, and more caring,
And tried to give you gladness for a space.
I would have brought more warmth into the place,
   If I had known.

If I had known what thoughts despairing drew you;
(Why do we never try to understand?)
I would have lent a little friendship to you,
And slipped my hand within your hand,
And made you stay more pleasant in the land,
   If I had known.

MARY CAROLYN DAVIES

TIME

Time

Time is
Too slow for those who Wait,
Too swift for those who Fear,
Too long for those who Grieve,
Too short for those who Rejoice;
But for those who Love
Time is
Eternity.
AUTHOR UNKNOWN

The Power of Littles

Great events, we often find,
  On little things depend,
And very small beginnings
  Have oft a mighty end.

Letters joined make words,
  And words to books may grow,
As flake on flake descending
  Form an avalanche of snow.

A single utterance may good
  Or evil thought inspire;
One little spark enkindled
  May set a town on fire.

What volumes may be written
  With little drops of ink!
How small a leak, unnoticed,
  A mighty ship will sink!

A tiny insect's labor
  Makes the coral strand,
And mighty seas are girdled
  With grains of golden sand.

A daily penny, saved,
  A fortune may begin;
A daily penny, squandered,
  May lead to vice and sin.

Our life is made entirely
  Of moments multiplied,
As little streamlets, joining,
  Form the ocean's tide.

Our hours and days, our months and years,
  Are in small moments given:
They constitute our time below—
  Eternity in heaven.

AUTHOR UNKNOWN

Even Such Is Time

Even such is Time, which takes in trust
   Our youth, and joys, and all we have;
And pays us but with age and dust,
   Which, in the dark and silent grave,
When we have wandered all our ways,
Shuts up the story of our days:
   And from which earth and grave and dust
   The Lord shall raise me up, I trust.

SIR WALTER RALEIGH

TRUTH

Truth

Truth is the trial of itself,
 And needs no other touch;
And purer than the purest gold,
 Refine it ne'er so much.

It is the life and light of love,
 The sun that ever shineth,
And spirit of that special grace,
 That faith and love defineth.

It is the warrant of the word,
 That yields a scent so sweet,
As gives a power to faith to tread
 All falsehood under feet.
BEN JONSON

from *An Essay on Criticism*

A little learning is a dangerous thing;
Drink deep, or taste not the Pierian spring:
There shallow draughts intoxicate the brain,
And drinking largely sobers us again.
Fired at first sight with what the Muse imparts,
In fearless youth we tempt the heights of Arts,
While from the bounded level of our mind
Short views we take, nor see the lengths behind;
But more advanced, behold with strange surprise
New distant scenes of endless science rise!

So please at first the towering Alps we try,
Mount o'er the vales, and seem to tread the sky,
The eternal snows appear already past,
And the first clouds and mountains seem the last;
But, those attained, we tremble to survey
The growing labors of the lengthened way,
The increasing prospects tire our wandering eyes,
Hills peep o'er hills, and Alps on Alps arise!

ALEXANDER POPE

Still to Be Neat

Still to be neat, still to be drest
As you were going to a feast;
Still to be powder'd, still perfum'd:
Lady, it is to be presum'd,
Though art's hid causes are not found,
All is not sweet, all is not sound.

Give me a look, give me a face
That makes simplicity a grace;
Robes loosely flowing, hair as free;
Such sweet neglect more taketh me
Than all th' adulteries of art;
They strike mine eyes, but not my heart.

BEN JONSON

VICE

Vice

Vice is a monster of so frightful mien,
As to be hated, needs but to be seen;
Yet seen too oft, familiar with her face,
We first endure, then pity, then embrace.
ALEXANDER POPE

Flattery

'Tis an old maxim in the schools,
That flattery's the food of fools;
Yet now and then your men of wit
Will condescend to take a bit.
JONATHAN SWIFT

Gambling

Of every vice pursued by those
In folly's by-paths rambling,
There's none so bad in its dread close,
As the vile vice of gambling.
It taints our morals, wastes our time
And fills us with vexation.
Destroys our wealth and youthful prime,
And mars our reputation.

Yet I'll aver, with my own eyes,
And I am not called stupid,
I caught sweet Fanny by surprise
A gambling with young Cupid!
Beneath the silent moon's soft beams
In fragrant flowery arbor,
That noted gambling house it seems,
Where players love to harbor.
The cunning god and simple fair,
Sat down to play at leisure
And staked such sums as might impair
A mighty monarch's treasure.
And first they played for locks of hair
And Fanny won the game.
Then cheeks and lips & skin so fair
Her luck was all the same.
Vex'd by the maid to be outdone
Then Cupid made a high bet,
Stak'd all his smiles—a mighty sum
With dimples for a by-bet.
But still she won, & Cupid crost
Made dreadful sad grimaces,
Not only his own smiles he lost,
But all his mother's graces.
Proud Fanny's air and looks and eyes
Of victory gave token,
Her winnings seemed a noble prize,
A bank not to be broken.
Beware sweet girl and go no more
To midnight arbors rambling,
But think how soon you may deplore,
The dreadful end of gambling.

Sly Cupid has but played the knave,
And let you come off winner;
This is the way all gamblers have,
With every new beginner.
Some sharper soon will with you sport,
By Cupid's malice sent hence,
Win all your winnings and leave naught,
But sorrow and repentance.

ROYALL TYLER

The Clod & the Pebble

"Love seeketh not Itself to please,
Nor for itself hath any care;
But for another gives its ease,
And builds a Heaven in Hell's despair."

So sang a little Clod of Clay,
Trodden with the cattle's feet;
But a Pebble of the brook,
Warbled out these metres meet:

"Love seeketh only Self to please,
To bind another to its delight;
Joys in another's loss of ease,
And builds a Hell in Heaven's despite."

WILLIAM BLAKE

VIRTUE

Virtue

Sweet day, so cool, so calm, so bright,
The bridal of the earth and sky;
The dew shall weep thy fall tonight,
     For thou must die.

Sweet rose, whose hue, angry and brave,
Bids the rash gazer wipe his eye;
Thy root is ever in its grave,
     And thou must die.

Sweet spring, full of sweet days and roses,
A box where sweets compacted lie;
My music shows ye have your closes,
     And all must die.

Only a sweet and virtuous soul,
Like seasoned timber, never gives;
But though the whole world turn to coal,
     Then chiefly lives.

GEORGE HERBERT

Solitude

Happy the man, whose wish and care
A few paternal acres bound,
Content to breathe his native air
     In his own ground.

Whose herds with milk, whose fields with bread,
Whose flocks supply him with attire;
Whose trees in summer yield him shade,
     In winter, fire.

Blest, who can unconcernedly find
Hours, days, and years slide soft away
In health of body, peace of mind;
     Quiet by day,

Sound sleep by night; study and ease
Together mixed, sweet recreation,
And innocence, which most does please
     With meditation.

Thus let me live, unseen, unknown,
Thus unlamented let me die,
Steal from the world, and not a stone
     Tell where I lie.

ALEXANDER POPE

The Tongue

"The boneless tongue, so small and weak,
Can crush and kill," declared the Greek.

"The tongue destroys a greater horde,"
The Turk asserts, "than does the sword."

A Persian proverb wisely saith,
"A lengthy tongue—an early death."

Or sometimes takes this form instead,
"Don't let your tongue cut off your head."

"The tongue can speak a word whose speed,"
Says the Chinese, "outstrips the steed";

While Arab sages this impart,
"The tongue's great storehouse is the heart."

From Hebrew with the maxim sprung,
"Though feet should slip, ne'er let the tongue."

The sacred writer crown the whole:
"Who keeps the tongue doth keep his soul."

PHILLIPS BURROWS STRONG

VISION

Composed upon Westminster Bridge
September 3, 1802

Earth has not anything to show more fair:
Dull would he be of soul who could pass by
A sight so touching in its majesty:
This city now doth, like a garment, wear
The beauty of the morning; silent, bare,
Ships, towers, domes, theaters, and temples lie
Open unto the fields, and to the sky;
All bright and glittering in the smokeless air.
Never did sun more beautifully steep
In his first splendor, valley, rock, or hill;
Ne'er saw I, never felt, a calm so deep!
The river glideth at his own sweet will:
Dear God! the very houses seem asleep;
And all that mighty heart is lying still!

WILLIAM WORDSWORTH

Upon Love

Love brought me to a silent grove,
   And showed me there a tree,
Where some had hanged themselves for love,
   And gave a twist to me.

The halter was of silk and gold,
   That he reached forth unto me:
No otherwise, than if he would
   By dainty things undo me.

619

He bade me then that necklace use;
    And told me too, he maketh
A glorious end by such a noose,
    His death for love that taketh.

'Twas but a dream; but had I been
    There really alone,
My desperate fears, in love, had seen
    Mine execution.
                              ROBERT HERRICK

A Dream Within a Dream

Take this kiss upon thy brow!
And, in parting from you now,
Thus much let me avow—
You are not wrong, to deem
That my days have been a dream;
Yet if Hope has flown away
In a night, or in a day,
In a vision, or in none,
Is it therefore the less *gone*?
All that we see or seem
Is but a dream within a dream.

I stand amid the roar
Of a surf-tormented shore,
And I hold within my hand
Grains of the golden sand—
How few! yet how they creep
Through my fingers to the deep,
While I weep—while I weep!

O God! can I not grasp
Them with a tighter clasp?
O God! can I not save
One from the pitiless wave?
Is *all* that we see or seem
But a dream within a dream?

EDGAR ALLAN POE

Our Revels Now Are Ended

(*from The Tempest*)

Our revels now are ended. These our actors,
As I foretold you, were all spirits and
Are melted into air, into thin air:
And, like the baseless fabric of this vision,
The cloud-capp'd towers, the gorgeous palaces,
The solemn temples, the great globe itself,
Yea, all which it inherit, shall dissolve
And, like this insubstantial pageant faded,
Leave not a rack behind. We are such stuff
As dreams are made on, and our little life
Is rounded with a sleep.

WILLIAM SHAKESPEARE

Kubla Khan

In Xanadu did Kubla Khan
  A stately pleasure-dome decree:
Where Alph, the sacred river, ran
Through caverns measureless to man
  Down to a sunless sea.
So twice five miles of fertile ground
With walls and towers were girdled round:
And here were gardens bright with sinuous rills,
Where blossomed many an incense-bearing tree,
And here were forests ancient as the hills,
Enfolding sunny spots of greenery.

But oh! that deep romantic chasm which slanted
Down the green hill athwart a cedarn cover!
A savage place; as holy and enchanted
As e'er beneath a waning moon was haunted
By woman wailing for her demon-lover!
And from this chasm, with ceaseless turmoil seething,
As if this earth in fast thick pants were breathing,
A mighty fountain momently was forced,
Amid whose swift half-intermitted burst
Huge fragments vaulted like rebounding hail,
Or chaffy grain beneath the thresher's flail:
And 'mid these dancing rocks at once and ever
It flung up momently the sacred river.
Five miles meandering with a mazy motion
Through wood and dale the sacred river ran,
Then reached the caverns measureless to man,
And sank in tumult to a lifeless ocean:
And 'mid this tumult Kubla heard from far
Ancestral voices prophesying war!

The shadow of the dome of pleasure
Floated midway on the waves;
Where was heard the mingled measure
From the fountain and the caves.
It was a miracle of rare device,
A sunny pleasure-dome with caves of ice!

A damsel with a dulcimer
In a vision once I saw:
It was an Abyssinian maid,
And on her dulcimer she played,
Singing of Mount Abora.
Could I revive within me
Her symphony and song,
To such a deep delight 'twould win me,
That with music loud and long,
I would build that dome in air,
That sunny dome! those caves of ice!
And all who heard should see them there,
And all should cry, Beware! Beware!
His flashing eyes, his floating hair!
Weave a circle round him thrice,
And close your eyes with holy dread,
For he on honey-dew hath fed,
And drunk the milk of Paradise.

SAMUEL TAYLOR COLERIDGE

Ode to a Nightingale

My heart aches, and a drowsy numbness pains
  My sense, as though of hemlock I had drunk,
Or emptied some dull opiate to the drains
  One minute past, and Lethe-wards had sunk:
'Tis not through envy of thy happy lot,
  But being too happy in thy happiness,—
    That thou, light-winged Dryad of the trees,
      In some melodious plot
Of beechen green, and shadows numberless,
  Singest of summer in full-throated ease.

O for a draught of vintage, that hath been
  Cooled a long age in the deep-delved earth,
Tasting of Flora and the country green,
  Dance, and Provençal song, and sun-burnt mirth
O for a beaker full of the warm South,
  Full of the true, the blushful Hippocrene,
    With beaded bubbles winking at the brim,
      And purple-stained mouth;
That I might drink, and leave the world unseen
  And with thee fade away into the forest dim:

Fade far away, dissolve, and quite forget
  What thou among the leaves hast never known,
The weariness, the fever, and the fret
  Here, where men sit and hear each other groan;
Where palsy shakes a few, sad, last gray hairs,
  When youth grows pale, and spectre-thin, and dies;
    Where but to think is to be full of sorrow
      And leaden-eyed despairs;

Where beauty cannot keep her lustrous eyes,
  Or new love pine at them beyond tomorrow.

Away! away! for I will fly to thee,
  Not charioted by Bacchus and his pards,
But on the viewless wings of Poesy,
  Though the dull brain perplexes and retards:
Already with thee! tender is the night,
  And haply the Queen-Moon is on her throne,
    Clustered around by all her starry fays;
      But here there is no light,
Save what from heaven is with the breezes blown
  Through verdurous glooms and winding mossy ways.

I cannot see what flowers are at my feet,
  Nor what soft incense hangs upon the boughs,
But, in embalmed darkness, guess each sweet
  Wherewith the seasonable month endows
The grass, the thicket, and the fruit-tree wild;
  White hawthorn, and the pastoral eglantine;
    Fast-fading violets covered up in leaves;
      And mid-May's eldest child,
The coming musk-rose, full of dewy wine,
  The murmurous haunt of flies on summer eves.

Darkling I listen; and for many a time
  I have been half in love with easeful Death,
Called him soft names in many a mused rhyme,
  To take into the air my quiet breath;
Now more than ever seems it rich to die,
  To cease upon the midnight with no pain,
    While thou art pouring forth thy soul abroad
      In such an ecstasy!
Still wouldst thou sing, and I have ears in vain—
  To thy high requiem become a sod.

Thou wast not born for death, immortal Bird!
   No hungry generations tread thee down;
The voice I hear this passing night was heard
   In ancient days by emperor and clown:
Perhaps the self-same song that found a path
    Through the sad heart of Ruth, when, sick for home
      She stood in tears amid the alien corn;
        The same that oft-times hath
Charmed magic casements, opening on the foam
   Of perilous seas, in faery lands forlorn.

Forlorn! the very word is like a bell
   To toll me back from thee to my sole self!
Adieu! the fancy cannot cheat so well
   As she is famed to do, deceiving elf.
Adieu! adieu! thy plaintive anthem fades
    Past the near meadows, over the still stream,
      Up the hill-side; and now 'tis buried deep
        In the next valley-glades:
Was it a vision, or a waking dream?
   Fled is that music:—do I wake or sleep?

JOHN KEATS

WAR

The Glories of Our Blood and State

The glories of our blood and state
   Are shadows, not substantial things;
There is no armour against fate;
   Death lays his icy hand on kings:
      Sceptre and Crown
      Must tumble down,
And in the dust be equal made
With the poor crookèd scythe and spade.

Some men with swords may reap the field,
   And plant fresh laurels where they kill:
But their strong nerves at last must yield;
   They tame but one another still:
      Early or late
      They stoop to fate,
And must give up their murmuring breath,
When they, pale captives, creep to death.

The garlands wither on your brow,
   Then boast no more your mighty deeds;
Upon Death's purple altar now
   See, where the victor-victim bleeds:
      Your heads must come
      To the cold tomb;
Only the actions of the just
Smell sweet, and blossom in their dust.

JAMES SHIRLEY

YOUTH

Nothing Gold Can Stay

Nature's first green is gold,
Her hardest hue to hold.
Her early leaf's a flower;
But only so an hour.
Then leaf subsides to leaf.
So Eden sank to grief,
So dawn goes down to day.
Nothing gold can stay.

ROBERT FROST

Good-bye My Fancy!

Good-bye my Fancy!
Farewell dear mate, dear love!
I'm going away, I know not where,
Or to what fortune, or whether I may ever see you again,
So good-bye my Fancy.

Now for my last—let me look back a moment;
The slower fainter ticking of the clock is in me,
Exit, nightfall, and soon the heart-thud stopping.

Long have we lived, joy'd, caress'd together;
Delightful!—now separation—Good-bye my Fancy.

Yet let me not be too hasty,
Long indeed have we lived, slept, filter'd, become really
    blended into one;
Then if we die we die together, (yes, we'll remain one,)
If we go anywhere we'll go together to meet what happens,
May-be we'll be better off and blither, and learn something,
May-be it is yourself now really ushering me to the true
    songs, (who knows?)
May-be it is you the mortal knob really undoing, turning—
    so now finally,
Good-bye—and hail! my Fancy.

WALT WHITMAN

Sweet and Low

Sweet and low, sweet and low,
    Wind of the western sea,
Low, low, breathe and blow,
    Wind of the western sea!
Over the rolling waters go,
Come from the dying moon, and blow,
    Blow him again to me;
While my little one, while my pretty one, sleeps.

Sleep and rest, sleep and rest,
    Father will come to thee soon;
Rest, rest, on mother's breast,
    Father will come to thee soon;
Father will come to his babe in the nest,
Silver sails all out of the west
    Under the silver moon:
Sleep, my little one, sleep, my pretty one, sleep.

ALFRED, LORD TENNYSON

In Reference to Her Children

I had eight birds hatched in one nest,
Four cocks there were, and hens the rest.
I nursed them up with pain and care,
Nor cost, nor labour did I spare,
Till at the last they felt their wing,
Mounted the trees, and learned to sing;
Chief of the brood then took his flight
To regions far and left me quite.
My mournful chirps I after send,
Till he return, or I do end:
Leave not thy nest, thy dam and sire,
Fly back and sing amidst this choir.
My second bird did take her flight,
And with her mate flew out of sight;
Southward they both their course did bend,
And seasons twain they there did spend,
Till after blown by southern gales,
They norward steered with filled sails.
A prettier bird was no where seen,
Along the beach among the treen.
I have a third of colour white,
On whom I placed no small delight;
Coupled with mate loving and true,
Hath also bid her dam adieu;
And where Aurora first appears,
She now hath perched to spend her years.
One to the academy flew
To chat among that learned crew;
Ambition moves still in his breast
That he might chant above the rest,
Striving for more than to do well,
That nightingales he might excel.

My fifth, whose down is yet scarce gone,
Is 'mongst the shrubs and bushes flown,
And as his wings increase in strength,
On higher boughs he'll perch at length.
My other three still with me nest,
Until they're grown, then as the rest,
Or here or there they'll take their flight,
As is ordained, so shall they light.
If birds could weep, then would my tears
Let others know what are my fears
Lest this my brood some harm should catch,
And be surprised for want of watch,
Whilst pecking corn and void of care,
They fall un'wares in fowler's snare,
Or whilst on trees they sit and sing,
Some untoward boy at them do fling,
Or whilst allured with bell and glass,
The net be spread, and caught, alas.
Or lest by lime-twigs they be foiled,
Or by some greedy hawks be spoiled.
O would my young, ye saw my breast,
And knew what thoughts there sadly rest,
Great was my pain when I you bred,
Great was my care when I you fed,
Long did I keep you soft and warm,
And with my wings kept off all harm,
My cares are more and fears than ever,
My throbs such now as 'fore were never.
Alas, my birds, you wisdom want,
Of perils you are ignorant;
Oft times in grass, on trees, in flight,
Sore accidents on you may light.
O to your safety have an eye,
So happy may you live and die.

Meanwhile my days in tunes I'll spend,
Till my weak lays with me shall end.
In shady woods I'll sit and sing,
And things that past to mind I'll bring.
Once young and pleasant, as are you,
But former toys (no joys) adieu.
My age I will not once lament,
But sing, my time so near is spent.
And from the top bough take my flight
Into a country beyond sight,
Where old ones instantly grow young,
And there with seraphims set song;
No seasons cold, nor storms they see;
But spring lasts to eternity.
When each of you shall in your nest
Among your young ones take your rest,
In chirping language, oft them tell,
You had a dam that loved you well,
That did what could be done for young,
And nursed you up till you were strong,
And 'fore she once would let you fly,
She showed you joy and misery;
Taught what was good, and what was ill,
What would save life, and what would kill.
Thus gone, amongst you I may live,
And dead, yet speak, and counsel give:
Farewell, my birds, farewell adieu,
I happy am, if well with you.

ANNE BRADSTREET

The Toys

My little son, who looked from thoughtful eyes
And moved and spoke in quiet grown-up wise,
Having my law the seventh time disobeyed,
I struck him, and dismissed
With hard words and unkissed,
—His mother, who was patient, being dead.
Then, fearing lest his grief should hinder sleep,
I visited his bed,
But found him slumbering deep,
With darkened eyelids, and their lashes yet
From his late sobbing wet.
And I, with moan,
Kissing away his tears, left others of my own;
For, on a table drawn beside his head,
He had put, within his reach,
A box of counters and a red-veined stone,
A piece of glass abraded by the beach,
And six or seven shells,
A bottle with bluebells,
And two French copper coins, ranged there with careful art,
To comfort his sad heart.
So when that night I prayed
To God, I wept, and said:
"Ah, when at last we lie with trancéd breath,
Not vexing Thee in death,
And Thou rememberest of what toys
We made our joys,
How weakly understood
Thy great commanded good,

Then, fatherly not less
Than I whom Thou hast molded from the clay,
Thou'lt leave Thy wrath, and say,
'I will be sorry for their childishness.'"

COVENTRY PATMORE

When I Was One-and-Twenty

When I was one-and-twenty
   I heard a wise man say,
"Give crowns and pounds and guineas
   But not your heart away;
Give pearls away and rubies
   But keep your fancy free."
But I was one-and-twenty,
   No use to talk to me.

When I was one-and-twenty
   I heard him say again,
"The heart out of the bosom
   Was never given in vain;
'Tis paid with sighs a-plenty
   And sold for endless rue."
And I am two-and-twenty,
   And oh, 'tis true, 'tis true.

A.E. HOUSMAN

There Was a Child Went Forth

There was a child went forth every day,
And the first object he look'd upon, that object he became,
And that object became part of him for the day or a certain
    part of the day,
Or for many years or stretching cycles of years.

The early lilacs became part of this child,
And grass and white and red morning-glories, and white
    and red clover, and the song of the phoebe-bird,
And the Third-month lambs and the sow's pink-faint litter,
    and the mare's foal and the cow's calf,
And the noisy brood of the barnyard or by the mire of the
    pond-side,
And the fish suspending themselves so curiously below
    there, and the beautiful curious liquid,
And the water-plants with their graceful flat heads, all
    became part of him.
The field-sprouts of Fourth-month and Fifth-month
    became part of him,
Winter-grain sprouts and those of the light-yellow corn,
    and the esculent roots of the garden,
And the apple-trees cover'd with blossoms and the fruit
    afterward, and wood-berries, and the commonest weeds
    by the road,
And the old drunkard staggering home from the outhouse
    of the tavern whence he had lately risen,
And the schoolmistress that pass'd on her way to the
    school,
And the friendly boys that pass'd, and the quarrelsome
    boys,

And the tidy and fresh-cheek'd girls, and the barefoot
    negro boy and girl,
And all the changes of city and country wherever he went.

His own parents, he that had father'd him and she that had
    conceiv'd him in her womb and birth'd him,
They gave this child more of themselves than that,
They gave him afterward every day, they became part of him.

The mother at home quietly placing the dishes on the
    supper-table,
The mother with mild words, clean her cap and gown, a
    wholesome odor falling off her person and clothes as she
    walks by.
The father, strong, self-sufficient, manly, mean, anger'd,
    unjust,
The blow, the quick loud word, the tight bargain, the crafty
    lure,
The family usages, the language, the company, the furni-
    ture, the yearning and swelling heart,
Affection that will not be gainsay'd, the sense of what is
    real, the thought if after all it should prove unreal,
The doubts of day-time and the doubts of night-time, the
    curious whether and how,
Whether that which appears so is so, or is it all flashes and
    specks?
Men and women crowding fast in the streets, if they are
    not flashes and specks what are they?
The streets themselves and the façades of houses, and
    goods in the windows,
Vehicles, teams, the heavy-plank'd wharves, the huge
    crossing at the ferries,
The village on the highland seen from afar at sunset, the
    river between,

Shadows, aureola and mist, the light falling on roofs and
    gables of white or brown two miles off,
The schooner near by sleepily dropping down the tide, the
    little boat slack-tow'd astern,
The hurrying tumbling waves, quick-broken crests, slap-
    ing,
The strata of color'd clouds, the long bar of maroon-tint
    away solitary by itself, the spread of purity it lies motion-
    less in,
The horizon's edge, the flying sea-crow, the fragrance of
    salt marsh and shore mud,
These became part of that child who went forth every day,
    and who now goes, and will always go forth every day.

WALT WHITMAN

Making a Man

Hurry the baby as fast as you can,
Hurry him, worry him, make him a man.
Off with his baby clothes, get him in pants,
Feed him on brain foods and make him advance.
Hustle him, soon as he's able to walk,
Into a grammar school; cram him with talk.
Fill his poor head full of figures and facts,
Keep on a-jamming them in till it cracks.
Once boys grew up at a rational rate,
Now we develop a man while you wait,
Rush him through college, compel him to grab,
Of every known subject a dip and a dab.

Get him in business and after the cash,
All by the time he can grow a mustache
Let him forget he was ever a boy,
Make gold his god and its jingle his joy.
Keep him a-hustling and clear out of breath,
Until he wins—nervous prostration and death.

NIXON WATERMAN

Where Did You Come From?

Where did you come from, Baby dear?
Out of the everywhere into here.

Where did you get your eyes so blue?
Out of the sky as I came through.

What makes the light in them sparkle and spin?
Some of the starry spikes left in.

Where did you get that little tear?
I found it waiting when I got here.

What makes your forehead so smooth and high?
A soft hand stroked it as I went by.

What makes your cheek like a warm white rose?
I saw something better than anyone knows.

Whence that three-corner'd smile of bliss?
Three angels gave me at once a kiss.

Where did you get this pearly ear?
God spoke, and it came out to hear.

Where did you get those arms and hands?
Love made itself into hooks and bands.

Feet, whence did you come, you darling things?
From the same box as the cherubs' wings.

How did they all come just to be you?
God thought of me, and so I grew.

But how did you come to us, you dear?
God thought of you, and so I am here.

GEORGE MACDONALD

On Going Home for Christmas

He little knew the sorrow that was in his vacant
    chair;
He never guessed they'd miss him, or he'd surely have
    been there;
He couldn't see his mother or the lump that filled her
    throat,
Or the tears that started falling as she read his hasty
    note;
And he couldn't see his father, sitting sorrowful and
    dumb,
Or he never would have written that he thought he
    couldn't come.
He little knew the gladness that his presence would
    have made,

And the joy it would have given, or he never would
    have stayed.
He didn't know how hungry had the little mother
    grown
Once again to see her baby and to claim him for her
    own.
He didn't guess the meaning of his visit Christmas
    Day
Or he never would have written that he couldn't get
    away.

He couldn't see the fading of the cheeks that once
    were pink,
And the silver in the tresses; and he didn't stop to
    think
How the years are passing swiftly, and next Christmas
    it might be
There would be no home to visit and no mother dear
    to see.
He didn't think about it—I'll not say he didn't care.
He was heedless and forgetful or he'd surely have
    been there.
Are you going home for Christmas? Have you written
    you'll be there?
Going home to kiss the mother and to show her that
    you care?
Going home to greet the father in a way to make him
    glad?
If you're not I hope there'll never come a time you'll
    wish you had.
Just sit down and write a letter—it will make their
    heartstrings hum
With a tune of perfect gladness—if you'll tell them
    that you'll come.

EDGAR GUEST

645

On Children

Your children are not your children.
They are the sons and daughters of Life's longing for
    itself.
They come through you but not from you,
And though they are with you yet they belong not to
    you.

You may give them your love but not your thoughts,
For they have their own thoughts.
You may house their bodies but not their souls,
For their souls dwell in the house of tomorrow, which
    you cannot visit, not even in your dreams.
You may strive to be like them, but seek not to make
    them like you.
For life goes not backward nor tarries with yesterday.

KAHLIL GIBRAN

To a New Daughter-in-Law

Forgive me if I speak possessively of him
    Who now is yours, yet still is mine;
Call it the silver cord disparagingly
    And weave new colors in an old design,
Yet know the warp was started long ago
    By faltering steps, by syllable and sound,
By all the years in which I watched him grow. . . .
    By all the seasons' turnings are we bound.

But now, I loose the cord, untie the knot,
    Unravel years so he is yours alone
And if there is a message I forgot
    Or something that could help you had you
        known,
    I shall be waiting, hoping you will see
    That him you love, is also *loved by me*.
AUTHOR UNKNOWN

To My Son

Do you know that your soul is of my soul such part,
That you seem to be fibre and cord of my heart?
None other can pain me as you, dear, can do,
None other can please me or praise me as you.

Remember the world will be quick with its blame
If shadow or stain ever darken your name,
"Like mother like son" is a saying so true,
The world will judge largely of "Mother" by you.

Be yours then the task, if task it shall be
To force the proud world to do homage to me,
Be sure it will say when its verdict you've won,
"She reaped as she sowed, Lo! this is her son."
MARGARET JOHNSTON GRIFFIN

Patty-Poem

She never puts her toys away;
Just leaves them scattered where they lay—
I try to scold her, and I say
  "You make me mad!"

But when to bed she has to chase,
The toys she left about the place
Remind me of her shining face,
  And make me glad.

When she grows up and gathers poise
I'll miss her harum-scarum noise,
And look in vain for scattered toys—
  And I'll be sad.

NICK KENNY

To Youth

This I say to you:
Be arrogant! Be true!
True to April's lust that sings
Through your veins. These sharp Springs
Matter most . . . After years
Will be time enough to sleep . . .
Carefulness . . . and tears . .

Now while life is raw and new,
Drink it clear, drink it deep!

Let the moonlight's lunacy
Tear away your cautions.
Be proud, and mad, and young, and free!
Grasp a comet! Kick at stars
Laughingly! Fight! Dare!
Arms are soft, breasts are white.
Magic's in the April night—

Never fear, Age will catch you.
Slow you down, ere it dispatch you
To your long and solemn quiet . . .
What will matter—then—the riot
Of the lilacs in the wind?
What will mean—then the crush
Of lips at hours when birds hush?
Purple, green and flame will end
In a calm, gray blend.

Only graven in your soul
After all the rest is gone
There will be ecstasies . . .
These alone . . .

JOHN WEAVER

How Old Are You?

Age is a quality of mind.
If you have left your dreams behind,
   If hope is cold,
If you no longer look ahead,
If your ambitions' fires are dead—
   Then you are old.

But if from life you take the best,
And if in life you keep the jest,
  If love you hold;
No matter how the years go by,
No matter how the birthdays fly—
  You are not old.

H.S. FRITSCH

ZEAL

The New Colossus

Not like the brazen giant of Greek fame,
With conquering limbs astride from land to land;
Here at our sea-washed, sunset gates shall stand
A mighty woman with a torch, whose flame
Is the imprisoned lightning, and her name
Mother of Exiles. From her beacon-hand
Glows world-wide welcome; her mild eyes command
The air-bridged harbor that twin cities frame.

"Keep ancient lands, your storied pomp!" cries she
With silent lips. "Give me your tired, your poor,
Your huddled masses yearning to breathe free,
The wretched refuse of your teeming shore.
Send these, the homeless, tempest-tost to me,
I lift my lamp beside the golden door!"

EMMA LAZARUS

INDEXES

INDEX OF FIRST LINES

A wind sways the pines, 149
A wise old owl lived in an oak, 493

Backward, turn backward, O Time, in your flight, 407
Beauty depends on simplicity-I mean the true simplicity, 49
Because, dear Lord, their way is rough and steep, 87
Because you come to me with naught save love, 353
Believe me, if all those endearing young charms, 338
Better than grandeur, better than gold, 224
Bless this house, O Lord, we pray, 478
Break, break, break, 394
Breathes there the man with soul so dead, 425
Build for yourself a strong box, 174
By the merest chance, in the twilight gloom, 360
By the rude bridge that arched the flood, 426

Call the roller of big cigars, 277
Come, fill the Cup, and in the fire of Spring, 496
Come, I will make the continent indissoluble, 425
Come, rest in this bosom, my own stricken deer, 321
"Come down, O maid, from yonder mountain height, 311
Come in the evening, or come in the morning, 320
Come live with me and be my love, 352

Darest thou now O soul, 559
Dear, why should you command me to my rest, 191
Dear gentle hands have stroked my hair, 411
Death, be not proud, though some have called thee, 17
Do all the good you can, 120
Does the road wind up-hill all the way?, 293
Don't, like the cat, try to get more out, 232
Don't you remember sweet Alice, Ben Bolt,—, 529
Do you know that your soul is of my soul such part, 647
Drink to me only with thine eyes, 351
Dull soul aspire, 561

If I should die, think only this of me, 427
If love were what the rose is, 357
If the red slayer think he slays, 439
If thou must love me, let it be for naught, 325
If we but knew what forces helped to mold, 32
If we knew the woe and heartache, 589
If you are on the Gloomy Line, 493
If you can keep your head when all about you, 97
If you can't be a pine on the top of the hill, 288
If you sit down at set of sun, 119
I had eight birds hatched in one nest, 635
I hate to be a kicker, 231
I have a rendezvous with Death, 164
I have found such joy in simple things, 227
I have had playmates, I have had companions, 4
I have never been rich before, 206
I have spread wet linen, 221
I'll hold my candle high, and then, 170
I love you, 201
I love your lips when they're wet with wine, 346
I met a traveler from an antique land, 445
I miss you in the morning, dear, 240
I must go down to the seas again, to the lonely sea, 40
I need so much the quiet of your love, 343
I never saw a man who looked, 160
In Flanders fields the poppies blow, 427
In Love, if Love be Love, if Love be ours, 332
In men whom men condemn as ill, 52
In summer, when the days were long, 330
In Xanadu did Kubla Khan, 622
I remember, I remember, 528
I said, "Let me walk in the fields," 179
I saw God. Do you doubt it?, 181
I seek in prayerful words, dear friend, 207
I see Thee in the distant blue, 177
I see them,-crowd on crowd they walk the earth, 271
I shot an arrow into the air, 205

'Tis an old maxim in the schools, 607
'Tis the human touch in this world that counts, 29
'Tis the last rose of summer, 5
To him who in the love of Nature holds, 154
To see a world in a grain of sand, 549
Tread lightly, she is near, 21
Truth is the trial of itself, 603
'Twas the night before Christmas, when all through the, 583
'Twixt failure and success the point's so fine, 442
Two roads diverged in a yellow wood, 91
Type of the antique Rome! Rich reliquary, 390

Under a spreading chestnut tree, 42
Under the wide and starry sky, 151
Used to wonder just why father, 196

Vice is a monster of so frightful mien, 607

We are the music-makers, 449
We have walked in Love's land a little way, 190
We will speak out, we will be heard, 52
What delightful hosts are they—, 151
What is song's eternity?, 145
What is to come we know not. But we know, 312
What was his creed?, 31
When Abraham Lincoln was shoveled into the tombs, 441
When a feller hasn't got a cent, 211
When all the world is young, lad, 6
Whenever Richard Cory went down town, 504
When I am dead, my dearest, 153
When I am dead and over me bright April, 159
When I consider how my light is spent, 169
When I go away from you, 356
When I have fears that I may cease to be, 149
When in disgrace with fortune and men's eyes, 343
When I was a beggarly boy, 275
When I was one-and-twenty, 639

INDEX OF AUTHORS

Index of Titles